Lecture Notes
in Business Information Processing   325

Series Editors

Wil van der Aalst
  RWTH Aachen University, Aachen, Germany
John Mylopoulos
  University of Trento, Trento, Italy
Michael Rosemann
  Queensland University of Technology, Brisbane, QLD, Australia
Michael J. Shaw
  University of Illinois, Urbana-Champaign, IL, USA
Clemens Szyperski
  Microsoft Research, Redmond, WA, USA

More information about this series at http://www.springer.com/series/7911

Mohamed Anis Bach Tobji · Rim Jallouli
Yamen Koubaa · Anton Nijholt (Eds.)

Digital Economy

Emerging Technologies and Business Innovation

Third International Conference, ICDEc 2018
Brest, France, May 3–5, 2018
Proceedings

 Springer

Editors
Mohamed Anis Bach Tobji ⓘ
University of Manouba
Manouba
Tunisia

Rim Jallouli ⓘ
University of Manouba
Manouba
Tunisia

Yamen Koubaa ⓘ
Brest Business School
Brest
France

Anton Nijholt ⓘ
University of Twente
Enschede
The Netherlands

ISSN 1865-1348   ISSN 1865-1356 (electronic)
Lecture Notes in Business Information Processing
ISBN 978-3-319-97748-5   ISBN 978-3-319-97749-2 (eBook)
https://doi.org/10.1007/978-3-319-97749-2

Library of Congress Control Number: 2018950101

This Springer imprint is published by the registered company Springer Nature Switzerland AG
The registered company address is: Gewerbestrasse 11, 6330 Cham, Switzerland

Preface

The Digital Economy also called the New Economy or the Internet Economy has grown fast in the past decade. Although a precise and universal definition that clarifies the boundaries and the measurement scales of the Digital Economy is lacking, many reports and scientific papers are published in several fields to highlight the role of digital enabling infrastructure over which organizations and people interact, communicate, and create value.

The International Conference on Digital Economy, ICDEc, was founded in 2016 to discuss innovative research and projects related to the supporting role of information system technologies in the digital transformation process, business innovation, and e-commerce.

ICDEc is a unique opportunity for researchers and experts to attend international networking sessions and reinforce collaborations to explore ideas, exchange thoughts, and implement joint research projects related to the use of digital platforms to communicate, collaborate, and transact business.

The third edition of the conference took place at the Brest Business School, France, during May 3–5, 2018. The theme of ICDEc 2018 was "Digital Economy: Emerging Technologies and Business Innovation." This edition offered a number of sessions discussing digital transformation, cloud education, smart and playable cities, digital marketing, e-banking, e-government, information system technologies, security, and competitive intelligence.

The 41 papers submitted to the ICDEc competitive sessions were reviewed using a double-blind peer- review process. Each paper received between three and six reviews; the average was 4.13 reviews per paper. The rate of acceptance was 36% and only 15 papers were selected with the help of PhD researchers and distinguished professors in the fields of emerging technologies and business innovation. The Program Committee members were from about 40 universities around the world. We express our appreciation for their contribution to the reviewing process.

All participants to ICDEc 2018 were invited to benefit from the insightful keynote speeches, the scientific sessions, as well as the cultural program in the beautiful castle "Chateau de Kerjean" and the social events (the banquet and the gala dinner).

We express our deepest gratitude to the country chairs, the Organizing and Finance Committees, as well as the Scientific and Program Committees for their support in making this conference successful. Special thanks go to the sponsors and scientific partners of the conference, mainly Brest Business School for hosting ICDEc 2018 and the International University of Beirut, BIU, for supporting the organization of this edition.

The intended audience of this book consists of researchers, research students, and practitioners in the fields of information system technologies, digital marketing, e-learning, e-government, e-health, e-banking, and competitive intelligence.

Mohamed Anis Bach Tobji
Rim Jallouli
Anton Nijholt
Yamen Koubaa

Organization

General Co-chairs

Rim Jallouli	University of Manouba, Tunisia
Yamen Koubaa	Brest Business School, France

Program Committee Co-chairs

Mohamed Anis Bach Tobji	University of Tunis, Tunisia
Anton Nijholt	University of Twente, The Netherlands
Rym Srarfi Tabbane	University of Manouba, Tunisia

Organizing Committee

Mickaël Cabon	ISEN Bretagne, France
Jihène El Ouakdi	University of Manouba, Tunisia
Fidel Ettien	Brest Business School, France
Bernard Gourvennec	IMT Atlantique, France
Philippe Lenca	IMT Atlantique, France
Mohammad Makki	Beyrouth International University, Lebanon
Ines Mezghani	ISET'COM, Tunisia
Jean Moussavou	Brest Business School, France

Finance Co-chairs

Dorra Guermazi	University of Manouba, Tunisia
Afef Herelli	University of Manouba, Tunisia
Karim Kamoun	University of Manouba, Tunisia

IT Chair

Nassim Bahri	One Way IT, Tunisia

Junior Committee

Chayma Maatougui	Ysatis Consulting, Tunisia
Rihab Melki	IHG Group, Tunisia

Country Chairs

Ana Pires	Federal University of Bahia, Brazil
Chiheb El Ouakdi	Laval University, Canada

Abdel-Badeeh Salem	Ain Shams University, Egypt
Yamen Koubaa	Brest Business School, France
Masayuki Maruyama	Kansai University of International Studies, Japan
Krishna Koppa	Jain University, India
Dyah Ismoyowati	Gadjah Mada University, Indonesia
Ali Afshar	Eqbal Lahoori Institute of Higher Education, Iran
Namjae Cho	Hanyang University, Seoul, South Korea
Kaouther Znaidi	College of Business Administration, University of Hail, KSA
Mohammad Makki	School of Business - Beyrouth International University, Lebanon
Dorota Jelonek	Czestochowa University of Technology, Poland
Rute Abreu	Instituto Politécnico da Guarda, Portugal
Sambil Charles Mukwakungu	Faculty of Engineering and Built Environment, South Africa
Che-Jen Su	Fu Jen University, Taiwan
Rim Jallouli	University of Manouba, Tunisia
Walid Trabelsi	IBM Ireland, UK
Samir R. Moussalli	Huntingdon College, USA

Program Committee

Chakor Abdellatif	Mohammed Fifth University, Morocco
Hana Abou Jreiche Al Haddad	Lebanese University, Lebanon
Ali Afshar	Eqbal Lahoori Institute of Higher Education, Iran
Abdullah Alqahtani	University of Dammam, Saudi Arabia
Md Atiqur Rahman Ahad	University of Dhaka, Bangladesh
Mohamed Karim Azib	University of Tunis El Manar, Tunisia
Afef Belghith	University of Manouba, Tunisia
Mariem Belkhir	University of Sfax, Tunisia
Montassar Ben Messaoud	University of Tunis, Tunisia
Hanen Borchani	SimCorp A/S, Denmark
Imen Boukhris	University of Manouba, Tunisia
Zaki Brahmi	Taibah University, KSA
Yousra Chabchoub	ISEP, France
Ismahène Chahbi	University of Manouba, Tunisia
Mouna Chebbah	University of Jendouba, Tunisia
Soumaya Cheikhrouhou	Université de Sherbrooke, Canada
Zaineb Chelly Dagdia	Aberystwyth University, UK
Houda Chihi	Innov'COM, Tunisia
Thouraya Daouas	University of Carthage, Tunisia
Ikbel Daly	University of Manouba, Tunisia
Belisle Deny	Université de Sherbrooke, Canada
Amine Dhraief	University of Manouba, Tunisia
Nabila El Jed	University of Manouba, Tunisia

Ines Thabet Karkar	University of Manouba, Tunisia
Imene Trabelsi Trigui	University of Sfax, Tunisia
Sajeh Zairi	University of Manouba, Tunisia

Additional Reviewers

Amna Abidi	University of Tunis, Tunisia
Rabie Beji	University of Tunis-El Manar, Tunisia
Khitem Ben Ali	University of Sfax, Tunisia
Oussama Ben Rhouma	University of Tunis-El Manar, Tunisia
Fatma Ezzahra Bousnina	University of Tunis, Tunisia
Sayda Elmi	University of Technology and Education, South Korea
Prabha Kiran	Jain University, India
Johannes Köstler	Institute of IT-Security and Security Law, Germany
Marwa Saidi	University of Tunis-El Manar, Tunisia
Gongxing Guo	Shantou University, China
Huan Liu	University of Groningen, The Netherlands
Jean-Michel Sahut	Idrac Business School, France
Hassene Seddik	University of Tunis, Tunisia

Organizers

 Association Tunisienne D'économie Numérique

 Brest Business School

 The International University of Beirut

Scientific and Organizing Partners

 École Supérieure D'économie Numérique

  Écoles D'ingénieurs Des Hautes Technologies Et Du Numérique

IMT Atlantique Bretagne Pays De La Loire

Sponsors

Connect Data

Wess E-Commerce

Minerva Consulting

Arab Tunisian Bank

Contents

E-Learning, E-Government and E-Health

Digital Marketing

The Role of Content Marketing Strategies in Traffic Generation: A Conceptual Model Development

Rihab Mhimed and Meriam Belkhir[(✉)]

Faculty of Economic Sciences and Management of Sfax, University of Sfax,
Sfax, Tunisia
rihabmhimed@gmail.com, belk.meriam@gmail.com

Abstract. Past research acknowledged the important role of content marketing strategies in generating traffic and brand's posts popularity. They have been focused mainly on how these content strategies drive the audience's response in terms of liking, commenting and sharing brand posts on Facebook. However, the characteristics of relevant content strategies that help to make those actions and the specific consumers' motivations that are stimulated by each action remain unclear. Our aim in this paper is to develop a conceptual model clarifying the effect of two main content marketing strategies, brand-oriented content and social-oriented content strategy, on generating traffic in social media, through the mediation of consumers' motivations to create traffic online.

Keywords: Content marketing strategies · Traffic generation · Social media
E-advertising · Consumers' motivations online

1 Introduction

Traffic generation remain a top priority for brands that post content on social media platforms, with 63% of marketers saying that generating traffic is on top of their company's marketing challenges (HubSpot 2017), and 73% of B2C content creators saying that creating more engaging content is their first and most challenging objective in their content marketing strategy (Pulizzi and Handley 2016). To address this challenge, a large number of companies employ some forms of content marketing, but the majority of them are still struggling with creating content that truly engages their customers and delivers results for the company (Pullizi 2012). To develop and curate appropriate content it is necessary to understand the target audience (Taylor et al. 2011) in order to address their needs and motivations.

Prior studies about content marketing strategies, consumer motivations, and traffic generation have been conducted separately. On one hand, a brand can create traffic for its content by including the characteristics of a popular brand content in their strategy like informational and entertaining content (Berger and Milkman 2012; De Vries et al. 2012; Chauhan and Pillai 2013; Sabate et al. 2014; Tafesse 2015). On the other hand, some other research suggested that identifying consumers' motivation to interact with the brand post on social media is the way to create more traffic. (Ho and Dempsey

M. A. Bach Tobji et al. (Eds.): ICDEc 2018, LNBIP 325, pp. 3–15, 2018.
https://doi.org/10.1007/978-3-319-97749-2_1

2010; Jahn and Kunz 2012; Rohm et al. 2013; Azar et al. 2016). However, the cause-effect relationship between content marketing strategies and traffic generation is still lacking. Indeed, although marketers receive advice regarding the execution of content delivery in social media (Ashley and Tuten 2015), they receive little guidance on how to create content including those characteristics and which content will stimulate which consumer's motivation to interact with it. So how the content marketing strategy can enhance online traffic?

The aim of this article is to develop a conceptual model of content marketing strategies for online traffic generation. Based on the S-O-R (stimulus-organism-response) model, we suggest that the best way to create traffic is through the mechanisms of stimulating the consumers' motivations to interact with the brand by two content marketing strategies: brand-oriented content strategy and social-oriented content strategy. This conceptual model proposal provides a new way of thinking to the development of an e-advertisement plan and to achieve an efficient differentiation not only in the marketplace, but in consumers' mind.

In this article, we first present the different definitions and meaning of content marketing strategy, and offer a review of past studies around traffic generation, motivations to interact and the S-O-R approach. Based on this literature review, we develop a model that establishes the relationship between content marketing strategies and traffic generation using the S-O-R model as a theoretical background in order to explore the potential role of consumer's online interaction motivations as a mediating mechanism.

2   Literature Review

2.1   Content Marketing Strategies

One of the first and most cited definition of content marketing is presented by Pulizzi and Barrett (2008, p. 8) who argue that content marketing is "the creation and distribution of educational and/or compelling content in multiple formats to attract and/or retain customers". But Holliman and Rowley (2014) detected some limits around this definition and they offered in their study, an empirical definition of digital content marketing that goes beyond creating and distribution of content to include content sharing: "B2B digital content marketing involves creating, distributing and sharing relevant, compelling and timely content to engage customers at the appropriate point in their buying consideration processes, such that it encourages them to convert to a business building outcome." (Holliman and Rowley 2014, p. 18). This definition more specific to the buying process and present the key characteristics of content of the potential business outcome.

The definitions of content marketing are relatively presented in the literature, but there is no precise definition that is specific to the digital context. After reviewing different definitions of content marketing from several researchers, listed in the Table 1 below, we present content marketing as the process of creating interesting and valuable content and sharing it through social Medias to respond to the audiences needs in order to engage them with the brand with a profitable perspective.

Table 1. Content marketing definitions in previous researches

Author, year	Definitions
Rowley (2008)	Content marketing can be defined as a management process where a firm identify, analyse and satisfy customer demand to gain profit with the use of digital content through electronic channels
Pulizzi (2013, p. 5)	"Content marketing is the marketing and business process for creating and distributing valuable and compelling content to attract, acquire, and engage a clearly defined and understood target audience- with the objective of profitable customer action"
Järvinen and Taiminen (2016)	Content marketing, as defined by the interviewees, refers to processes of creating and delivering content (i.e., text messages, pictures, videos, animations) to target customers in ways that add value and engages them in relationships with the company
Du Plessis (2015)	Content marketing is a strategic brand storytelling technique aimed at changing consumers' inactive behaviour through unobtrusive, engaging brand conversations in earned media

With respect to content marketing strategy, Joe Gollner[1] suggests that "content strategy is a process that incorporates content acquisition, content delivery, content engagement, and content management" (Gollner 2014). Halvorson (2010) also defined the content strategy as a practice of planning for the creation, delivery and governance of useful and usable content. Tafesse (2015, p. 4) concluded that "research has mainly been focused on how content strategy drives the audiences' response in terms of liking, discussing and sharing brand posts". The result of his study declares that the content strategy is all about managing a brand post with different characteristics including vividness, interactivity, content type, novelty and consistency in order to increase audience response in terms of liking, commenting and sharing brand posts: the measures of traffic generation on Facebook.

2.2 Online Traffic Generation

According to Volle et al. (2015), traffic online reflects both the general interest of the public for the merchant -it is a measure of attractiveness and therefore of performance- but also the potential sales that it can engender. At constant conversion rates, the creation of traffic is one of the essential means of generating revenues. Gaining traffics on social media platforms is one of the first and most challenging objective for many brands that has established a content marketing strategy (Pulizzi and Handley 2016). In this case, generating traffic online is at the centre of a strategic thinking, but some of the efforts to achieve this objective take off while others fail. Consequently, understanding what drives people to interact with the brand's content can help organizations and policy makers avoid consumer backlash and craft contagious content (Berger and Milkman 2012).

---

[1] A specialist in digital content technologies.

With respect to the characteristics of content that create traffic, Berger and Milkman (2012) argue that emotional appeals are more likely the type of content to be shared than informational appeals content, and that sharing emotional content generate valuable virality that really benefits the brand sharing and can boost product adoption and sales. De vries et al. (2012) also determined possible drivers for brand post popularity on brand's fans pages, which are: brand post characteristics (vividness, interactivity), content of the brand post (information, entertainment), the position of the brand post and the valence of comments on the brand post written by brand fans. Results showed that vivid and interactive brand post characteristics enhance the number of likes and the number of comments can be enhanced by the interactive brand post characteristic like posts that contain questions. Likewise, Tafesse (2015) analysed brand posts characteristics from pages created by the brands on Facebook. They studied characteristics, beside vividness and interactivity were, novelty, brand consistency and content type (entertainment, informational, transactional). Out of the five characteristics, two were fully related to audience response (novelty and brand consistency), two were marginally related (interactivity and content type). Unlike the study of De vries et al. (2012), vividness does not affect audience response in terms of liking and sharing the brand's posts.

2.3 Consumers' Motivations to Interact with the Brand Content

In the context of media use, motivations are understood as the incentives that drive people's selection and use of media and media content (Rubin 2002). They have been shown to influence website effectiveness, attitudes towards brands and advertisements, and purchase behaviour (Rodgers 2002; Ko et al. 2005). To examine questions of "how" and "why" individuals use media in satisfying particular needs, Katz et al. (1973) proposed the uses and gratifications theory (U&G) which is based on four gratification categories: diversion, personal relationships personal identity and surveillance.

After examining several studies, we adapted a scale from a recent study done by Azar et al. (2016) who applied the uses and gratification theory proposed by Katz (1973). Their study aimed to summarise and extend the main motivations associated with the use of social networks. They identified five main motivations that might influence consumers' interactions with a brand precisely on Facebook: social influence, search for information, entertainment, trust and reward.

- **Social influence:** Previous research has widely shown that people purchase goods or services to make favourable impressions on others or to connect with others. Indeed, in social media, consumers use brands as a means to create a self-identity, and when they link themselves to a brand via Facebook 'likes', this allows them to create an impression on others and increase their social involvement (Azar et al. 2016).
- **Search for information:** The literature points out that information seeking is an important motive for individuals to use SNS, to participate in Facebook groups or in online brand communities, and that social media has become a primary source for consumers searching for reliable information (Enginkaya and Yılmaz 2014).

- **Entertainment:** The entertainment motivation covers gratifications that are linked to escaping from problems or daily routines, relaxing, feeling emotional relief, or cultural or aesthetic enjoyment (Muntinga et al. 2011).
- **Trust:** Brand trust is the degree to which a community member believes that the brand keeps its promises regarding performance (Füller et al. 2008). Trust is a fundamental driver of virtual community members' intentions to exchange information with other members (Ridings et al. 2002).
- **Reward:** According to previous research on social media, people join brand communities in order to gain economic benefits such as discounts, or to take part in raffles and competitions (Gummerus et al. 2012) or obtain material extrinsic rewards such as gifts and prizes (Martins and Patrício 2013).

Tsimonis and Dimitriadis (2014, p. 2) acknowledged that "there is a lack of studies examining the motivations, the expected benefits and the strategy that firms use for their corporate fan pages in a social medium like Facebook, Twitter, or YouTube". They found, along with other studies, that some of the main actions of a brand in their social media pages are: interacting with fans, providing advice and useful information, creating/enhancing relationships with customers, brand awareness and customer engagement. Nevertheless, they didn't identify the characteristics of the best strategies that help to make those actions neither the specific consumers' motivations that are stimulated by each action. This study intends to contribute to fill this research gap by developing a conceptual model that constructs the relationship between content marketing strategies and traffic generation, including their relationship with the characteristics of popular content and the consumers' motivations to interact with the brand online.

2.4 The S-O-R Model

One of the most important theoretical backgrounds for basic psychological and psychiatric concepts is the S-O-R (stimulus-organism-response) functionalist approach that was proposed by Woodworth in 1954, who extended the strictly Stimulus-Response (S-R) behaviorists approach. This model consists on the moderation between the stimulation and human behavior (reaction, action) by an organismic component, so the stimulus can affect the response differently depending on the state of the organism. The structures and processes that constitute the organism can be biological (sense organs, nervous system, muscular system) or psychological, such as perception, emotion and motivation (Buxbaum 2016).

The S-O-R model is mainly oriented for psychological and psychiatric studies, but it is also used in marketing to address different aspects of consumer behavior. For example, Russell and Mehrabian (1976), replicated the SOR model in the context of environmental stimulation, based on emotional induction. In that context, the atmosphere (stimulus) influences the internal or emotional states of individuals (organism), generating behavioral responses (response) to the physical environment. This version of the SOR model is most used in marketing research, to address mainly the environmental variables in consumer research, such as the influence of the atmosphere of the point of sale (real and virtual) on consumer behavior (Lemoine 2003, 2008). However, the S-O-R model, as much as we know, has never been applied in the social media context. This article proposes that the content marketing strategy (stimuli) will enhance traffic (response) by the means of consumes' motivations (organism) to interact with the brand's content.

3 Conceptual Model Development

While Majority of the researchers who studied content marketing considered the content marketing strategy as a one unit to work with, for all types of consumers (e.g. Cvijikj and Michahelles 2013; De Vries et al. 2012; Sabate et al. 2014; Tafesse 2015); Gao and Feng (2016) argued that users' motivation will influence how they accept and process information they receive. Thus they expected that Social media users would be attracted by different content strategies and classified the brand content strategies on social media into three types: brand content, brand-extended content and social-oriented content. In this article, we took Gao and Feng's (2016) study as a base for our content strategies and develop them further. Through a survey of brand home pages on Renren and Sina Weibo (Chinese social media sites), Gao and Feng (2016) classified the brand content strategies on social media into three complementary strategies:

- **Strategy n°1**: Consist on posting brand content only, such as information about the brand, its products and services, the company that owns the brand, and activities and events of the brand.
- **Strategy n°2**: Consist on posting brand and brand-extended content, such as related knowledge, news, and product category information. The aim could be linking the brand/product to current happenings and facilitating consumers' learning about the brand/product.
- **Strategy n°3**: Consist on posting brand content, brand-extended content, and social-oriented content. Social-oriented content refers to the messages that are not related to the brand/product but are provided to elicit social interactions with users or among users.

While the boundaries of the first and the third strategies seem to be clearly defined, strategy n°2 seem to have fuzzy boundaries that make it difficult to clearly distinguish it from the first strategy. For this reason, we will consider only two content strategies as explanatory variables: brand-oriented content strategy and social-oriented content strategy. We argue in this paper that the content's characteristics of each content strategy contribute to traffic generation by stimulating different kinds of motivations to interact with the brand. The proposed conceptual model of this paper is presented in Fig. 1.

3.1 Brand-Oriented Content Strategy

The first level of the content marketing strategy consists on posting content that is limited to the brand itself, such as information about the brand, its products and services, the company that owns the brand, and activities and events of the brand. According to Ashley and Tuten (2015) as well as Gao and Feng (2016), at the simplest level, content strategies can be distinguished as primarily functional/informational. Besides, this strategy also includes transactional information referring to activities and events of the brand that are mainly related to products promotions. This leads us to identify to characterize this strategy level as mainly informational and transactional.

Informational Content, Motivations to Interact and Traffic Generation
Brand posts are regarded as informative when the brand post contains information about the company/brand and/or its products (De Vries et al. 2012). Informational content contain all the product specifications and technical details that inform the audience about product attributes, product reviews and product recommendations (Tafesse 2015). This type of content help consumers in their search for reliable information about the brand, throughout their brand information processing. Furthermore, consumers read content to make more well-informed buying decisions, or to get 'inspiration' and new ideas (Muntinga et al. 2011). According to De vries et al. (2012), the pursuit of information explains why people consume brand-related content. Hence, if a brand post contains information about the brand or product, then the brand fans' motivations to participate or consume the content are met. Additionally, research shows that people tend to have positive attitudes toward informative ads on social networks (Taylor et al. 2011). Jahn and Kunz (2012) also found that acquiring valuable functional content on the brand fan page is one of the most important drivers for attracting new fans to the page. Therefore brand-oriented content strategy might enhance traffic by stimulating the motivation to search for information through posting informational content. Thus we argue that:

H1a: Brand-oriented content strategy will enhance traffic by stimulating the motivation to search for information.

Transactional Content, Motivation to Interact, and Traffic Generation
According to previous research on social media (Azar et al. 2016), people join brand communities in order to gain economic benefits such as discounts, or to take part in raffles and competitions (Gummerus et al. 2012) or obtain material extrinsic rewards (Martins and Patrício 2013). Therefore, the brand content strategy should focus on offering rich details about the brand's activities and events such as price promotions, loyalty programs and distribution points, potentially reward the audience with economic value (Cvijikj and Michahelles 2013; De Vries et al. 2012; Muntinga et al. 2011). Tafesse (2015) categorised this kind of content as transactional content where brands post about all the sales related details. The beneficial reasoning that consumers might get by following a brand, is explained by the motivation of opportunity seeking as stated by Enginkaya and Yılmaz (2014) or even by the motivation of remuneration, as stated by Muntinga et al. (2011) for being associated with a financial incentive.

Moreover, according to Azar et al. (2016), this type of transactional content will stimulate "brand profiteers" who are particularly susceptible to promotions and incentives, which are their primary motivations to interact with brands on Facebook. They will mainly like posts about events, posts containing announcements about special offers, posts that explicitly promote the brand's products and posts related to special dates. Those brand profiteers main motivation to engage in voyeuristic behaviour is reward. Therefore brand-oriented content strategy might enhance traffic by stimulating the motivation of reward through posting transactional content. Thus we argue that:

H1b: Brand-oriented content strategy will enhance traffic by stimulating the motivation of reward.

3.2 Social-Oriented Content Strategy

Social-oriented content refers to the messages that are not related to the brand/product and include daily greetings, funny jokes, or weather condition (Gao and Feng 2016). These are examples of entertaining content that Tafesse (2015) categorised it as the humour and artistic works that offer the audience enjoyment and pastime. So the first characteristic of the content in this strategy is entertaining content. Besides, social-oriented strategy aims to show its human involvement and satisfy users' needs for social-interactions with brands. The content shared in this strategy are also provided to elicit social interactions with users or among users, and discussions about different topics to encourage users to share their thoughts (Gao and Feng 2016). Social-interaction gratification is often related to the tendency to affiliate with others, to achieve a sense of belonging, and to avoid remaining alone. Chung and Austria (2010) found that needs for social-interaction significantly affect users' attitudes toward product messages on social media. Based on these studies, we can identify two of the main characteristics for this strategy: entertainment and social-interactive

Entertaining Content, Motivation to Interact, and Traffic Generation

The entertainment value of a social networking site is an important factor for using it (De Vries et al. 2012). Entertainment leads people to consume, create or contribute to brand-related content online (Muntinga et al. 2011). Swani et al. (2013) examined the message strategies most likely to promote online WOM, and their findings support the idea that entertaining content is more likely to stimulate likes and become viral. Their findings support the idea that entertaining content is more likely to stimulate likes and become viral. Likewise, Jahn and Kunz (2012) showed that brand fan pages should deliver entertaining content in order to attract users to the pages and stimulate the usage intensity. For example, entertaining ads that are perceived to be fun, exciting, cool, and flashy – do have a positive effect on attitude toward the ad (Taylor et al. 2011), attitude toward the brand, and the desire to return to the website (Raney et al. 2003). Jahn and Kunz (2012) showed that brand fan pages should deliver entertaining content in order to attract users to the pages and stimulate the usage intensity. Gummerus et al. (2012) found that entertainment enhances satisfaction with the Facebook brand community and brand loyalty. Enginkaya and Yılmaz (2014) argued that entertainment is critical to create online consumer-involvement with a brand. De vries et al.'s (2012) study proves that, if a brand post is entertaining, brand fans' motivations to participate or consume the content are met. The results showed that brand fans have more positive attitudes toward entertaining brand posts compared to non-entertaining brand posts, and generate higher popularity even more than informational and transactional content. Therefore we suggest that consumers who seek for entertainment when they use social media, will interact with the brand that offer entertaining content. We propose:

H2a: Social-oriented content strategy will enhance traffic by stimulating the motivation of entertainment.

Social-Interactive Content, Motivations to Interact and Traffic Generation

As presented by De Vries et al. (2012, p. 3), interactivity is "the degree to which two or more communication parties can act on each other, on the communication medium, and on the messages and the degree to which such influences are synchronized". Interactivity is characterized by two-way communication between companies and customers, as well as between customers themselves; put differently, it characterizes many-to many communication (Goldfarb and Tucker 2011; Hoffman and Novak 1996). Brand post characteristics differ in the degree of interactivity. For example, a brand post with only text is not at all interactive, while a link to a website is more interactive (Fortin and Dholakia 2005) since brand fans can click on that link. Moreover, a question acts as a highly interactive brand post characteristic because it begs an answer from brand fans. Research shows inconclusive findings (no effect versus positive effect) regarding interactivity on outcome measures, such as attitude toward an ad, which might be explained by the considered degrees of interactivity (Liu and Shrum 2002). Since the objective of brand posts is to motivate brand fans to react, De vries et al. (2012) confirmed that higher degrees of interactivity will generate more likes and comments. According to them, managers who specifically want to enhance the number of comments should post a highly interactive brand post characteristic at the brand post, such as a question. This result is intuitive because answering a question is only possible by placing a comment. The social-interactive content is the most appealing content for 'brand companions' to interact with brand-related content on Facebook. Indeed, their primer motivations to do so is social influence (Azar et al. 2016). Therefore we assume that consumers who are motivated by social influence will be stimulated by social-interactive content. We propose:

H2b: Social-oriented content strategy will enhance traffic by stimulating the motivation of social influence.

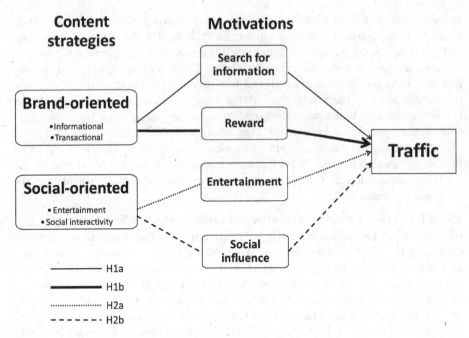

Fig. 1. Conceptual model.

4 Theoretical Implications

This study enriches the marketing literature by providing more insights into the content marketing strategy in the context of creating traffic online. In addition, the conceptual model helps clarify the subject of both suggested content strategies and identify the important variables that are stimulated by each one of them. We defined and discussed the major role of content marketing strategies in creating traffic by the mean of mediation of consumers' motivation to interact with the brand's content. Such relationships haven't been exposed in previous studies.

5 Conclusion

Various research tried to illustrate the relationship between content marketing strategy and traffic generation (e.g. Cvijikj and Michahelles 2013; De Vries et al. 2012; Sabate et al. 2014; Tafesse 2015), but they failed to generalize a relevant content marketing strategy that effectively enhance traffic. Our objective was to develop a conceptual model clarifying the effect of two main content marketing strategies, brand content and social content strategy, on generating traffic in social media, through the mediation of consumers' motivations to create traffic online. First, we explored the consumers' motivations to interact with the brand. Second we restricted the characteristics of popular content and we attributed them to the convenient content strategy. Finally, we determinate which content strategy will address better to which consumers' motivation to interact with the brand proposing that: The brand content strategy will enhance traffic by addressing the motivation of search for information when posting informational content and by addressing the motivation of reward when posting transactional content. The social content strategy will enhance traffic by addressing the motivation of entertainment when posting entertaining content and by addressing the motivation of social influence when posting social interactive content. By including the characteristics of a popular content in them, and defining their effect on consumers' motivations to interact, our framework offer theoretically stronger and more reliable content marketing strategies than the strategies in past researches. In addition, it will be easier and clearer for the managers to consider these strategies in their marketing strategy to create traffic on social media.

6 Limitations and Future Studies

Although this article represents a substantial attempt at conceptualization of the content marketing strategy in the traffic generation context, the significant relationship between the variables should be tested via an empirical research. A quantitative study based on experimental design will be very relevant to test our hypothesis.

References

Ashley, C., Tuten, T.: Creative strategies in social media marketing: an exploratory study of branded social content and consumer engagement. Psychol. Market. **32**(1), 15–27 (2015)

Azar, S.L., Machado, J.C., Vacas-de-Carvalho, L., Mendes, A.: Motivations to interact with brands on Facebook-towards a typology of consumer–brand interactions. J. Brand Manag. **23**(2), 153–178 (2016)

Berger, J., Milkman, K.L.: What makes online content viral? J. Market. Res. **49**(2), 192–205 (2012)

Buxbaum, O.: Key Insights into Basic Mechanisms of Mental Activity. Springer, Heidelberg (2016). https://doi.org/10.1007/978-3-319-29467-4

Chauhan, K., Pillai, A.: Role of content strategy in social media brand communities: a case of higher education institutes in India. J. Product Brand Manag. **22**(1), 40–51 (2013)

Chung, C., Austria, K.: Social media gratification and attitude toward social media marketing messages: a study of the effect of social media marketing messages on online shopping value. In: Proceedings of the Northeast Business & Economics Association (2010)

Cvijikj, I.P., Michahelles, F.: Online engagement factors on Facebook brand pages. Soc. Netw. Anal. Mining **3**(4), 843–861 (2013)

De Vries, L., Gensler, S., Leeflang, P.S.: Popularity of brand posts on brand fan pages: an investigation of the effects of social media marketing. J. Interact. Market. **26**(2), 83–91 (2012)

Du Plessis, P.: Borkowski's Textbook on Roman Law. Oxford University Press, Oxford (2015)

Enginkaya, E., Yılmaz, H.: What drives consumers to interact with brands through social media? A motivation scale development study. Procedia-Soc. Behav. Sci. **148**, 219–226 (2014)

Fortin, D.R., Dholakia, R.R.: Interactivity and vividness effects on social presence and involvement with a web-based advertisement. J. Bus. Res. **58**(3), 387–396 (2005)

Füller, J., Matzler, K., Hoppe, M.: Brand community members as a source of innovation. J. Product Innov. Manag. **25**(6), 608–619 (2008)

Gao, Q., Feng, C.: Branding with social media: user gratifications, usage patterns, and brand message content strategies. Comput. Hum. Behav. **63**, 868–890 (2016)

Goldfarb, A., Tucker, C.: Online display advertising: targeting and obtrusiveness. Market. Sci. **30** (3), 389–404 (2011)

Gollner, J.: Content strategy: fast and good, Content Philosopher (2014). http://www.gollner.ca/2014/07/content-strategy-fast-and-good.html

Gummerus, J., Liljander, V., Weman, E., Pihlström, M.: Customer engagement in a Facebook brand community. Manag. Res. Rev. **35**(9), 857–877 (2012)

Halvorson, K.: Content Strategy for the Web. New Riders, Berkeley (2010)

Ho, J.Y., Dempsey, M.: Viral marketing: motivations to forward online content. J. Bus. Res. **63** (9–10), 1000–1006 (2010)

Hoffman, D.L., Novak, T.P.: Marketing in hypermedia computer-mediated environments: conceptual foundations. J. Market. **60**(3), 50–68 (1996)

Holliman, G., Rowley, J.: Business to business digital content marketing: marketers' perceptions of best practice. J. Res. Interact. Market. **8**(4), 269–293 (2014)

Hubspot: The Ultimate List of Marketing Statistics (2017). https://www.hubspot.com/marketing-statistics

Jahn, B., Kunz, W.: How to transform consumers into fans of your brand. J. Serv. Manag. **23**(3), 344–361 (2012)

Järvinen, J., Taiminen, H.: Harnessing marketing automation for B2B content marketing. Industr. Market. Manag. **54**, 164–175 (2016)

Katz, E., Blumler, J.G., Gurevitch, M.: Uses and gratifications research. Public Opin. Q. **37**(4), 509–523 (1973)

Ko, H., Cho, C.-H., Roberts, M.S.: Internet uses and gratifications: a structural equation model of interactive advertising. J. Advertising **24**(2), 57–70 (2005)

Lemoine, J.F.: Vers une approche globale de l'atmosphère du point de vente. Revue française du Market. **194**(4), 83 (2003)

Lemoine, J.F.: L'influence de l'atmosphère des sites web marchands sur les réponses des internautes. In: Proceedings of the 24ème congrès international de l'association française du marketing (2008)

Liu, Y., Shrum, L.J.: What is interactivity and is it always such a good thing? Implications of definition, person, and situation for the influence of interactivity on advertising effectiveness. J. Advertising **31**(4), 53–64 (2002)

Martins, C.S., Patrício, L.: Understanding participation in company social networks. J. Serv. Manag. **24**(5), 567–587 (2013)

Muntinga, D.G., Moorman, M., Smit, E.G.: Introducing COBRAs: exploring motivations for brand-related social media use. Int. J. Advertising **30**(1), 13–46 (2011)

Pulizzi, J.: What Content Marketing's History Means for Its Future. Content Marketing Institute, Cleveland (2013)

Pulizzi, J., Barrett, N.: Get Content, Get Customers. Voyager Media, Bonita Springs (2008)

Pulizzi, J., Handley, A.: B2C Content Marketing: 2016 Benchmarks, Budgets, and Trends—North America (2016)

Pulizzi, J.: The rise of storytelling as the new marketing. Publishing Res. Q. **28**(2), 116–123 (2012)

Raney, A.A., Arpan, L.M., Pashupati, K., Brill, D.A.: At the movies, on the web: an investigation of the effects of entertaining and interactive web content on site and brand evaluations. J. Interact. Mark. **17**(4), 38–53 (2003)

Ridings, C.M., Gefen, D., Arinze, B.: Some antecedents and effects of trust in virtual communities. J. Strateg. Inf. Syst. **11**(3–4), 271–295 (2002)

Rodgers, S.: The interactive advertising model tested: the role of motives in ad processing. J. Interact. Advertising **2**(2), 22–33 (2002)

Rohm, A., Kaltcheva, V.D., Milne, G.R.: A mixed-method approach to examining brand-consumer interactions driven by social media. J. Res. Interact. Market. **7**(4), 295–311 (2013)

Rowley, J.: Understanding digital content marketing. J. Market. Manag. **24**(5–6), 517–540 (2008)

Rubin, A.M.: The uses-and-gratifications perspective of media effects. In: Bryant, J., Zillmann, D. (eds.) Media Effects: Advances in Theory and Research (2002)

Russell, J.A., Mehrabian, A.: Environmental variables in consumer research. J. Consumer Res. **3**, 62–63 (1976)

Sabate, F., Berbegal-Mirabent, J., Cañabate, A., Lebherz, P.R.: Factors influencing popularity of branded content in Facebook fan pages. Eur. Manag. J. **32**(6), 1001–1011 (2014)

Swani, K., Milne, G., Brown, B.: Spreading the word through likes on Facebook: evaluating the message strategy effectiveness of Fortune 500 companies. J. Res. Interact. Market. **7**(4), 269–294 (2013)

Tafesse, W.: Content strategies and audience response on Facebook brand pages. Market. Intell. Plan. **33**(6), 927–943 (2015)

Taylor, D.G., Lewin, J.E., Strutton, D.: Friends, fans, and followers: do ads work on social networks? How gender and age shape receptivity. J. Advertising Res. **51**(1), 258–275 (2011)

Tsimonis, G., Dimitriadis, S.: Brand strategies in social media. Market. Intell. Plan. **32**(3), 328–3440 (2014)

Volle, P., Isaac, H., Charfi, A.A.: Création de trafic sur les sites web marchands: enjeux et arbitrages entre visibilité et réputation/generation of traffic on merchant websites: a question of trade-off between visibility and online reputation. Revue Française du Marketing **253**, 27 (2015)

Exploring Readers' Perception
of Professional Blogs

Inga Fischer[✉]

TH Köln/University of Applied Sciences,
Steinmüllerallee 1, 51643 Gummersbach, Germany
iklesch@gmail.com

Abstract. This explorative study is focused on blog readers who read or follow professional and personal blogs. The purpose of this research is to investigate how blog readers perceive and anticipate both blogs in general and professional blogs. In particular, the main interest of the research is to investigate the influence of monetising activities in blogs on authenticity of the blog authors and credibility of their blogs. The insights into the motivations and attitudes of the readers demonstrate the need of best practices on finding the balance between monetisation and self-presentation of the authors in their blogs. This study reveals a few issues that should serve as a motivation for the future research in the field of professional blogging.

Keywords: Blog readers · Content monetisation · Authenticity
Credibility · Professional blogs

1 Introduction

Although professional blogging is a widely spread and well-known activity that became a source of income for many popular individual bloggers, there is very little research on personal experiences of reading such blogs. This research intends to begin to fill the gap in existing knowledge by exploring the experiences of blog readers and their perception of the aspects that define blogging as a professional activity.

Originally, blogs appeared as online diaries. People shared information about their private lives, hobbies, interests and knowledge with the online world. Some authors started growing their audience. The readers reached out for authentic content, shared the same opinion, or had the same problems as the authors. Communities of like-minded people emerged around many popular blogs. Koltsova et al. [10] explore the differences of such *blog celebrities* compared to regular unpopular bloggers. Hendrick [6] investigates a few communities that emerged around popular blogs and topics. Popular bloggers soon had an opportunity to monetise their blogs (or better said to monetise their audience?).

There are different ways to monetise a blog [4]. The most recently emerged monetisation measures are discussed in [8, 18]. Different bloggers employ different

© Springer Nature Switzerland AG 2018
M. A. Bach Tobji et al. (Eds.): ICDEc 2018, LNBIP 325, pp. 16–27, 2018.
https://doi.org/10.1007/978-3-319-97749-2_2

monetising activities and do it in the way that best fits to their blog topic. However, every blogger struggles to achieve a balance between building a brand and staying authentic at the same time [14]. Sometimes employing monetising measures in a blog provokes a negative reaction from readers [7]. Surely, it is clear that the role of the audience is important in the activity of blogging [1]. Therefore, it is logical to refer to the readers for the best solution to finding the balance between monetisation and authenticity.

2 Objectives

The main objective of this study is to investigate the attitude of blog readers towards aspects of professional blogging. The given study aims to clarify the following questions:

1. What kind of blogs do blog readers follow nowadays?
2. How aware are blog readers of monetising practices in blogs?
3. What are blog readers' attitudes to monetising practices in blogs?
4. How do blog readers perceive authenticity and credibility in professional blogs?

3 Related Work

3.1 Definitions and Scope

For the scope of this research, based on the definitions and descriptions provided in [3,5,11,16], the following definition of the term *blog* was formulated. **A blog is an online medium that allows individuals or groups of authors to advocate their own cause through publishing news and articles in the form of blog entries sorted by the publication date (newest at the top), categorised by topics and/or tags, and encourages discussion and feedback through comments.** Blogs are seen here as a channel for communication with an audience, where authors have their own agenda. The personal agenda of the author(s) is the key element of a blog. The structural aspect of a blog is essential for differentiating blogs from, for instance, information websites, where the focus lies on the structure, and not on the timeline. The timeline of blog entries is primary to their categorisation. This definition provides the necessary foundation for understanding blogs, nevertheless, the comprehension of the whole concept is inconsequential without understanding who stands behind the blog.

Indeed, it is hard to define the border between a blog and an online magazine. Regardless of the number of authors, there should be a core, an aspect holding the author(s) and their audience together. This aspect is the authenticity of the author(s). As Nardi et al. [1] note, without authenticity blogs will lose their readership, as the audience expects authenticity from bloggers. **A blogger is the person who authenticates the agenda of a blog.**

The term **professional blog** adds one essential feature to the above for-mulated definition of a blog: commercialisation of content. According to [12], professional blogs are commercialised blogs that (potentially) offer a source of income to their writers.

3.2   Blog Reading Practices

Baumer et al. [1] explore reading practices in general and the role of the reader in the activity of blogging. Kaye [9] examines motivations for reading blogs. Nardi et al. [11], Rieh et al. [15], and Peterson [13] focus on the side of the bloggers' activity and their perception of their audience.

Recent research of professional blogging has analysed either the content of blogs themselves [12] or the content of discussions in forums [7]. It was not possible to find any research where the readers and their perception of blogs were studied directly. Therefore, in the given study it was decided to ask blog readers to share their opinion about blogging and, in particular, professional blogging and monetisation in blogs.

3.3   Authenticity and Credibility in Professional Blogs

van Nuenen in [12] discusses the issues of authenticity and self-branding in pro-fessional travel blogs. He considers authenticity to be the main aspect attracting audiences to blogs. Petersen [13] discusses *mommy blogging* as one of the most authentic blogging practices. However, when bloggers choose to become profes-sional they face the challenge of finding a balance between monetisation and authenticity. Hunter [7] explores the conflict between the audience and popu-lar *mommy bloggers*. She argues that with the development of blogging into a professional practice, *authenticity* was transformed into a *performance*. By per-formance she means the activity of presenting a form of entertainment, "acting" as if on the stage. She sees commercialisation as the reason for this transfor-mation. van Nuenen [12] also notices such development: "The entanglement of commercial interests in personal stories creates tension: it could potentially cause harm to the credibility of bloggers in the eyes of their readers" [12].

4   Research Method

4.1   Methodology Choice

Braun and Clarke [2] affirm that qualitative surveys are appropriate for lite-projects, such as student academic research. They argue that qualitative surveys can especially be used for research about experiences, understandings, percep-tions, and practice of the participants. Therefore, the most suitable method of research for this study was considered to be a qualitative survey.

4.2   Limitations of the Chosen Method

Any findings or conclusions made on the basis of the given survey do not claim to be statistically significant. There was no statistical analysis conducted. The survey was intended to produce the data for a descriptive analysis of the given topic. Therefore, the results cannot be used to make a general statement about blog readers.

Besides, Braun and Clarke [2] acknowledge that survey data is usually thinner than, for example, interview data, and the depth of responses depends greatly on the participants motivation. This survey, in fact, delivered a diverse depth of responses. Some open-ended questions received too few responses and could not be used to make any conclusions. However, in general a high response rate was achieved, and enough of relevant data could be collected.

Additionally, a major limitation of qualitative surveys is a lack of flexibility that sometimes leads to misunderstanding of questions [2]. Misunderstanding of questions in this survey could not be avoided. Moreover, mother tongue of many participants was not English. Despite the efforts taken during the piloting phase, there was no way to guarantee the elimination of question misunderstanding.

4.3   Sample Profile

The recruitment of the participants was accomplished mainly through social media, particularly, Facebook. Besides, a few fellow students took part in this survey. Thirty-five blog readers answered the survey questions (Table 1). The participants needed between fifteen and forty minutes for filling out the survey. The amount of information received from different respondents was uneven, because longer answering time led to more informative answers. Most of the participants were rather frequent blog readers, who did not have their own blog. However, a few respondents who had been reading blogs frequently also had their own blogs and posted there regularly. Most of the respondents were students between 18 and 30 with rather low income. More female than male respondents participated in this survey. Instead of learning respondents' nationality it was decided to enquire about the country of residence, because the place of living, not the birth place, is more important in considering the access to, or the quality and the sort of information sources. Due to the implemented recruiting method and the residency of the researcher herself, most of the participants live in Germany. Otherwise, there is a great variety of countries represented in the sample.

5   Findings and Discussion

5.1   Blog Readers' Profile

The survey demonstrates that frequent blog readers are more aware of what kind of blogs they read. Besides, they are able to reflect better on their reading behaviour. Some respondents do not differentiate considerably between blogs and social media platforms. Nardi et al. [11] discussed in 2004 that one of the bloggers'

Table 1. Profile of the survey sample

P	Blog reading	Own blog	Age	Country	Gender	Occupation	Education	Income
P01	From time to time	Not yet	25	Mexico	Female	Employed full-time	Bachelor	less than 15000
P02	I think so	Not yet	25	Germany	Male	Student	Bachelor	less than 15000
P03	I think so	Not yet	22	Singapore	Prefer not to answer	Student	Diploma	15000 - 24999
P04	From time to time	Used to have	26	Netherlands	Female	Student	Bachelor	less than 15000
P05	From time to time	No	24	USA	Female	Student	N/A	more than 45000
P06	From time to time	No	24	Italy	Female	Student	Bachelor	less than 15000
P07	From time to time	No	22	UK	Female	Student	Bachelor	Prefer not to answer
P08	I think so	No	40	USA	Female	Employed full-time	Bachelor	Prefer not to answer
P09	I think so	No	25	Germany	Male	Student + part-time job	Bachelor	less than 15000
P10	I think so	No	27	UAE	Female	Student	Bachelor	Prefer not to answer
P11	I think so	No	48	Germany	Female	Student	Master	Prefer not to answer
P12	Rather frequently	No	29	Germany	Female	Employed full-time	Master	15000 - 24999
P13	Rather frequently	No	19	Germany	Male	Student + part-time job	High School	less than 15000
P14	Rather frequently	No	23	Germany	Female	Student + part-time job	Bachelor	15000 - 24999
P15	Rather frequently	No	26	Germany	Male	Student + part-time job	Bachelor	less than 15000
P16	Rather frequently	No	26	Germany	Male	Student + part-time job	Bachelor	less than 15000
P17	Rather frequently	No	30	Germany	Male	Student	N/A	less than 15000
P18	From time to time	Yes, post very rarely	39	Germany	Male	Employed part-time	Master	15000 - 24999
P19	Rather frequently	Yes, post regularly	52	USA/ Slovenia/ France	Male	Employed full-time	University undergraduate	25000 - 45000
P20	Rather frequently	Yes, post regularly	26	Spain	Female	Self-employed	College	less than 15000
P21	From time to time	Yes, post from time to time	21	New Zealand	Female	Student	University undergraduate	less than 15000
P22	Rather frequently	Yes, post regularly	29	USA	Female	Self-employed	Bachelor	15000 - 24999
P23	Rather frequently	Yes, post regularly	34	Australia	Male	Self-employed	College	Prefer not to answer
P24	Rather frequently	Yes, post regularly	20	India	Male	Student	N/A	N/A
P25	Rather frequently	Yes, post regularly	55	Australia	Female	Unemployed, not currently looking for work	Bachelor	less than 15000
P26	Rather frequently	No	43	Germany	Female	Employed full-time	N/A	Prefer not to answer
P27	I think so	Yes, post from time to time	42	Germany	Female	Employed full-time	Phd	25000 - 45000
P28	Rather frequently	No	42	Finland	Male	Employed full-time	College	15000 - 24999
P29	I think so	No	28	Germany	Female	Student + part-time job	Bachelor	15000 - 24999
P30	From time to time	Not yet	25	Germany	Female	Employed part-time	Bachelor	less than 15000
P31	From time to time	No	25	Germany	Female	Student	Bachelor	less than 15000
P32	I think so	No	24	Germany	Female	Student	Master	less than 15000
P33	Rather frequently	Yes, post very rarely	29	Germany	Male	Employed full-time	Master	15000 - 24999
P34	I think so	No	25	Germany	Female	Student + part-time job	Bachelor	less than 15000
P35	From time to time	No	25	Germany	Female	Student	Bachelor	15000 - 24999

motivations for blogging is to "update others on activities and whereabouts". With the functionality of social media, like Instagram and Facebook, one does not need a blog for updates anymore.

Some respondents listed online magazines as blogs, like TheVerge (P09, P16) or ComputerBase (P15). The transformation of many blogs into a new kind of mass media was discussed by Wall [17]. The fact that some blog readers tend to see no difference between an online magazine and a blog confirms that the border between traditional media and blogs is vague. The role of blogs, therefore, is comparable with the role of online magazines and newspapers nowadays. Blogging cannot be considered only a social activity, like Nardi et al. [11] argued. It has undergone a significant transformation in the last decade and gained new qualities and aspects. Besides, the survey revealed that the respondents read mostly monetised content. This fact tells us that blog readers are used to commercialised content and read a lot of online media, including blogs, that are monetised.

5.2 Motivations for Reading

Kaye [9] identified more than sixty different motivations for reading blogs and grouped them into broader categories:

1. Convenient Information Seeking
2. Anti-traditional Media Sentiment
3. Expression/Affiliation
4. Guidance/Opinion Seeking
5. Blog Ambiance
6. Personal Fulfillment
7. Political Debate
8. Variety of Opinion
9. Specific Inquiry

The most popular motivations from her list were chosen as answer options for the respondents of the given survey. The participants were also offered the possibility to add their own answers. Despite this, none of the respondents added their own option. It seems that this list of motivations covered the range of the respondents' motivations for reading blogs. The Fig. 1 shows the breakdown of different motives readers have for following blogs.

Nardi et al. [11] talk about blogging as a social activity, and blogs as journals, or diaries. Among the participants of their study, many used blogs as "a record of events in their lives for themselves and others" [11]. However, blog readers rarely look to read diaries nowadays. They want to learn something new or have some entertainment. Besides, the major motivations to read blogs included finding life hacks and tutorials, authentic stories and experiences, and specific information of interest. 22 of 35 respondents have indicated authentic stories/experiences/opinions as one of the motivations for reading blogs. The fact, that so many respondents indicated this motivation, confirms the importance of blog authenticity for the readers.

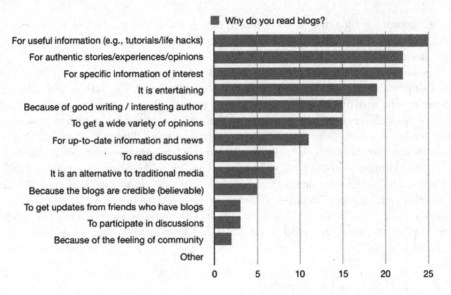

Fig. 1. Motivations for reading blogs

The least popular motivations for reading blogs appeared to be:

- To get updates from friends who have blogs (3 respondents)
- To participate in discussions (3 respondents)
- Because of the feeling of community (2 respondents)

These motivations reflect the nature of blogs as a social activity. Nardi et al. [11] and Baumer et al. [1] write about blogging as a social activity connecting bloggers and their readers through responsibilities they feel to each other and, therefore, forming communities around blogs. According to the answers of the respondents, the demand has changed from a social to a more pragmatic kind of activity.

5.3   Readers' Perception of Professional Blogging

Most of the participants had no doubt that blogging should be considered to be a profession. From the argumentation in favour of blogging being a profession the following topics could be identified:

- Writing a blog is like working for mass media or writing a book
- If you can earn money/make living blogging, it is a job/profession
- It takes time/effort writing quality content/generating ideas
- Blogging is a passion that brings revenue
- Blogging can be both a hobby and a profession

If the answers on the question about participants' attitude to blogging as a profession were relatively consistent, and could be grouped into a few categories, the question how the readers distinguished between professional and hobby blogs brought a great variety of answers. A few aspects mentioned by the participants stood out: advertising, sponsorship, frequency of the posts, blogging style, design, and quality of the content. That could mean that these aspects are the most noticeable for readers and that they have a predominant influence on the reader's perception of blogs (Fig. 2).

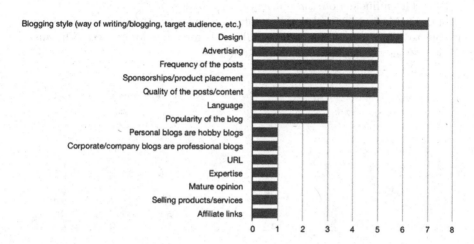

Fig. 2. A list of aspects that allow readers to distinguish between a hobby and a professional blog.

5.4 Readers' Attitude to Monetising in Blogs

P18: I assume that professional bloggers live from advertisement. If there is no monetisation, I doubt a person has blogging as his profession.

In fact, monetisation of a blog is the usual way for bloggers to transform their hobby into a profession [4]. Most of the participants reported to be aware that authors monetise their blogs. Moreover, most of the respondents expressed understanding towards monetising of blogs. Even though a few of them expressed "negative, but with understanding" attitude, there were more respondents who actually expressed a positive attitude towards monetising.

When blogging emerged as a social activity as Nardi et al. [11] describe it, the technology was still mostly perceived as a way of publishing a personal diary on the web. When popular bloggers realised the power of the audience, a conflict between authenticity/credibility and monetisation emerged [7]. Nowadays, monetisation of blogs is a usual matter, and the readers accept it the way they accept advertisements on TV. However, the fact that the bloggers struggle to find the balance between authenticity/credibility and monetisation cannot be ignored. Indeed, receiving renumeration for their activities, bloggers are able to make better quality content. However, the very appearance of sponsored posts can be perceived as a decrease of content quality throughout the blog. Due to the limitations discussed in Sect. 4.2 opinions on monetising measures were scarce. Nevertheless, there are some responses that provide deeper insights on this topic:

P12: It depends whether the authors declare about the blog being a way of making money, declaring whether they are actually advertising something...

P18: The influence on the authenticity depends on the character of the blogger. Money can widen the number of topics, as the blogger might be able to afford things he couldn't afford before. [...] More money means more money for design, also better quality.

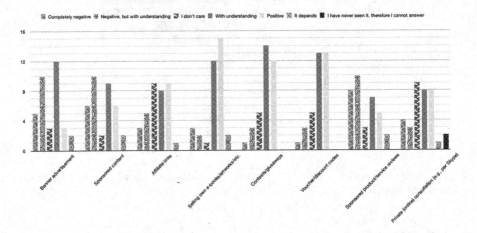

Fig. 3. Overview of the responses: what is your attitude towards the following monetising measures in blogs?

The blog readers opinions on different monetising measures are shown in Fig. 3. In general, the readers seem to be accustomed to various monetising measures. They probably know them not only from blogs, but from other online platforms/newspapers/magazines, etc. P23 indicated that donations could be another way of monetising a blog. Indeed, bloggers often use donation buttons to support their projects, travels and activities. Donation as a monetising measure should not be omitted from discussion in the future research.

Even though the readers perceive some monetising measures as unfavourable, they indicate certain aspects of blogs that can minimise or even eliminate the general negative influence of monetising. It is important that the author stays authentic and trustworthy:

P21: As long as the blogger is being truthful and legit with what they are advertising I don't mind if they do it.

P16: [...] for me it is important to read not only about the 'good' sides of a product but the negative stuff as well. I just want an honest opinion.

5.5 Readers' Attitude to Labelling of Monetised Content

Being honest and trustworthy implies revealing and labelling sponsored content. Figures 4 and 5 demonstrate how perception of authenticity of the author, credibility of the blog, quality of the content, topic of the interest, and design of the blog are influenced by monetising activities and labelling sponsored content respectively. Comparing the visuals provided in Figs. 4 and 5 there is an obvious difference in negative vs positive perception concerning the aspect of authenticity, credibility and quality. The survey revealed that in readers' perception monetising as an activity does not influence major elements of a professional blog, which is demonstrated in Fig. 4. However, Fig. 4 demonstrates either none or very little positive attitude to monetising activities. There are fewer respondents who think that monetising influences any of the aspects mentioned above positively than those respondents who consider that monetising has a rather negative effect.

Figure 5 reveals that more respondents consider labelling of monetised content contributing positively to authenticity of the author, credibility of the blog, and quality of the content. Even aspects such as topic of the interest, and design of the blog received more answers that scale the reader's attitude as positive. Therefore, clear labelling of monetised content has an apparent positive affect on authenticity of the author, credibility of the blog, and quality of content, as can be seen from comparing the blog readers' responses in Figs. 4 and 5.

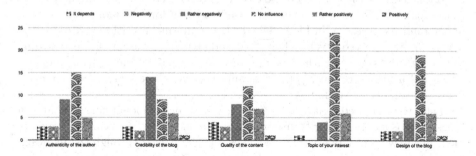

Fig. 4. Overview of the responses: how do *monetising activities* affect different aspects of your perception of the blog?

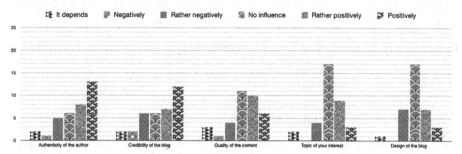

Fig. 5. Overview of the responses: which aspects of your perception could be influenced positively/negatively by *clear labelling* of monetised content?

6 Conclusions

6.1 Authenticity and Credibility in Professional Blogs

Regarding the role of blogging in modern media and the state of the blogosphere it can be concluded: the blogosphere grows and evolves steadily. In the last years it became more commercial, since many bloggers who have big audiences have chosen to monetise their blogs. During this development some blogs have transformed into online magazines, which sometimes results in confusion during the attempt to differentiate professional blogs from other types of online media.

The qualitative survey helped to collect some insights on the kind of information the readers are looking for in blogs, on readers' awareness and perception of monetising practices in blogs and their influence on major aspects of blogging, such as authenticity of the author and credibility of the blog. The survey data confirms that blogging has transformed from a mainly social activity into a mainly professional and commercial activity, and readers are aware of and even demand this change. Blog readers do not look for community or a source of information from their friends, but read blogs for useful information (e.g., life hacks), authentic stories and opinions, and entertainment, which they find mostly in professional monetised blogs.

In the process of the commercialisation of blogs, authenticity and credibility play a crucial role. It seems that monetisation triggers different reactions from the audience, both negative and positive. However, the majority of the readers (participants of the given survey) are used to some form of monetisation, and understand its necessity in blogs. On the one hand monetisation gives bloggers many opportunities to develop their blogs and attract a wider audience according to their interests. On the other hand, it discourages part of the existing audience which has a feeling of loosing the real authenticity of the stories and getting a fake performance instead.

The survey showed that despite general acceptance of monetising measures in blogs there is a demand for transparency and authenticity. The call for improvement in the ways of monetisation becomes especially clear through the following feedback:

> P19: "In general terms, the main problem is that most bloggers are marketers first and journalists second. That's painfully apparent with far too many travel/lifestyle bloggers and a major turn off."

Besides, clear labelling of sponsored content seems to have a positive affect on authenticity of authors, credibility of blogs, and quality of content as discussed in Sect. 5.5.

6.2 Outlook for the Future Research

This study serves as an inspiration for the further research of blogging as a professional activity. Topics to be examined in the future include: sponsored content and its labelling, acceptance of monetising measures, awareness of sponsored content, sponsorship and trust. Due to its significant length and variety of covered topics, the survey has delivered rather vague and indefinite results. These results can be used to formulate hypotheses for various future studies.

References

1. Baumer, E., Sueyoshi, M., Tomlinson, B.: Exploring the role of the reader in the activity of blogging. In: Proceedings of the SIGCHI Conference on Human Factors in Computing Systems, CHI 2008, pp. 1111–1120. ACM (2008)
2. Braun, V., Clarke, V.: Successful Qualitative Research: A Practical Guide for Beginners. SAGE Publications, Thousand Oaks (2013)
3. Dean, J.: Blog Theory: Feedback and Capture in the Circuits of Drive. Polity, Cambridge (2010)
4. Firnkes, M.: Blog Boosting: mitp Business. mitp/bhv (2012)
5. Garden, M.: Defining blog: a fool's errand or a necessary undertaking. J. Theory Pract. Crit. **13**(4), 483–499 (2012)
6. Hendrick, S.: Beyond the blog. Ph.D. thesis, Umeå University, Department of language studies (2012)
7. Hunter, A.: Get off my internets: the audience commodity and the mommy blog backlash. In: Proceedings of the 2015 International Conference on Social Media & Society, SMSociety 2015, pp. 12:1–12:9. ACM, New York (2015)
8. Johansen, I.K., Guldvik, C.S.: Influencer marketing and purchase intentions: how does influencer marketing affect purchase intentions? Master's thesis (2017)
9. Kaye, B.K.: Going to the blogs: toward the development of a uses and gratifications measurement scale for blogs. Atl. J. Commun. **18**(4), 194–210 (2010)
10. Koltsova, O., Koltcov, S., Alexeeva, S.: Do ordinary bloggers really differ from blog celebrities? In: Proceedings of the 2014 ACM Conference on Web Science, WebSci 2014, pp. 166–170. ACM (2014)
11. Nardi, B.A., Schiano, D.J., Gumbrecht, M.: Blogging as social activity, or, would you let 900 million people read your diary? In: Proceedings of the 2004 ACM Conference on Computer Supported Cooperative Work, CSCW 2004, pp. 222–231. ACM (2004)
12. van Nuenen, T.: Here i am: authenticity and self-branding on travel blogs. Tour. Stud. **16**(2), 192–212 (2016)
13. Petersen, E.J.: Empathetic user design: understanding and living the reality of an audience. Commun. Des. Q. Rev. **4**(2), 23–36 (2017)
14. Rettberg, J.: Blogging: Digital Media and Society. Wiley, Hoboken (2013)
15. Rieh, S.Y., Jeon, G.Y.J., Yang, J.Y., Lampe, C.: Audience-aware credibility: from understanding audience to establishing credible blogs. In: Proceedings of the 8th International Conference on Weblogs and Social Media, ICWSM (2014)
16. Scott, D.: Die neuen Marketing- und PR-Regeln im Social Web: Wie Sie mit Social Media und Content Marketing, Blogs, Pressemitteilungen und viralem Marketing Ihre Kunden erreichen. mitp Business, mitp/bhv (2014)
17. Wall, M.: Blogs of war. Journalism **6**(2), 153–172 (2005)
18. Wojdynski, B.W., Evans, N.J.: Going native: effects of disclosure position and language on the recognition and evaluation of online native advertising. J. Advert. **45**, 157–168 (2015)

Co-design and Chronic Regulatory Focus: A Cross-cultural Study and Suggestions for Future *e*-Marketing Practices

Olfa Ammar[(⊠)], Safa Garbout[(⊠)], and Imen Trabelsi Trigui[(⊠)]

Faculty of Economic Sciences and Management of Sfax, Sfax, Tunisia

Abstract. Today, to get optimal and effective solutions, firms go toward co-creation and crowdsourcing activities especially the virtual ones. The technological and e-marketing revolutions greatly explain the spread of those collaborative practices. Special interest of this study is on consumer perceptual and behavioral responses toward co-designed packaging in order to assess the worthiness of conducting an online co-design experience. For this reason, based on categorization and regulatory focus theories, we developed a research model to understand consumer's perceptual and psychological effects on his responses toward co-designed packaging. A cross-cultural study through an online experiment brings to light unpredicted findings and new insights for co-design and consumer psychology literatures, as well as, for e-marketers and professionals.

Keywords: Online co-design · Packaging typicality · Regulatory orientation
Quality perception · Purchase intention

1 Introduction

Nowadays, we could not neglect the rising number of internet users and connected consumers, which has greatly supports the advancement of digital marketing activities. Some researchers (Dennis et al. 2009) have confirmed the specification and distinctiveness of e-consumer in comparison to an ordinary one regarding his attitudes, interests and online behavior. This is in line with previous studies' conclusions (Chaffey et al. 2013, 2014), which have proved that e-marketing practices affect consumers' perceptions toward the firm, the brand, the product, etc. and guide his decision-making and actions on web interfaces. The revolution of digital marketing and technological progress have supported the advancement of co-creation and crowdsourcing experiences and possibilities (Labrecque et al. 2013). Today, empowering the consumer in new product/service development is much easier with the development of information-communication technologies. Those collaborative and participatory activities fuel online and offline marketing strategies and impact consumers' online and offline behaviors (Gatautis and Vitkauskaite 2014; Harrison and Waite 2015). Hence, co-creation presents a new way for marketers to differentiate themselves in the marketplace and in the eyes of the consumer, particularly, when it comes to new product development. Nishikaw et al. (2017) have emphasized on the weight of marketing the product as "customer-ideated" in boosting the product's market performance up to 20

© Springer Nature Switzerland AG 2018
M. A. Bach Tobji et al. (Eds.): ICDEc 2018, LNBIP 325, pp. 28–47, 2018.
https://doi.org/10.1007/978-3-319-97749-2_3

percent. This is what we address in this research with special focus on co-design activity. We believe that when it comes to develop new packaging design, using an online co-design strategy would be interesting to engage the consumer in memorable experience and to obtain new packaging that fits consumers' preferences and their consumption needs. However, before launching such virtual experience, we need to investigate consumers' perceptions and response toward the co-designed packaging. Definitely, the design features are an important determinant of product marketplace by capturing consumer's attention and inducing favorable impression and response (Bloch 1995; Rettie and Brewer 2000; Henderson and Cote 2004; Silayoi and Speece 2004). However, packaging attractiveness may be not limited to the design characteristics; it may be also related to how the design was developed, which may affect product's evaluation and consumer's response.

In previous researches (Zeithaml 1988; Ophuis and Van Trijp 1995), consumer perceptions of product's quality have been considered as key determinants of consumer's judgement, his purchase behavior and product choice. From the other side, studies from different research streams admitted that individual's personality traits and, precociously, his regulatory orientation influence their perceptions and attitudes when evaluating and choosing a product (Werth and Foerster 2007; Hassenzahl et al. 2008). In fact, according to Higgins (1997, the theory of regulatory focus describes and analyses individuals' perceptions and their motivations to achieve their goals (Werle et al. 2012; Kurman et al. 2015, Werth and Foester 2007). Reasoning on person's autonomy and self-reported preferences, Kurman et al. (2015) acknowledged that individuals' regulatory orientation is a major explanatory variable of psychology differences across cultures. Accordingly, this study develops a cross-cultural analysis to capture individuals differences from culture to another when interpreting and responding to product packed in co-designed packaging.

The main objective of this research is to dig deeper into co-designed product and consumer psychology to determine whether the information about the packaging designer and its perceived typicality coupled with consumer's regulatory orientation, shape his perception toward products' overall quality, as well as, his purchase intention. Hence, the main questions that we seek to respond on are: Does consumer's response toward co-designed packaging and the related product differs across cultures? What role plays a consumer's regulatory orientation in this subject? And how these can be integrated in a conceptual framework?

Answering those questions will help us expand the literature of crowdsourcing and co-design paradigms, as well as, the regulatory focus theory. Moreover, this paper induces knowledge to online consumer participation in new product development. From managerial perspective, this study is in helping firms that look to launch new product and to apply an online co-design strategy, better understand how consumer's regulatory orientation and co-designed products shape consumers' evaluation and responses to it. Indeed, input from the target consumers is crucial and information about their expectations and what will be the resulting behavioral response can help companies before going along new strategy of new product development.

2 Theoretical Background

Working on co-design research stream, we should take into account participants' creativity and imagination that could lead to standard and "typical" designs or unique, exceptional and "atypical" ones. In research on packaging design, this brings us to consider different shapes of packaging that could result from co-design experience. Taking into account this specific point, we go with previous researches findings (Luo et al. 2008; Becker et al. 2011; Wang 2013; Westerman et al. 2013) that attested that different packaging characteristics influence consumer's perceptions, attitudes and behavioral response toward the product. Luo et al. (2008) go a bit further and proved that consumer use objective and subjective packaging criteria to evaluate a product and to decide on product's purchase. They maintained that subjective attribute differs from individual to another as it could be interpreted and perceived in various own ways such as packaging ease of use, aesthetic appearance, emotional appealing, innovation, etc. in contrast to objective attributes that include its technical and physical configurations (e.g. packaging color, material, shape, background image, etc.). Consequently, in addition to packaging objective characteristic, such as its shape, consumer may use his perception toward this shape typicality when evaluating the product. Indeed, drawing on categorization theory, Schoormans and Robben (1997) proved that deviation in packaging designs affect consumer typicality perception and the way he categorizes those stimuli. In the same vein, Loken et al. (2006) maintained that individuals always compare a product with its predecessor of the reference group to build interpretation that lead to different evaluation and judgement. Hence, identifying to what extent the product fits the original category is a matter of perspective. In this study, we focus on the effect of different packaging designs (typical vs. atypical) and their perceived typicality on product evaluation (e.g. perceived overall quality (Becker et al. 2011)) and consumer's purchase intention. In addition, Luo et al. (2008) admitted that objective attributes affect consumer perception of the subjective one, which in turn, influence product's evaluation and consumer behavioral intention. Accordingly, we hypothesize:

H1: the packaging typicality (typical vs. atypical) effect on product's perceived quality is mediated by consumer perception toward the packaging typicality degree.
H2: the packaging typicality (typical vs. atypical) effect on consumer's purchase intention is mediated by consumer perception toward the packaging typicality degree.

Previously, Veryzer and Hutchinson (1998) admitted that when combining an aesthetic design feature with other product information, consumer's evaluation and purchase intention could be different. With the emergence of crowdsourcing and co-creation activities, different studies investigated consumer perception and behavioral response toward crowdsourced product that are marketed as "customer-ideated" (Nishikawa et al. 2017) in comparison with other conventional and standard ones. It was proved that such product creates value for the consumer and affects his judgement toward the product and his behavioral intention and decision (e.g. purchase intention, willingness to pay, etc.). Indeed, being co-created or developed by professional designer is a product related information that may lead to consumer's perceptions and response deviation and adaptation.

From different perspective, Bless and Wänke (2000) proved that an information could be typical and atypical, depending on the extent it fits the target category. Consumer judgement could be based on the current information, which could influence consumer's evaluation, attitudes and behavioral intention toward the product. Accordingly, we suggest a third extrinsic factor, in addition to objective and subjective attributes, that influence packaging perceived typicality, the quality inference and consumer purchase intention. It is the information about the packaging designer, if it was a "co-designed" packaging or "developed by professional designer". Indeed, adding further information, that could be a distinctive and different one in the product category, may have an influence on packaging design's typicality interpretation (objective and subjective typicality). Subsequently, we need to investigate the extent to which the designer information influence the effect of packaging typicality on its typicality perception, on products' quality inference and purchase intention. We need to identify the condition of which the information of packaging designer may influence the way that other attribute is processed. Accordingly, we hypothesize packaging typicality and its perceived typicality degree effects by the designer information interaction:

H3a: When the packaging is co-created (vs. developed by professional designer), the impact of its typicality on consumer perception toward the typicality degree becomes stronger (vs. insignificant).

H3b: When the packaging is co-created (vs. developed by professional designer), the effect of its typicality on the product perceived quality becomes greater (vs. insignificant) through the packaging perceived typicality.

H3c: When the packaging is co-created (vs. developed by professional designer), the effect of its typicality on consumer purchase intention becomes greater (vs. insignificant) through the packaging perceived typicality.

In order to understand deeply the role of consumer's psychology on shaping his perception and behavior toward co-designed packaging, we relied on social psychology and human behavior literatures, where Higgins (1997, 2000) acknowledged that individuals are behaviorally motivated by approach–avoidance strategies with emotional sensitivities. According to Higgins (1997), regulating those different directions of approach and avoidance behaviors is called regulatory focus. Indeed, consumer's regulatory focus is a motivational orientation that guides his thoughts, feelings, choices and goals. People focused promotion engage in approach-related behavior and they are more concerned with aspiration and sensitive to positive outcomes. In Contrast, preventive consumer engage in avoidance-related behaviors and rely on reason to choose the product in order to be away from the negative end sates (Crowe and Higgins 1997; Pham and Higgins 2005; Pham and Avnet 2009; Boesen-Mariani et al. 2010). In recent years, there is a great interest on the role of this psychological trait on decision making especially on alternatives' evaluation (Higgins 2006). Based on Higgins's (2000) researches, consumer motivation and information processing are influenced by his regulatory orientation, which affects the type of information sought to utilize before decision-making.

Conducting an online marketing campaign through crowdsourcing activity attract peoples from different regions and, especially, with various imagination and innovativeness. Consequently, being co-designed is a novel issue that could be a sign of creativity and uniqueness or a mark of uninventiveness and unoriginality. Different researches (Amabile 1996; Baas et al. 2011; Herman and Reiter-Palmon 2011) proved that an individual regulatory orientation could be a motivational factor of his creativity and, no matter a person's orientation (promotion versus prevention); he is able to enhance creativity and promote creative performance. Baas et al. (2011) admitted that prevention-oriented is positively related to the creativity despite his anxiety and fear feelings when he made decisions (Friedman and Förster 2001, 2002; Baas et al. 2008, 2011). Other studies has argued that the promotion orientated consumer, as an extraverted person, can choose a risky and creative alternative (Higgins 1997, 2000) using his emotions and intuition. Going for creative and original concepts and products is related to flexible thinking that is associated with flexible information processing and faculty of new pathways exploration (Baas et al. 2011). Holding similar level of creativity proved that both promotion and prevention oriented people develop cognitive flexibility and information processing that help them go for innovative and unusual alternative, such us an atypical co-designed packaging. In cognitive psychology, different studies have proved the effect of person's mood and affective states on category processing and interpretative thinking that founds his attitudes and intentions (Loken 2006). It has been revealed that preventive consumer places greater importance on mood, that facilitate his cognitive flexibility, than does a promotion oriented consumer (Pula et al. 2014). We can deduce the role of consumers' psychological orientation on his perception toward the packaging typicality and the way he develops associations and interprets designs' related information, which, in turn, affect his perception and behavioral intention toward the product. In accordance to this study's objectives, we believe that the information about the packaging designer and the packaging typicality degree would be evaluated and judged differently from consumer to another in correspondence to his regulatory orientation. Accordingly, we hypothesize packaging's designer information effects by consumer regulatory orientation interaction:

H4a: packaging typicality by designer information interaction effect on consumer perception toward the typicality degree is moderated by consumer's regulatory orientation.
H4b: packaging typicality by designer information interaction effect on product perceived quality is moderated by consumer's regulatory orientation.
H4c: packaging typicality by designer information interaction effect on consumers' purchase intention is moderated by consumer's regulatory orientation.

From this intensive literature review, we present below the research model that helps us respond to this research questions and objectives (Fig. 1).

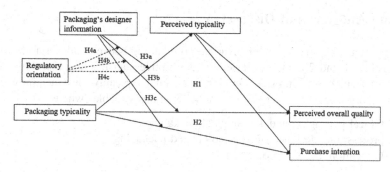

Fig. 1. Research model

3 Research Method

Participant and design:
To conduct a cross-cultural study and collect data, we used Qualtrics panel to recruit respondents from Denmark (n = 374) and Tunisia (n = 138) and we choose olive oil product to work on. We conduct an online experiment as it provides a strong and effective causal interpretation. Precisely, we used a dichotomous manipulation of packaging typicality where one appears more natural and ordinary olive oil packaging relative to the second one that look more unusual and atypical olive oil packaging. As well as, we change the related information for each packaging as a stimulus. Hence, the design differences were combined with the packaging designer information. Besides, for manipulation check, we tested the packaging typicality before launching the experimentation in order to guarantee the divergence efficiency between the two designs. Participants were randomly assigned to one condition of our 2 (typicality: typical vs. atypical) × 3 (no information, expert designer, co-designed) designs. Subsequently, the online experimental procedure is about evaluating six packaging designs displayed in Annex 1. As we mentioned above, it is a cross-cultural comparative study where we compare six different independent groups.

Material and procedure:
To assess product's overall quality perception and consumer's purchase intention, we used single items. Indeed, giving the exploratory nature of the study, we simply need a "snap shot" of consumers' perception of the overall quality and their response toward different packaging designs rather than a comprehensive analysis. In relation to regulatory focus measurement, we used the composite scale of Haws et al. (2010) to ascertain individual differences in promotion and prevention concerns. It comprises ten items (five each for promotion and prevention focus) with high reliability (Cronbach's α = 0.801). All the items were valued on a Likert scale from 1 to 7.

4 Data Analysis and Discussion

We begin our data analysis with bivariate correlations between all variables of this study. Tables 1 and 2 contains all details (descriptive statistics and Pearson's coefficients) for Danish and Tunisian samples. Packaging typicality, designer information and regulatory orientation were coded as dichotomous variables where:

0 = typical packaging and 1 = atypical packaging
0 = professional designer and 1 = co-created packaging
0 = prevention and 1 = promotion

Examining Tables 1 and 2, we notice that for both samples the packaging typicality and its perceived typicality degree are negatively correlated. Which implies that the more the packaging is atypical, the more it is perceived different to standard bottle of olive oil product category. Hence, we validate our manipulation.

Focusing on Danish consumers' response and perceptions, we obtained negative and significant inter-correlation between packaging typicality and product perceived overall quality. This implies that olive oil packed in atypical packaging is perceived of high quality than in typical one. In the other side, we got significant positive correlation between consumer purchase intention and his perception toward product quality and its packaging perceived typicality. Subsequently, when it comes to olive oil buying, Danish consumer based on his perception toward the packaging typicality degree. Indeed, the more the bottle is perceived similar to standard packaging of the product's category, the more he intend to buy the product. In addition, being correlated positively and significantly to typicality perception, the more the consumer is involved in olive oil category, the more he perceives the packaging typical to the product category. In contrast, in regards to atypical design, Danish consumer identifies himself as less knowledgeable toward olive oil.

Table 1. Summary of inter-correlations, means, and standard deviations for all study variables for Danish sample.

	M	SD	Packaging typicality	Designer information	Regulatory orientation	Perceived typicality	Perceived quality	Purchase intention	Knowledge	Involvement
Packaging typicality	.49	.501	1							
Designer information	1.5	.501	−.021	1						
Regulatory orientation	.62	.485	−.062	−.013	1					
Perceived typicality	3.51	1.88	−.462**	−.040	−.020	1				
Perceived quality	4.27	1.58	−.212**	−.079	.017	.055	1			
Purchase intention	4	1.64	.062	−.036	−.006	.194**	.619**	1		
Knowledge	4.14	1.53	−.111*	.052	.040	.131	.023	.051	1	
Involvement	3.61	1.12	−.026	.001	.073	.178**	.052	.080	.444**	1

N = 374; *p < .05; **p < .01

We got different results with Tunisian sample. Indeed, consumer's perception toward product quality was correlated positively and notably with his perception toward the packaging typicality. Hence, in opposition with Danish individual, the more the packaging is perceived typical, the more Tunisian consumer perceives the olive oil of high quality. In the same vein, consumers' purchase intention was correlated positively and significantly with his perception toward the product's quality and to its packaging perceived typicality too. For both samples, we got significant and positive inter-correlation between consumer's knowledge and involvement as regards to olive oil product, which signifies that the more the individual is involved in this product category, the more he considers himself knowledgeable and well informed toward it.

The absence of direct effects of packaging designer information and consumers' regulatory orientation brings around the possibility of their interactions effects. Subsequently, we conduct ANOVA univariate analysis to detect means differences between groups when manipulating different factors. Packaging typicality, designer information and consumers' regulatory orientation were retained as fixed factors and product perceived overall quality/purchase intention as dependent variables. Conducting experiment and cross-cultural study necessitate controlling for some variables in order to be the same between experiments and groups. In this study, we controlled consumers' involvement and knowledge toward olive oil as, in the current context, the more the product is important, the more consumer perception and response vary accordingly.

Table 2. Summary of inter-correlations, means, and standard deviations for all study variables for Tunisian sample.

	M	SD	Packaging typicality	Designer information	Regulatory orientation	Perceived typicality	Perceived quality	Purchase intention	Knowledge	Involvement
Packaging typicality	.52	.501	1							
Designer information	1.51	.502	.130	1						
Regulatory orientation	.72	.450	.083	.173	1					
Perceived typicality	3.83	1.91	−.452**	−.158	−.059	1				
Perceived quality	4.88	1.66	−.098	.119	.123	.372**	1			
Purchase intention	4.26	1.84	−.164	.093	.014	.317**	.596**	1		
Knowledge	5.44	1.45	−.038	−.120	−.071	.057	.111	.019	1	
Involvement	6.10	.867	−.037	−.047	−.118	−.053	.129	.123	.365**	1

N = 138; **p < .01

Univariate analysis results:

For Danish consumer, only one of the tested interactions has a significant effect on product perceived quality. Indeed, consumer regulatory orientation × information about packaging designer has a great influence on consumer's perception toward the product's quality $(F(1, 347) = 6.695, p = .010)$. However, packaging typicality × consumer regulatory orientation $(F(1, 347) = .058, p = .809)$ and packaging typicality × information about packaging designer $(F(1, 347) = .008, p = .927)$ interactions have no effect on product's perceived quality.

Focusing on means differences (see Table 3), Danish consumer with promotion orientation perceives product in typical packaging that was developed by professional design of highest quality (MDK-promotion = 4.12) than the co-designed one (MDK-promotion = 3.76). Similarly, in the case of atypical packaging, promotion consumer highlights product quality in packaging designed by professional designer (MDK-promotion = 5) greater than in the co-designed packaging (MDK-promotion = 4.21). On the contrary, and mainly for atypical packaging, Danish preventive consumer weigh up product quality in co-designed packaging (MDK-prevention = 4.82) than the one developed by professional designer (MDK-prevention = 4.31). For Tunisian consumer, none of the three interactions has an effect on his quality perception toward olive oil quality. In fact, all interactions come up with p > .05.

Table 3. Summary of means differences of packaging typicality, designer information and regulatory orientation interaction for Danish and Tunisian samples.

Packaging design × Designer information × Regulatory orientation						
Dependent variables: perceived quality					Purchase intention	
Packaging typicality	Designer information	Regulatory orientation	Means		Means	
			DK	TN	DK	TN
Typical	Professional	0	3.75	4.43	3.67	4
		1	4.12	5.2	3.97	4.4
	Consumer	0	3.88	4.71	3.93	5.11
		1	3.76	5.31	3.64	4.96
Atypical	Professional	0	4.31	4.12	3.95	4.31
		1	5	4.56	4.25	4
	Consumer	0	4.82	5.1	4.2	4.14
		1	4.21	5.17	3.8	4.13

However, compared to Danish population, Tunisian consumers highly evaluate olive oil quality in co-designed packaging than in standard packaging developed by professional design. Remarkably, in the case of atypical design, consumers' with promotion or prevention orientation consider the product of greatest quality when it is packed in co-designed packaging (MTN-promotion = 5.17; MTN-prevention = 5.1) than in the professional one (MTN-promotion = 4.56; MTN-prevention = 4.12).

When it comes to purchase intention, the interaction Danish consumer regulatory orientation × designer information marginally affect consumers' purchase intention (F (1, 347) = 3.219, p = .074). This wasn't the case for the rest of interactions including packaging typicality × consumer regulatory orientation $(F(1, 347) = .036, p = .850)$ and packaging typicality × information about packaging designer $(F(1, 347) = .041, p = .839)$. Regarding means differences, Danish consumer with promotion orientation has greater intention to purchase an olive oil packed in bottle conceived by professional designer (MDK-promotion = 4.25) higher than an olive oil in a co-designed bottle (MDK-promotion = 3.8) no matter its typicality level but mainly for atypical packaging.

On the contrary, in the case of atypical design, Danish preventive consumer intend to purchase olive oil in co-designed packaging (MDK-prevention = 4.2) than in a standard bottle developed by professional designer (MDK-prevention = 3.95). The same for typical designs where the co-designed packaging always attract Danish preventive consumers (MDK-prevention = 3.93) more than professional designers' packaging (MDK-prevention = 3.67). For Tunisian population, all of the interactions come up with $p > .05$, which means that they have no effect on consumer's purchase intention. However, unlike Danish population, typical co-designed packaging incites Tunisian consumers' purchase intention (MTN-promotion = 4.96; MTN-prevention = 5.11) more than the atypical one (MTN-promotion = 4.13; MTN-prevention = 4.14). Hence, for typical packaging, Tunisian preventive and promotion consumers go for co-designed one. Conversely, for atypical packaging, preventive consumer shows more protective behavioral intention and he is more interested to purchase the one developed by professional designer (MTN-prevention = 4.31) while consumer with promotion orientation go to some extent for co-designed packaging (MTN-promotion = 4.13).

From above, it is clearly that in some cases (especially with Danish sample) our findings controvert with regulatory orientation theory's basic notions. Indeed, we realized that an individual oriented promotion is not always concerned with advancement and that prevention focused individual is more likely to take chances and adopts innovations. This corresponds to Baas et al. (2011) findings that attested that preventive individuals develop creative ideas and perceptions when they are cognitively stimulated and energized. This is in line with this study design where consumers were cognitively activated by packaging atypicality and the related designer information.

In order to check the differences with the control group, other Anova analyzes were conducted with other independent Boolean variables comparing the condition control with the condition "designed by processional designer" {0 = control group; 1 = designed with professional} and the condition "co-designed" {0 = control group; 1 = co-designed}.

In Danish sample, we found that the participant with both the condition co-designed or designed with professional, highly evaluate olive oil quality than the control group {M professional designer = 4, 389 > M co-designed = 4,153 > M control = 4, 066}. For Tunisian consumer, they perceived the quality of olive oil product when it is packed in co-designed packaging higher than the control group and the group exposed to condition designed by professional {M Co-designed = 5.07 > M control = 4.79 > M professional designer = 4.68}.

When it comes to purchase intention, we found also that the control group has an intention less than the other groups {M control = 3.809 < M co-designed = 3.933 < M professional designer = 4.048}. However, unlike to Danish population, the Tunisian participant have a different intention. Thus the control group has an effect more highly than the other group {M control = 4.735 > M co-designed = 4.454 > M professional designer = 4.096}. This result explain that the Tunisian consumer is indifferent to the information putted in olive oil packaging in contrast to the Danish consumer.

Process Macro results:

To analyze our research model and to detect the significant direct and indirect effects, we use Process Macro (Hayes 2013). For data analysis, we focus on p values and confidence intervals, which should not cross zero, of each variable and interaction. In the research model, we have moderated moderated mediation. We start with the mediation assessment that corresponds to model 4 in Process Macro. In this case, packaging design, typicality perception and overall quality perception/purchase intention correspond respectively to X, M and Y of model 4. Certainly, with consumer's knowledge and product involvement as control variables.

Beginning with product perceived quality, we get significant model with Danish sample (R2DK = .076, FDK(4, 369) = 6.51, p < .01) where both of packaging typicality (t(369) = 5.03, p < .01, [.581; 1.33]) and its perceived typicality degree (t (369) = 2.85, p < .01, [.049; .268]) affect Danish consumers' perception toward overall product quality. The significance of total effect model (R2DK = .049, FDK (3, 370) = 6.47, p < .01) proves that the perceived typicality plays the role of a partial mediator as the direct effect of packaging typicality on quality perception remains significant with the presence of typicality perception. In contrast to Tunisian sample, where the packaging typicality has no direct effect on overall quality perception (t (133) = 1.04, p = .3, [−.297; .956]), we got a complete mediation. Indeed, the insignificance of total effect model (R2TN = .03, FTN(3, 134) = 1.5, p = .21) is opposed to the significance of packaging typicality effect on its perceived typicality (t (134) = −5.88, p < .01, [−2.31; −1.15]), which in turn, influence product perceived quality (t(133) = 3.96, p < .01, [.183; .547]). Therefore, we confirm H1 for Danish and Tunisian samples.

Both of packaging typicality (t(369) = 3.36, p < .01, [.262; .1]) and its perceived typicality (t(369) = 4.4, p < .01, [.133; .347]) predicts Danish consumer purchase intention (R2DK = .07, FDK(4, 369) = 6.2, p < .01). However, the overall model is not significant (R2DK = .01, FDK(3, 370) = 1.42, p = .23), which implies that packaging perceived typicality does not mediate the effect of packaging typicality on consumer purchase intention. Similarly, we did not get a significant mediation with Tunisian sample (R2TN = .04, FTN(3, 134) = 1.42, p = .12). Even the packaging typicality, in contrast to its perceived typicality degree (t(133) = 2.9, p < .01, [.098; .519]), has no effect on Tunisian consumer purchase intention (t(133) = −.156, p = .87, [−.771; .658]). Subsequently, we disprove H2 for both samples. Greatly, our findings go in line with Roest and Rindfleisch (2010) study's results, which proved that products/services' cues affect their perceived typicality that, in turn, influence consumer overall quality perception and his purchase intention.

We end with total model analysis. In particular, we focus on total (direct and indirect effects) and the moderated moderated mediation effects of this research model, which corresponds to model 12 in Process Macro templates (Hayes 2013), where:

Y: perceived overall quality/purchase intention
X: packaging design
M: perceived typicality
W: designer information
Z: regulatory orientation

The first objective of this study was to verify the effect of the packaging designer information on consumer perception toward its typicality degree and if there was any effect of consumer's psychological orientation. Beginning with Danish consumer perception toward the packaging's typicality degree, the findings revealed a major effect of the packaging typicality (t(337) = −8.86; p < .00) but no significant effects of the tested interactions, which was different to Tunisian consumer reactions (see Table 4 in Annex 2). Indeed, Tunisian sample's perception toward the packaging typicality degree was significantly influenced by the interaction of the packaging typicality, the information about its designer and consumer's regulatory orientation (t(112) = 2.31; p = .02 < .05) in addition to the direct effect of the packaging typicality (t(112) = −6; p < .00). Those findings attested that the moderating role of packaging's designer information on packaging typicality effect on its typicality perception is dependent on a second moderator, which is consumer regulatory orientation. Hence, the effect of packaging typicality on its perceived typicality degree depends on both the packaging's designer and consumer's psychological orientation. This prove the importance of Tunisian's regulatory focus when dealing with the information about the packaging's designer. From above, we validate H4a only for Tunisian sample and we reject the H3a for both samples.

Focusing on the direct and interactions effects, the results showed a significant direct effect of packaging perceived typicality degree on both Danish and Tunisian consumers' responses toward the product (see Tables 5 and 6 in Annex 2). Additionally, the packaging typicality significantly influence Danish consumers' perception toward the overall product quality and their purchase intention, which was not the case for Tunisian consumer. This confirms the findings obtained from mediation analysis and prove that Tunisian consumer do not give importance to olive oil packaging design unlike the Danish sample. Here comes the weight of cultural differences and consumer involvement in olive oil category where, as it has been proven in previous research (Deliya and Parmar 2012), individual with low involvement tend to focus on products' extrinsic cues more than the one with high involvement degree.

One of the primary goals of this study is to investigate the weight of the packaging's designer information on consumers' responses. The results indicated a meaningful positive effect of such information on Tunisian consumers' quality assessment of the product (Coef. = .615; t(111) = 2.1; p = .03 < .05) without any significant effect of their psychological orientation. On the other hand, Danish consumers' perception toward the overall product quality depends on the negative effect of the interaction of the packaging designer information and consumers' regulatory orientation (Coef. = −.856; t(336) = −2.56; p = .01 < .05). Hence, the weight of such information depends on individuals' psychological orientation among Danish samples, which is not the case for Tunisian consumer.

Those results did not yield to sufficient evidence about the moderating roles of packaging's designer information and consumers' regulatory focus. Consequently, we move to the next stage of this research involving the moderated moderated mediation. Here, the effect of packaging typicality on consumer responses (overall quality perception and purchase intention) through its perceived typicality degree by the moderating role of the designer information is assumed to be dependent on consumer regulatory orientation that plays the role of a second moderator.

The results revealed that our research model fit our data with consumer's perception toward the product's overall quality for both samples (R2DK = .097, FDK (10, 336) = 3.6, p < .00; R2TN = .266, FTN (10, 111) = 4.07, p < .00) and his purchase intention (R2DK = .081, FDK (10, 336) = 2.88, p < .01; R2TN = .190, FTN (10, 111) = 3.2, p < .01) (for more details, see Table 5 in Annex 2).

In order to investigate the moderated moderated mediation validity, we went along Hayes (2018) instructions. Starting with Tunisian sample's perception toward the overall product's quality, with whom we got significant effect of individual's regulatory orientation as a second moderator in the first stage of data analysis, the index of moderated moderated mediation = 1.51 (different form zero) with 95% bootstrapped CI that is entirely above zero [.332; 3.147]. Consequently, we attest that the moderation of the indirect effect by the packaging designer information differs between preventive and promotion oriented consumer. Specifically, among promotion individuals, the indirect effect of packaging typicality on consumers' perception toward the product quality through its perceived typicality changed by .626 (the index of conditional moderated mediation) as the designer information change by 1 unit with CI above zero [.109; 1.39]. Hence, the designer information positively moderate the indirect effect of packaging typicality among promotion focused Tunisian consumers. However, we could not conclude definitely that the designer information moderates the indirect effect of the packaging typicality among preventive consumer, because the rated 95% bootstrapped CI for the related index cross zero [−2.18; .144]. In addition, the indirect effect of packaging typicality differs between preventive and promotion consumer only for a packaging developed by professional designer (Index of conditional moderated mediation = −1.026; CI = [−2.32; −.09]) and not for the co-designed one (CI = [−2.18; .144]) as the related CI include zero. Those results meet the one obtained for Tunisian consumer purchase intention. Indeed, the significance of the index of moderated moderated mediation = 1.33 with positive 95% bootstrapped CI = [.35; 2.95] prove that the moderation effect of packaging designer information on the indirect effect depends on the influence of consumer's regulatory focus that plays the role of a second moderator. In particular, the indirect effect of packaging typicality on promotion oriented consumer's purchase intention through its perceived typicality changed by .553 as the designer information change by 1 unit with CI above zero [.089; 1.27], which was not the case for preventive oriented consumer (CI = [−2.01; .083]). This effect was merely significant for packaging developed by professional design (Index of conditional moderated mediation = −.907; CI = [−2.15; −.094]) and not for the co-designed one (CI = [−.168; 1.24]), the same as overall quality perception. However, the findings revealed insignificance moderated moderated mediation among Danish consumers, which prove that the indirect effect of the packaging typicality on consumers' responses toward the product through the packaging's perceived typicality degree is not affected by the moderator role of packaging designer information neither by consumers' regulatory orientation that plays the role of a second moderator. Consequently, we validate H4b and H4c for Tunisian sample and not for the Danish one.

Taking a closer look to the effect of different level of the packaging's designer information (professional designer vs. co-designed) we focus on the index of conditional moderated mediation indicated. The findings with Tunisian population revealed that only when the packaging is created by a professional designer that its prototypicality significantly influence the overall assessment of the product's quality (Index = −1.026, CI = [−2.32; −.091]) and consumer's purchase intention (Index = −.907, CI = [−2.15; −.094) through the packaging perceived typicality. In contrast to the Danish population where the packaging designer information has no significant effect on consumers' responses. Hence, we disapprove the stated hypothesis H3b and H3c for both samples.

This research findings could be explained by the fact that Tunisian consumer belongs to one of the leaders of olive oil exporters and consumer perceptions and his purchase decision depends on other factors such as the product's price, taste, organoleptic characteristics, the manufacturer, etc. far critical than the packaging typicality and the information about its designer. That is why, the effects of those two last attributes depended on individual's regulatory focus, which is a motivational principle affecting the way of how peoples response their environment. Besides, we defend the fact that packaging typicality perception, which is a subjective evaluation, influence on Tunisian consumer's quality perception and purchase intention with no effect of packaging typicality, which is an objective judgement. Indeed, in order to suffice his annual consumption rate, Tunisian consumer purchase olive oil in bulk (e.g. from the manufacturer) or in a big container and not in a bottle with limited quantity. That is why, Tunisian sample respond according to what he perceive (packaging typicality perception) regardless the reality (actual packaging typicality). In contrast with Danish sample where olive oil purchase intention simply depends on its bottle typicality (perceived and objective typicality). The unfamiliarity toward this product makes Danish sample to base on bottle appearance to decide on olive oil purchase.

5 Managerial Implications

This paper presents a template to e-marketers that attempt to go through crowdsourcing, and specifically, co-design experiences. Indeed, it provides an overview of consumers' response and behavioral intention toward a co-designed packaging, which serves as basis to recognize the worthiness of such participatory activities in the eyes of the consumer. What's more is that this study takes into account consumers' psychological orientation (promotion vs. prevention), which is exceptionally enriching to get the whole picture of what could affect individuals' reactions toward co-created products. Specifically, our findings greatly help Danish e-marketers that reflect on marketing a crowdsourced product in Denmark via virtual channels, in the way that they should take into account Danish consumers' psychological orientation. The absence of such effect on Tunisian consumer would inspires Tunisian e-marketers to plan for and work on the real co-design experience that would fire up consumer's interest and stimulate his attitudes and feelings.

6   Conclusion

This paper sheds the light on consumers' psychological specificities effects in his perception and behavioral response toward different packaging designs with various typicality degrees (typical vs. atypical). We acknowledged that packaging typicality affects consumer typicality perception, which in turn, influence his overall quality perception and behavioral intention. Those findings lined up with previous studies, but the absence of direct effect of packaging typicality on overall quality inference and behavioral intention for Tunisian sample, in contrast to Danish one, proves that in the case of olive oil, there are other factors deeply influence Tunisian consumer's judgement.

This study fuels future researches in digital marketing, co-creation, co-design and consumer psychology streams. Indeed, one of the main purposes of this research is to investigate the effect of crowdsourced product on consumer perception and behavioral response. Applying this to packaging design, we obtained for Tunisian samples significant direct effect of the information that the packaging was crowdsourced or developed by professional design when assessing the products' quality. This effect was greatly significant with the presence of consumer regulatory orientation. This is a further proof that individual regulatory orientation influences information interpretation and a first step in considering consumers' psychology when examining crowdsourcing impacts and values for the consumer. Nevertheless, individual regulatory orientation effects was not validated with Danish sample. This does not exclude the role of consumer psychology in affecting consumers' response, but the product nature and the context of the study are critical factors that shape consumer perception and behavioral intention greater than his prevention or promotion-orientation. Consequently, our findings are limited by the choice of the product, which is one this research weakness. In addition, in some of previous studies (Semin et al. 2005, Shah and Higgins 2001; Van-Dijk and Kluger 2004), consumer's regulatory orientation is experimentally framed, without applying a measurement scale. Such method could be extremely significant in detecting promotion and prevention oriented individuals.

From above, further researches could address those limitations and improve our contributions by examining crowdsourced product and consumer regulatory fit using other product and employing other research methodology. In fact, co-creation in general and co-design in particular are useful and emerging marketing trends, however, the nature of the product under investigation (olive oil) and the difference of product importance among different cultures could to some extent explain the insignificance of the packaging designer information in shaping consumer quality perception and purchase intention toward the product.

Annex 1: Stimulus

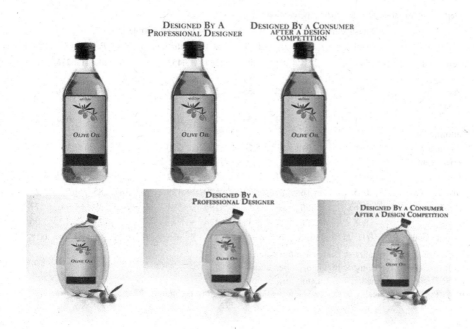

Annex 2: Process Macro's Results

Table 4. Summary of Process Macro results for perceived typicality of Danish and Tunisian samples.

Dependent variable: perceived typicality

	Danish sample					Tunisian sample				
	Coefficient	T	P	LLCI	ULCI	Coefficient	T	P	LLCI	ULCI
Packaging typicality	−1.67	−8.86	**.00**	**−2.04**	**−1.3**	−1.817	−5.96	**.00**	**−2.42**	**−1.21**
Designer information	−.224	−1.21	.22	−.587	.139	−.379	−1.24	.21	−.98	.22
Regulatory orientation	−.217	−1.11	.26	−.600	.165	−.108	−.296	.76	−.828	.613
Int_1	−.328	−.889	.37	−1.055	.398	.454	.757	.45	−.735	1.643
Int_2	−.173	−.443	.65	−.940	.595	−.628	−.877	.38	−2.04	.791
Int_3	−.215	−.550	.58	−.982	.553	.746	1.02	.30	−.696	2.18
Int_4	.031	.039	.96	−1.51	1.57	3.335	2.31	**.02**	**.484**	**6.18**
For all model, R^2 = .229, $F(9, 337)$ = 11.735, p = .00						R^2 = .281, $F(19, 112)$ = 6.517, p = .00				

Int-1: Packaging typicality × designer information
Int-2: Packaging typicality × regulatory orientation
Int-3: Designer information × regulatory orientation
Int-4: Packaging typicality × designer information × regulatory orientation

Table 5. Summary of Process Macro results for overall quality perception of Danish and Tunisian samples.

Dependent variable: Overall quality perception										
	Danish sample					Tunisian sample				
	Coefficient	T	P	LLCI	ULCI	Coefficient	T	P	LLCI	ULCI
Perceived typicality	.149	2.53	**.01**	**.033**	**.264**	.453	4.56	**.00**	**.256**	**.65**
Packaging typicality	.943	4.73	**.00**	**.551**	**1.33**	.549	1.6	.11	−.136	1.23
Designer information	−.201	−1.16	.24	−.540	.138	.615	2.1	**.03**	**.034**	**1.2**
Regulatory orientation	.119	.715	.47	−.209	.448	.520	1.5	.13	−.166	1.2
Int_5	−.081	−.240	.81	−.749	.586	.337	.586	.56	−.803	1.47
Int_6	−.055	−.164	.87	−.710	.600	−.129	−.187	.85	−1.5	1.24
Int_7	−.856	−2.56	**.01**	**−1.51**	**−.198**	−.591	−.860	.39	−1.95	.77
Int_8	−.808	−1.21	.22	−2.11	.498	−1.7	−1.22	.22	−4.47	1.06
For all model, $R^2 = .097$, $F(10, 336) = 3.596$, $p = .00$						$R^2 = .266$, $F(10, 111) = 4.07$, $p = .00$				

Int-5: Packaging typicality × designer information
Int-6: Packaging typicality × regulatory orientation
Int-7: Designer information × regulatory orientation
Int-8: Packaging typicality × designer information × regulatory orientation

Table 6. Summary of Process Macro results for purchase intention of Danish and Tunisian samples.

Dependent variable: purchase intention										
	Danish sample					Tunisian sample				
	Coefficient	T	P	LLCI	ULCI	Coefficient	T	P	LLCI	ULCI
Perceived typicality	.24	4.23	**.00**	**.128**	**.350**	.400	3.8	**.00**	**.191**	**.608**
Packaging typicality	.635	3.21	**.001**	**.247**	**1.02**	.195	.519	.6	−.551	.942
Designer information	−.097	−.55	.58	−.445	.250	.521	1.584	.11	−.131	1.172
Regulatory orientation	.029	.167	.86	−.311	.369	.024	.06	.95	−.76	.812
Int_5	−.01	−.03	.97	−.700	.679	−.850	−1.3	.2	−2.15	.456
Int_6	−.027	.08	.93	−.704	.650	−.041	−.052	.96	−1.61	1.53
Int_7	−.6	−1.74	.08	−1.27	.078	−.421	−.525	.6	−2.01	1.16
Int_8	−.13	−.18	.85	−1.48	1.23	−.477	−.311	.75	−3.52	2.57
For all model, $R^2 = .081$, $F(10, 336) = 2.88$, $p = .002$						$R^2 = .190$, $F(10, 111) = 3.199$, $p = .001$				

Int-5: Packaging typicality × designer information
Int-6: Packaging typicality × regulatory orientation
Int-7: Designer information × regulatory orientation
Int-8: Packaging typicality × designer information × regulatory orientation

References

Avnet, T., Higgins, E.T.: How regulatory fit affects value in consumer choices and opinions. J. Mark. Res. **43**(1), 1–10 (2006)

Baas, M., De Dreu, C.K., Nijstad, B.A.: A meta-analysis of 25 years of mood-creativity research: hedonic tone, activation, or regulatory focus? Psychol. Bull. **134**(6), 779 (2008)

Baas, M., De Dreu, C.K., Nijstad, B.A.: When prevention promotes creativity: the role of mood, regulatory focus, and regulatory closure. J. Pers. Soc. Psychol. **100**(5), 794 (2011)

Becker, L., van Rompay, T.J., Schifferstein, H.N., Galetzka, M.: Tough package, strong taste: the influence of packaging design on taste impressions and product evaluations. Food Qual. Prefer. **22**(1), 17–23 (2011)

Bless, H., Wänke, M.: Can the same information be typical and atypical? How perceived typicality moderates assimilation and contrast in evaluative judgments. Pers. Soc. Psychol. Bull. **26**(3), 306–314 (2000)

Bloch, P.H.: Seeking the ideal form: product design and consumer response. J. Mark. **59**, 16–29 (1995)

Boesen-Mariani, S., Gomez, P., Gavard-Perret, M.L.: Regulatory focus: a promising concept for marketing research. Recherche et Applications en Marketing (English Edition) **25**(1), 87–106 (2010)

Chaffey, D., Ellis-Chadwick, F., Isaac, H., Volle, P., Mercanti-Guérin, M.: Marketing Digital. Pearson, London (2014)

Chaffey, D., Smith, P.R., Smith, P.R.: eMarketing eXcellence: Planning and Optimizing Your Digital Marketing. Routledge, Abingdon (2013)

Crowe, E., Higgins, E.T.: Regulatory focus and strategic inclinations: promotion and prevention in decision-making. Org. Behav. Hum. Decis. Process. **69**(2), 117–132 (1997)

Deliya, M.M.M., Parmar, M.B.J.: Role of packaging on consumer buying behavior–Patan district. Glob. J. Manag. Bus. Res. **12**(10) (2012)

Dennis, C., Merrilees, B., Jayawardhena, C., Tiu Wright, L.: E-consumer behaviour. Eur. J. Mark. **43**(9/10), 1121–1139 (2009)

Franke, N., Schreier, M., Kaiser, U.: The "I designed it myself" effect in mass customization. Manag. Sci. **56**(1), 125–140 (2010)

Friedman, R.S., Förster, J.: The influence of approach and avoidance motor actions on creative cognition. J. Exp. Soc. Psychol. **38**(1), 41–55 (2002)

Friedman, R.S., Förster, J.: The effects of promotion and prevention cues on creativity. J. Pers. Soc. Psychol. **81**(6), 1001 (2001)

Gatautis, R., Vitkauskaite, E.: Crowdsourcing application in marketing activities. Procedia-Soc. Behav. Sci. **110**, 1243–1250 (2014)

Harrison, T., Waite, K.: Impact of co-production on consumer perception of empowerment. Serv. Ind. J. **35**(10), 502–520 (2015)

Hassenzahl, M., Schöbel, M., Trautmann, T.: How motivational orientation influences the evaluation and choice of hedonic and pragmatic interactive products: the role of regulatory focus. Interact. Comput. **20**(4–5), 473–479 (2008)

Haws, K.L., Dholakia, U.M., Bearden, W.O.: An assessment of chronic regulatory focus measures. J. Mark. Res. **47**(5), 967–982 (2010)

Hayes, A.F.: Introduction to Mediation, Moderation, and Conditional Process Analysis: A Regression-Based Approach. Guilford Publications, New York (2013)

Hayes, A.F.: Partial, conditional, and moderated moderated mediation: quantification, inference, and interpretation. Commun. Monogr. **85**(1), 4–40 (2018)

Henderson, J.L.G., Cote, J.A.: Impression management using typeface design. J. Mark. **68**, 60–72 (2004)

Herman, A., Reiter-Palmon, R.: The effect of regulatory focus on idea generation and idea evaluation. Psychol. Aesthet. Creat. Arts **5**(1), 13 (2011)

Higgins, E.T.: Beyond pleasure and pain. Am. Psychol. **52**(12), 1280 (1997)

Higgins, E.T.: Making a good decision: value from fit. Am. Psychol. **55**(11), 1217 (2000)

Kurman, J., Liem, G.A., Ivancovsky, T., Morio, H., Lee, J.: Regulatory focus as an explanatory variable for cross-cultural differences in achievement-related behavior. J. Cross Cult. Psychol. **46**(2), 171–190 (2015)

Labrecque, L.I., vor dem Esche, J., Mathwick, C., Novak, T.P., Hofacker, C.F.: Consumer power: evolution in the digital age. J. Interact. Mark. **27**(4), 257–269 (2013)

Loken, B.: Consumer psychology: categorization, inferences, affect, and persuasion. Annu. Rev. Psychol. **57**, 453–485 (2006)

Loo, R.: A caveat on using single-item versus multiple-item scales. J. Manag. Psychol. **17**(1), 68–75 (2002)

Luo, L., Kannan, P.K., Ratchford, B.T.: Incorporating subjective characteristics in product design and evaluations. J. Mark. Res. **45**(2), 182–194 (2008)

Nishikawa, H., Schreier, M., Fuchs, C., Ogawa, S.: The value of marketing crowdsourced new products as such: evidence from two randomized field experiments. J. Mark. Res. **54**(4), 525–539 (2017)

Ophuis, P.A.O., Van Trijp, H.C.: Perceived quality: a market driven and consumer oriented approach. Food Qual. Prefer. **6**(3), 177–183 (1995)

Pham, M.T., Higgins, E.T.: The state of the art and theoretical propositions. In: Inside Consumption: Consumer Motives, Goals, and Desires, vol. 8 (2005)

Pham, M.T., Avnet, T.: Contingent reliance on the affect heuristic as a function of regulatory focus. Org. Behav. Hum. Decis. Process. **108**(2), 267–278 (2009)

Pula, K., Parks, C.D., Ross, C.F.: Regulatory focus and food choice motives. Prevention orientation associated with mood, convenience, and familiarity. Appetite **78**, 15–22 (2014)

Rettie, R., Brewer, C.: The verbal and visual components of package design. J. Prod. Brand Manag. **9**(1), 56–70 (2000)

Roest, H., Rindfleisch, A.: The influence of quality cues and typicality cues on restaurant purchase intention. J. Retail. Consum. Serv. **17**(1), 10–18 (2010)

Schoormans, J.P., Robben, H.S.: The effect of new package design on product attention, categorization and evaluation. J. Econ. Psychol. **18**(2), 271–287 (1997)

Semin, G.R., Higgins, T., de Montes, L.G., Estourget, Y., Valencia, J.F.: Linguistic signatures of regulatory focus: how abstraction fits promotion more than prevention. J. Pers. Soc. Psychol. **89**(1), 36 (2005)

Silayoi, P., Speece, M.: Packaging and purchase decisions: an exploratory study on the impact of involvement level and time pressure. Br. Food J. **106**(8), 607–628 (2004)

Wang Edward, S.T.: The influence of visual packaging design on perceived food product quality, value, and brand preference. Int. J. Retail Distrib. Manag. **41**(10), 805–816 (2013)

Sweeney, J.C., Soutar, G.N.: Consumer perceived value: the development of a multiple item scale. J. Retail. **77**(2), 203–220 (2001)

Van-Dijk, D., Kluger, A.N.: Feedback sign effect on motivation: is it moderated by regulatory focus? Appl. Psychol. **53**(1), 113–135 (2004)

Veryzer Jr., R.W., Hutchinson, J.W.: The influence of unity and prototypicality on aesthetic responses to new product designs. J. Consum. Res. **24**(4), 374–394 (1998)

Werth, L., Foerster, J.: How regulatory focus influences consumer behavior. Eur. J. Soc. Psychol. **37**(1), 33–51 (2007)

Werle, C.O.C., Boesen-Mariani, S., Gavard-Perret, M.L., Berthaud, S.: Preventing youth obesity: the efficacy of the social risk argument on eating intentions and behaviors. Recherche et Application en Marketing (English Edition) **27**(3), 3–27 (2012)

Westerman, S.J., et al.: The design of consumer packaging: effects of manipulations of shape, orientation, and alignment of graphical forms on consumers' assessments. Food Qual. Prefer. **27**(1), 8–17 (2013)

Zeithaml, V.A.: Consumer perceptions of price, quality and value: a means-end model and synthesis of evidence. J. Mark. **52**, 2–22 (1988)

The Practices of Nonprofit Organizations in the New Age of Social Media: A Qualitative Study of Donors' Receptiveness

Emna Haddar and Meriam Belkhir[(✉)]

Faculty of Economic Sciences and Management of Sfax, University of Sfax,
Sfax, Tunisia
emna.haddar1993@gmail.com, belk.meriam@gmail.com

Abstract. Social media platforms have engendered new avenues for social participation, which enables non-profit organizations and their core stakeholders to build a fruitful relationship. Yet, emerging challenges have hindered them from taking advantages of all features offered by the new media namely with reference to potential donors' receptivity to online charitable presence. Therefore, a critical examination of opportunities and challenges associated with nonprofit and donor' use of these media is needed. Our study examines donors' receptiveness toward online charitable activities. To achieve this aim, we designed a qualitative study using in-depth individual interviews. Our findings reveals the perceived benefits of the integration of social media in nonprofit' work and explore barriers that prevent effective use of these platforms in non-profit practices.

Keywords: Charitable organizations · Facebook · Social media use
Donation behaviors · Online charity

1 Introduction

Social welfare services provided by nonprofit organizations have always been vital to our society [4]. Feeding starving people, advocating for children's education or treating sick and disabled, however could not be achieved without support from donors. Since donors are crucial to the survival of charitable activities, organizations struggle to broaden their donor base and to persuade them to get involved [2]. With the advent of social media, nonprofit managers have gained significant capabilities to effectively do so [14].

Compared to the traditional media, features offered by these platforms allow them to reach a wide audience, spread awareness about its missions and attract stakeholders with significantly low cost [17, 19]. Nevertheless, merely having a social media presence does not guarantee the effectiveness of charitable activities. Charities need to understand the interactive nature of this new media that changed consumer preference and reactions. Consumers are no more the passive recipients of online content; indeed, they become content generators, empowered by technological advances that enable them to be more selective in their choices [26].

© Springer Nature Switzerland AG 2018
M. A. Bach Tobji et al. (Eds.): ICDEc 2018, LNBIP 325, pp. 48–63, 2018.
https://doi.org/10.1007/978-3-319-97749-2_4

Given the potential of social media for improving nonprofit work, scholars have devoted efforts to the study of the organizational use of social media and its impact on stakeholders engagement [15, 16, 18]. Previous studies yielded interesting findings regarding the importance of social media in advancing charitable activities and fostering online civic engagement [25]. Yet, they have not explored public receptivity toward online philanthropic communications. Although, researchers assume implicitly that stakeholders prefer dialogical interaction with nonprofit organizations, a scrutiny of several charities' Facebook pages reveals a lack of public engagement with the digital content available (low number of likes, comment and shares). Questions like what do stakeholders think about online presence of charitable organizations? What do they appreciate about charities social media content? And what are the barriers that prevent them from engaging with organizations remained unanswered.

To fill these gaps in literature, we explores in this paper donors receptiveness to online content provided by charities on their Facebook walls. We seek to highlight benefits and challenges associated with the utilization of social media by charitable organizations from a donors' perspective. Understanding social media users' preferences of some forms of philanthropic online content over other and the barriers that hinder them from participating will help charities managers develop effective online communication strategies, overcome obstacles of users' involvement and persuade potential donors to support the organization.

This paper is structured as follows: We begin with an overview of recent studies on online nonprofit practices. Next, we describe our qualitative methodology before presenting research findings. We end with a discussion of theoretical and practical implications for researchers and nonprofit managers.

2 Literature Review

2.1 Charitable Practices Before the Advent of Social Media

The proper functioning of society depends on institutions able to provide charitable services. Charities attempt to foster social change and to address issues ranging from health to environmental matters. Hence, donors' contributions are essential for funding charitable activities [6, 7]. However, "opening a donor's wallet" remains a challenge not only for nonprofit managers but also for social scientists who have always been interested in understanding helping behaviors and examining factors that affect charitable giving [2, 3, 8]. Extrinsic factors (age/gender/income) and intrinsic ones (individuals' egoistic or altruistic motives) are key determinants of charitable giving [3, 9]. Furthermore, factors that influence individuals' perceptual reactions such like message framing, portrayal of the beneficiary can greatly be effective in stimulating donation [3, 27]. Charities inputs affect also donor decision process. Researchers have demonstrated for example the role of charity brand image, relationship commitment and trust in persuading people to donate [10, 11]. Another challenging factor should be taken into consideration is the role of media. Sargeant [3] states that "donors responses will vary according to the type of media used for solicitation. For example, DRTV[1] or DRPA[2] medium engender a direct response from donors whereas donors solicited through face to face fundraising tend to develop a personal connection with the charity as they are committed to donate a regular gift each month" [3]. Therefore, selecting the appropriate media to recruit donors is a critical step for charitable organizations before creating their communication strategies [12]. Traditionally, managers have been relying on variety of techniques such telemarketing, direct mail, door to door distribution. However, one common problem associated with the implementation of the mentioned methods is that they require considerable human and financial resources in order to generate high donor responses rate. These resources would be helpful in funding immediate needs of victims rather be spent on administration and marketing costs. Such inefficient spending can negatively affect donors perception of charity perfor- mance and hence their intention to donate [28]. With the advent of social media platforms and due to their relatively low cost of operation, nonprofit managers have made attempts to use these platforms to involve stakeholders in their fundraising efforts. Social media have proved to be effective in civic participation and helped nonprofit organizations create a fruitful relationship with potential donors [1, 25]. However, this new media raises many challenges associated not only with the tech- nological aspect of the platforms but also with new sophisticated consumer behaviors. When encountering any type of promotional messages, consumers differ in their receptiveness of the message [39]. Hence the following question: how social media users respond to charitable messages on their Facebook feeds?

Social Media Platforms: Opportunities and Challenges for Charitable Organizations

The impact of social media on people' lives cannot be denied. Checking twitter feeds, sharing personal details with Instagram followers or scrolling Facebook homepage have become a daily practices. Since their growing importance in affecting people attitudes and shaping their preferences, nonprofit organizations have adopted this new means of communications in order to keep in touch with their stakeholders and to reach a new audience. However, the adoption of social media without assessing their real value and knowing potential challenges that may be faced could engender undesirable outcomes.

Social Media Opportunities for Charitable Organizations

Reaching a wide audience from different geographical areas seems to be the major reason for the integration of social media in nonprofit practices [17, 20, 35]. Social media platforms are witnessing a widespread use among consumers as a mean of communication and information exchange. This type of opportunity is very helpful in spreading awareness about a charity' activities which in turn leads to other benefits such public trust and engagement [1]. Otherwise, Information posted on Facebook walls about the organization' daily operations such as links about its history or its next

---

[1] DRTV: Direct Response Television Advertising.

[2] DRPA: Direct Response Press Advertising.

missions or pictures of victims who have been helped may enhance the perceived performance of the organization, foster potential donor trust and thus their willingness to support [1, 15].

The decentralized structure of this media and its ability to connect with stakeholder in a near real time have opened new avenues for dialogic interaction and relationship building [14, 21, 36]. This aspect have gained significant interest from researchers [see 15, 17, 19, 22, 23]. Twitter allow charitable organizations to send and receive public and private messages which may open conversation with followers. Conversations are important since they can create a personal connection with users and hence their commitment to the organization [24]. In a recent study in which tweets of cancers charities were analyzed, it was shown that personalized tweets not only support the psychological needs of patients but also help fostering the interest of followers of the organization [37]. Facebook by its nature affords different types of interaction with an organization' post including: expressing liking for the content, allowing supporters to share the organization' post around their community which may affect their peers' attitude or engaging in a productive conversation by adding comments. This amount of interactivity is vital to develop a meaningful online relationship with stakeholders [19, 23].

Collecting donations is the main objective of nonprofit organizations. However, an effective implementation of charitable fundraising often requires considerable marketing costs that don't match their limited funding. The low cost of social media services has taken away this obstacle. No matter an organization' size or resources, it can create a network of followers and gather them around the cause [1, 16]. Gofundme is an application offered by Facebook used to create campaigns and to collect money online.

Social Media Challenges for Charitable Organizations

A successful integration of social media in nonprofit' activities could not be achieved without addressing several challenges that arise or become more prominent in such online environment. A part of this challenge is inherent to the technological structure of these platforms. Facebook for example use algorithms to choose what content appears on the newsfeed of users. Usually, content rated highly by users (high number of like, shares, comment) are more likely to be selected and pushed to social media users, while content with low numbers of like, shares and comments could not appears on the newsfeed [29, 30]. Charitable organizations therefore need to attract users to their Facebook pages and engage them with the content. Part of this challenge deals also with the behavioral responses from consumers. Social media platforms have altered roles of consumers from passives recipients to editors and creators of information, allowing them to decide what content is most relevant to them and what is not. This kind of consumer empowerment is radically challenging the traditional patterns of communication between nonprofit organizations and donors [26].

With the growing reliance on social media by organizations to promote their activities, users became exposed to a huge number of promotional messages, an oversaturation that lead them to avoid this increasing and undesired clutter [31, 38]. This avoidance depends however on the goal of social media use and users' purpose [38]. In other words, online users are more task-oriented. If the goal of media use is for information acquisition and community learning, a user' engagement with a nonprofit messages will be higher. Yet, this is not the same case with those who look for entertainment in social sites [25]. This type of users will consider a charity message as inappropriate to the medium and interruptive and they are likely to avoid the message.

Concerns about privacy and security could also hinder potential donors from giving [32]. Online charitable giving require giving personal information or asking for credit card detail from those who decide to donate online which may lead them to hesitate to get involved. Indeed, social media platforms allowed nonprofit organization dissemi-nate their promotional messages with relatively low cost and helped some charitable causes went viral and reach a new audience (ex. Ice bucket challenge and Kony 2012), but a viral messages does not necessarily mean a real contributions to the cause. Social media platforms raise new concerns for charities namely "slacktivism". By definition slacktivism is the "willingness to perform a relatively costless, token display of support for a social cause, with an accompanying lack of willingness to devote significant effort to enact meaningful change" [33].

3   Methodology

In this study, we opted for a qualitative research due to the exploratory character of the study and the sensitivity of charitable giving topic which is susceptible to social desirability problems [13]. Therefore, 20 in-depth interviews were conducted with potential donors who have a social media presence. These qualitative procedures enable us to explore donors' receptiveness to online content provided by charities in social media sites.

The in-depth interviews were conducted in Tunisia. Statics[3] indicates that more than a half of the Tunisian population use social networking sites with Facebook as the most popular (68.34%) followed by Twitter (2.33%), and Instagram (0.28%). There-fore, we choose Facebook as the well suited platform for our research context. Par-ticipants were recruited conveniently through Facebook and through personal contact and the ages ranged from 20 to 40 years. In choosing the participants, two criteria were followed. Facebook participants were selected according to their engagement with charitable online content. Participants who expressed their engagement with nonprofit organizations on Facebook (Liking or sharing or commenting charities updates on Facebook) were invited through private messages to participate in our study. Those participants are likely to be potential donors in the future because these online practices of support can lead to more meaningful forms of support as noted by Kristofferson et al. [33]. Whereas participants recruited through personal contact were selected according to their educational level and their household income. Participants with high level education and relatively high household income were called to participate in the interviews as they are more likely to donate [5] (see Table 1 for sample characteristics). The data collection was performed along three months from November 2017 to January 2018.

---

[3] http://gs.statcounter.com/social-media-stats/all/tunisia accessed on March, 2018.

Table 1. Sample characteristics

Characteristics	Frequency
Age	
20–25	4
26–30	10
31–35	4
36–40	2
Sex	
Male	7
Female	13
Education	
Less than college	3
College	6
University	11
Occupation	
Non workers	2
Students	5
Full time workers	13
Internet experience	
Less than 3 year	8
More than 3 year	12
Social activities	
Active members	13
Non active members	7

The interviews were based on a predefined interview guide and participants were asked through open-ended questions (see appendix for details about the interview guide). Interviews ranged in length from 25 mn to 75 mn with an average time of 28 mn. All interviews were conducted face to face and taped recorded before being transcribed. All the transcripts were analyzed by authors. Themes were generated through the use of open, axial and selective coding [41] and then verified by an expert to ensure their reliability.

4   Findings

4.1   Charities' Social Media Use and Donors Receptiveness

Results indicated that social media platforms have become embedded in daily practices. This daily life invasion led participants to cite Facebook as one of the main information sources that helps them identify people who may need help or support. They expressed being receptive to posts from charities used to collect all kind of material and non-material support. Receptiveness to social media charity posts reflects consumers' predisposition to accept, and/or to interact with a charity appeal present on these online platforms. This receptiveness is expressed through participants' discourses for whom it becomes more than evident to receive such information on Facebook. For instance, one of the participants stated: "If there wasn't Facebook, how would I know about needy people? How could I know that charities need my support? I'm not very active in real life but I'm always connected online."

On the other hand, some participants even value the integration of social media platforms in charitable work as a good way to provide permanent information about charity appeal. An interviewee said: "It's really better to see donation appeals on the newsfeed, if I couldn't give this time, I will support you next time or someone else will see it and then he support you immediately."

For other participants, having a social media presence is a necessary condition for charitable organizations to assess credibility and effectiveness of their operations as stated in the following quote "I assess the eligibility of the organization according to their status updates on Facebook ... If a charitable organization do not have a social media accounts and do not post who guarantee its performance."

Throughout all the interviews, participants manifested their receptiveness to charity appeal on social media. However, the intensity of such receptiveness may be increased or decreased depending on the opportunities or challenges that may be perceived by the consumers.

4.2   Perceived Pros Associated with Charities Social Media Use

Our current findings highlight several benefits perceived by potential donors when it comes to social media use in nonprofit practices. These benefits are related to the capacity of social media to reach new and widespread audience, to facilitate communication, and to ensure visibility continuity (Table 2).

Enhanced Reaching Capacity

The use of social media by charities allowed them to ostensibly increase their capacity to reach new audience as well as widespread ones.

- **New audience reach:** Participants highlighted that the proliferation of social media use especially younger users constitute one of the main benefits of online charities' appeal. They said that younger generations are the most exposed to online charitable messages given they are always connected to social networking sites and they no longer spend enough time to read, view or listen to traditional media. This is noted by a participant who said: *"As a young person, I'm always connected online. I check Facebook newsfeeds more than watching TV or listening to the radio, so when I encounter a charitable event on Facebook probably I will be interested but if charities are not addressing me through Facebook I will not even heard about its activities"*. Additionally, some interviewees pointed out the value of targeting younger people through Facebook in order to drive campaign success. This new audience is very helpful because young people can stimulate new forms of helping that are crucial to organization's survival such as spending time, effort, and spreading information as evidenced in the following verbatim: *"sometimes I can't give money but I can volunteer or at least I can help them by spreading the message among my online community."*

- **Widespread audience.** The capacity of social media to spread content to a variety of audiences that goes beyond the traditional domain of the charitable organization was acknowledged by the majority of participants. They emphasized the fact that online content can be accessed by all social media users and can bring supporters from broader communities. A participant said: *"Facebook provide charities with the ability to attract users not only from their surrounding context but also from other different regions or even other countries and the message that traditionally reaches only a limited number of donors could reach a thousand of social media users."*

Improved and Facilitated Communication

The role of social media in facilitating charities' communication was the frequently cited by potential donors. Two aspects were indicated: ease of access to charity contact information and the ease of engaging interaction with the organization as well as other interested stockholders.

- **Contact information access.** When deciding to give to charity, donors often ask for additional information from the organization, therefore they may look for contact information such address, telephone numbers or bank account numbers. Participants said that this kind of information became more accessible on Facebook compared to traditional media. This is demonstrated through the following statement: *"If I decide to give money to the organization and I still need for some information, telephone numbers or the organization' locations are always available in their Facebook pages."*
- **Possibilities to engage interaction with charity association and other stake-holders.** In social media environment, a successful relationship building is essential step for donors before giving any type of help, therefore they prefer engage in a conversation with the organization and Facebook give them the tool to effectively do so. Facebook facilities open dialogue without devoting too much effort. Participants indicated the ease of the task through features like private messages or comments. For instance, an interviewee said: *"you don't even need to call them on telephone number or devote physical efforts simply you can send them a private message or write a comment and they will answer you."*

Continued Visibility and the Role of Facebook Features

Some of social media features, and especially Facebook, have interesting features that contribute to increased content visibility (charities appeal) and mainly to the continuity of their appearance. According to participants, these features allow them to be updated and to nurture their interest.

- **Facebook updates.** Facebook allows charitable organizations to attract users with permanent updates about daily activities, next events, and achievements. Unlimited content is available for users to assess the effectiveness of the organization. Interviewees expressed their preferences for seeing such status updates as they can evaluate the transparency and the accountability of the organization, which may help them deciding whether to engage or not in a given charity campaign. A participant said: *"when I see photos of sufferer people on my Facebook newsfeed, I sympathize and I want to help ... When I see charities updates about their missions and their achieved goals, It gives me positive vibes, it ensures the transparency of the organization and thus enhance my willingness to give next time."*

- **Reminder features.** Facebook also provides donors with specific features that enable them to be attracted to a charitable content. Participants said that one of the advantages that social media has over the traditional media, is their ability to keep them involved with charities and to remind them whenever there is new information as evidenced in this statement: *"when someone write a comment or when the schedule of the event is getting closer Facebook, reminds me. And it's helpful."*
- **WOM effect and peer pressure.** Before making decisions either for donating or volunteering, donors used to rely on alternative medium such as friend recommendations or word of mouth. In social media environment, these became more obvious. When asked, participants claimed that seeing their friends involved with online charitable acts or reading positive comments on charity Facebook pages affect positively their willingness to help. One of the interviewee expressed this idea by saying: *"Sometimes, I hesitate to contribute but when I notice that many people are interested or especially when my friends are interested in the charitable event and write a positive comment to the organization, it encourage me to get involved and contribute too."*

4.3 Perceived Cons Associated with Social Media Use by Charities

Participants discussed problems associated with social media deployment by nonprofit organizations and different barriers that hinder them from engaging with online charitable content. These barriers relate to distrust, unethical disclosure of private lives, media clutter problem, and inadequate communication actions (Table 2).

Distrust Risk

This aspect seems to be the main problem that prevents users from participation in online charity supporting activities. Trust has always played a role in donation decision process while its lack seems to affect negatively donor intention. After the advent of social media platforms, distrust became even more prominent as a consequence of many factors including:

- **Rapid increase in the number of organizations.** Participants are skeptical about claims made in online donation request. Some participants indicated that they do not trust these charities especially if they don't know any of the members or it are not a well-known organization. An interviewee said: *"in Facebook there is a lot of nonprofit organizations among them a fake ones that try to collect money for their personal purposes or even for unethical reasons, who guarantee that this charity is not a one of them?"*
- **Fake reviews or negative WOM**[4] is another factor that affects people distrust. As we noted above, social media users rely on electronic word of mouth to dampen the riskiness of their decision. Interviewees stated that encountering negative WOM about the organization can prevent them from giving. This is demonstrated in the following quote *"I don't trust this appeal especially when I see negative comments, I know it could be just fake and bad people that try to disrupt the charity' work ... anyway I hesitate to give my money."*

---

[4] WOM: word of mouth.

(a) **Disclosure of sufferers lives and conspicuous donations**

Another charitable act commonly unappreciated by potential donors is the disclosure of sufferers' lives. Disclosing personal information about the recipients of the aid or showing their pictures can affect negatively people willingness to donate. This practice was rejected by the majority of participants. For example, one of them stated *"I hate when charities publish photos of people who need help ... even though is helpful in assessing organization performance but they could put it otherwise like showing the aide not the persons."*

Media Clutter

Due the low cost of social media, many organizations are present online. Each organization posts a variety of content trying to spread information about its needs. However, having a plenty of donation request in the newsfeed could turn off potential donors. This is demonstrated through participant statement who said: *"seeing too much donation appeal on my newsfeed...perturbs me, I'm not able to decide who deserve my donation so I decide simply not to give."*

Inadequate and Ineffective Communication Actions

One of the main purposes of social media consumption is to facilitate communication among consumers. The new media give them the capacity to interact easily. Therefore, nonprofit organizations need to use the fullest capacities offered by social media devices to guarantee their effectiveness. However, when leveraged ineffectively, they can lead to undesirable outcomes. Inadequate communication actions like unclear or uncompleted information or lack of interactivity could constitute another set of barriers that hinder users from engaging with charitable organizations online.

- **Unclear or uncompleted information.** As we mentioned earlier, potential donors are in need for detailed information that encourage them to contribute, therefore a lack of it may lead to undesirable responses as stated by a participant: *"when I decide to give money but I didn't found neither clear information about the charity' needs, nor telephone numbers to call them to ask questions, nor the organization' address how am I supposed to give them my money."*
- **Lack of interactivity.** Social networking sites were developed to open discussion between organizations and their stakeholders where they interact in a two way communication. The absence of interactivity can be an obstacle to a fruitful engagement. Participants indicated that when their questions are neglected they tend to develop a negative image about the whole organization as evidenced in the following quote *"personally I don't like it when I write a comment asking for any kind of information and they do not reply me... It's a lack of responsibility".*

Table 2. Perceived opportunities and challenges associated with charities' social media use

Pros associated with charities' social media use	Cons associated with charities' social media use

1. *Reaching audience*
   1.1 Reaching a wide audience
   1.2 Reaching a new audience and new forms of support
 2. *Facilitating communication*
   2.1 Contact information access
   2.2 Enhancing interactivity
 3. *Benefiting from Facebook features*
   3.1 Updates features and discloser
   3.2 Reminder features
   3.3 Peer to peer effect and positive WOM
	1. *Distrust*
	   1.1 Unknown charities
	   1.2 A huge number of organizations
	   1.3 Fake accounts, reviews, negative WOM
	 2. *Disclosure*
	   2.1 Disclosure of sufferers' lives
	   2.2 Disclosure of charitable donation or conspicuous donation behavior
	 3. *Social media clutter*
	 4. *Inadequate communication actions*
	   4.1 Unclear and incomplete information
	   4.2 Lack of interactivity

5　Discussion and Conclusion

Addressing increasing social issues with decreasing funding from both donors and government leaves charities with no choice but adopting social media platforms in their practices. Although scholars have shown interest in assessing the value of social media in charitable work, they neglected donors' receptiveness to this online practice. To see what opportunities and challenges these new media can bring to nonprofit organizations, we have explored donors' perspectives on social media use by nonprofit organizations. This study indicates the crucial role played by social media in enhancing nonprofit performance. We attempted to address the relatively under-researched concept of donor's receptivity. In this research, we focus on the extent to which donors are receptive to nonprofit appeals on social media. As the literature offers little guidance, we therefore conceptualized donor's receptiveness as individual's predisposition to respond favorably and their willingness to accept charitable messages on social media sites. Charities' social media presence is not only accepted but highly valued by donors. Users in this research highlighted how important are social media in charitable campaigns and how it enables them learning more about altruistic causes and engaging with their community. This is consistent with the work by Gil de Zúñiga [25] who reported that social media platforms are used as an informational tool by individuals seeking for civic engagement.

In terms of opportunities and challenges: Spreading awareness about charitable causes, needs and missions seems to be a key factor that determine the performance of the organization and social media make it more effective. Facebook philanthropic events, informational posts about social causes, photographs of mission accomplished posted on Facebook pages help promoting charitable contributions. Users express their willingness to support charities after encountering such content on their newsfeed even though they are not very involved in charitable acts. In line with previous studies, participants are looking for more transparency from organizations. Nonprofit managers can adopt disclosure strategies like updates about their daily activities, pictures of charitable assistance, detailed information about intervention which is helpful in building trust and stimulating charitable giving. Increasing details about the output of the charitable organization help foster confidence in organization's ability to fulfill its promises. Charities updates on Facebook should include tangible information about the aid and pictures of accomplished missions. However, managers should be aware that too much disclosure may lead to undesirable responses from donors. Photographs of disabled, private information about sufferer people or photos of kids who have been helped is considered as violation of privacy or a kind of conspicuous donation behavior which may affect negatively people views about the organization' ethics. Therefore, managers should avoid pictures of recipients of the aid; instead photographs of the material assistance are more beneficial. Managers need to choose carefully their communication tactics and create messages that enhance positive image of organization.

Social media also enable nonprofit organizations to reach a large market of potential donors and to target especially younger generation. The usage of social media platforms has become stapled in daily life with a hundred millions of people log onto Facebook as of this writing, 50% among them aged 18–24 years who check their newsfeed every morning. Through online content, charities can expand their limited donors' base to include a widespread network of people from different categories of age, social class and regional groups. Youth are the most exposed to online donation appeal, even though their limited financial resources, they can afford other types of help like volunteering, providing foodstuff clothes or even share the content within their online community. Charitable organizations shouldn't miss out this opportunity and try to tailor their donation request according to their target. When creating their donation requests, nonprofit managers need to take into consideration the characteristics of their target. Although some social media users are interested in charitable activities, imposing a specific kind of help can hinder people from supporting the organization. Managers should note that charitable appeals that target a different audience and suggest a several categories of help are accepted more favorably by social media users.

Dynamic communication is a key step in organization's growth, charities need to the greater capacities offered by social media to facilitate conversation. Donors are looking for interactive dialogue with organizations in order to get more informed about the organization, and to build a fruitful relationship to ensure the safety of their donations. Facebook allow them to access to contact information such telephone numbers, organization' location and charity members accounts. Complete information with detailed description about current activities helps users educate more about the organization and its members, contrary to incomplete information that may prevents potential donors from getting involved. Managers need to make available on their Facebook pages an adequate profile with clear information. Photographs of the charity' members, the logo of the organization, telephone and contact numbers and different addresses such locations on Google maps, bank and RIP accounts should be included in Facebook profile of the organization. Furthermore, interactive features offered by Facebook (likes, comments, sending private messages or sharing content) have opened new possibilities for donors' to express their support. Social media facilitated direct communication between donors and organizations without devoting much time and effort. However, charities need to realize that neglecting private messages or not replying to comments could signal a lack of interactivity and seriousness from the charity part, which in turn leads to negative perceptions from users. Nonprofit managers should lend attention to their Facebook pages; they need to respond to users questions in a near real time. In addition, they should note that personalized responses are valuable by users. It would be beneficial for charitable organizations to nominate a responsible to oversee their social networking sites.

Compared to traditional media that restrict organizations to a limited time and content, social media allow nonprofit organizations to daily updates online content. This is even enhanced by reminder features provided on Facebook (notifications and Facebook calendar) that keep donors in touch with new information. Yet, managers should be aware that excessive online content tend to be avoided by users [26]. Charitable managers should take care of another aspect that may encourage or prevent donors from giving, namely e-WOM. Electronic word of mouth (e-WOM) is considered as reliable information, therefore friend recommendation and positive e-WOM encourage users to engage with charities which is not the same case with negative e-WOM about the organization or one of their members that may prevent potential donors from making charitable contributions. Nonprofit organizations need to encourage their supporters to share content with their online community and to involve friends with charitable activities. Managers also should be attentive to negative reviews from social media users and try to address these problems with effective responses and clarifications.

While social media platforms became the shapers of the nonprofit landscape, strategic use of these platforms for attracting donors remained unclear. The main focus of previous studies has been on understanding why and how nonprofit organizations are using the features provided to engage stakeholders [34]. However, Saxton and Waters [40] argued that researchers neglected to examine donors' preferences and responses to online content. In this study, we attempted to address this gap by exploring donors' receptiveness to nonprofit practices in social media sites. In this research, we have provided insights into how social media users perceive charities' communication strategies. Therefore, nonprofit managers would be able to identify whether their target audience are receptive to their messages and whether they meet or falling below their expectations and thereby tailor their communications to better appeal to those consumers. This study shed light on opportunities that Facebook would offer for both charitable organizations and their stakeholders. Managers shouldn't miss out these opportunities and should try to exploit the fullest benefits of the new media. Our findings also help us understand different barriers that may prevent potential donors from getting involved in charitable online practices. Nonprofit organizations need to take into consideration these problems when implementing their communications strategies to guarantee the success of their charitable campaigns.

6   Limitations and Future Research

While our study reveals interesting findings with regard to the benefits and problems associated with charitable organizations' use of social media platforms, we acknowledge the study's limitations. Since this is an exploratory study at preliminary stage, the size of our sample as well as its variety is limited. Indeed, the majority of participants were young active members which are more familiar with nonprofit organizations and volunteering activities so our findings ought to be regarded as tentative. Therefore, additional studies are needed to examine older participants' receptiveness and other socio professional categories. Future research can also investigate type of charitable content that may attract social media users and may generate favorable responses from donors. They can also examine factors that may enhance donors' trust on social media platforms.

Appendix

Interview guide

Introductory phase

1-What do you think about "People solidarity" nowadays?

2-According to you what are the different forms of helping people?

3-How do you know about "people who need help", at any level?

Centering phase

1-Do you ever heard about or do you knows some pages/ accounts aimed at charity donation?

-If yes, can you describe some of them (What do they ask for? How do they ask for donations?

-If no, participants were given 10 min to see examples of charitable Facebook pages

Depth phase

1-As a potential donor what are the opportunities offered by social media to engage you in civic participation?

2-According to you, what kind of benefits can we expect from using social media for charity donations? Can you give me some examples? How it is different form a classic way (any other way of donation)?

3- As you have told me above there is several challenges for the proliferation of social media, what do you think about challenges or problems that faces you when encounter a nonprofit post on social media? Something that you don't appreciate about social media? What are the barriers of your civic engagement after reading a post of a charitable organization?

4- Can you give a concrete example

Conclusion phase

-Do you have anything else to add

-Thank you for your collaboration

References

1. Lovejoy, K., Saxton, G.D.: Information, community, and action: how nonprofit organizations use social media. J. Comput.-Mediat. Commun. **17**(3), 337–353 (2012)
2. Bendapudi, N., Singh, S.N., Bendapudi, V.: Enhancing helping behavior: an integrative framework for promotion planning. J. Mark. **60**, 33–49 (1996)
3. Sargeant, A.: Charitable giving: towards a model of donor behaviour. J. Mark. Manag. **15**(4), 215–238 (1999)
4. Anheier, H.K.: Nonprofit Organizations: An Introduction. Routledge, Abingdon (2006)
5. Schlegelmilch, B.B., Diamantopoulos, A., Love, A.: Characteristics affecting charitable donations: empirical evidence from Britain. J. Mark. Pract.: Appl. Mark. Sci. **3**(1), 14–28 (1997)
6. Shanahan, K.J., Hopkins, C.D., Carlson, L., Raymond, M.A.: Depictions of self-inflicted versus blameless victims for nonprofits employing print advertisements. J. Advert. **41**(3), 55–74 (2012)
7. Chang, C.: Guilt regulation: the relative effects of altruistic versus egoistic appeals for charity advertising. J. Advert. **43**(3), 211–227 (2014)
8. De Bruyn, A., Prokopec, S.: Opening a donor's wallet: the influence of appeal scales on likelihood and magnitude of donation. J. Consum. Psychol. **23**(4), 496–502 (2013)
9. Batson, C.D.: Prosocial motivation: is it ever truly altruistic? In: Advances in Experimental Social Psychology, vol. 20, pp. 65–122. Academic Press (1987)
10. Michel, G., Rieunier, S.: Nonprofit brand image and typicality influences on charitable giving. J. Bus. Res. **65**(5), 701–707 (2012)
11. Sargeant, A., Lee, S.: Trust and relationship commitment in the United Kingdom voluntary sector: determinants of donor behavior. Psychol. Mark. **21**(8), 613–635 (2004)
12. Sargeant, A., Ewing, M.: Fundraising direct: a communications planning guide for charity marketing. J. Nonprofit Public Sect. Mark. **9**(1–2), 185–204 (2001)
13. Lee, Z., Sargeant, A.: Dealing with social desirability bias: an application to charitable giving. Eur. J. Mark. **45**(5), 703–719 (2011)
14. Guo, C., Saxton, G.D.: Tweeting social change: how social media are changing nonprofit advocacy. Nonprofit Volunt. Sect. Q. **43**(1), 57–79 (2014)
15. Waters, R.D., Burnett, E., Lamm, A., Lucas, J.: Engaging stakeholders through social networking: how nonprofit organizations are using Facebook. Public Relat. Rev. **35**(2), 102–106 (2009)
16. Nah, S., Saxton, G.D.: Modeling the adoption and use of social media by nonprofit organizations. New Media Soc. **15**(2), 294–313 (2013)
17. Ingenhoff, D., Koelling, A.M.: The potential of web sites as a relationship building tool for charitable fundraising NPOs. Public Relat. Rev. **35**(1), 66–73 (2009)
18. Campbell, D.A., Lambright, K.T., Wells, C.J.: Looking for friends, fans, and followers? Social media use in public and nonprofit human services. Public Adm. Rev. **74**(5), 655–663 (2014)
19. Phethean, C., Tiropanis, T., Harris, L.: Engaging with charities on social media: comparing interaction on Facebook and Twitter. In: Tiropanis, T., Vakali, A., Sartori, L., Burnap, P. (eds.) INSCI 2015. LNCS, vol. 9089, pp. 15–29. Springer, Cham (2015). https://doi.org/10.1007/978-3-319-18609-2_2
20. Greenberg, J., MacAulay, M.: NPO 2.0? Exploring the web presence of environmental nonprofit organizations in Canada. Glob. Media J. **2**(1), 63 (2009)
21. Waters, R.D., Jamal, J.Y.: Tweet, tweet, tweet: a content analysis of nonprofit organizations' Twitter updates. Public Relat. Rev. **37**(3), 321–324 (2011)

22. Briones, R.L., Kuch, B., Liu, B.F., Jin, Y.: Keeping up with the digital age: how the American Red Cross uses social media to build relationships. Public Relat. Rev. **37**(1), 37–43 (2011)
23. Cho, M., Schweickart, T., Haase, A.: Public engagement with nonprofit organizations on Facebook. Public Relat. Rev. **40**(3), 565–567 (2014)
24. Lovejoy, K., Waters, R.D., Saxton, G.D.: Engaging stakeholders through Twitter: how nonprofit organizations are getting more out of 140 characters or less. Public Relat. Rev. **38**(2), 313–318 (2012)
25. Gil de Zúñiga, H., Jung, N., Valenzuela, S.: Social media use for news and individuals' social capital, civic engagement and political participation. J. Comput.-Mediat. Commun. **17**(3), 319–336 (2012)
26. Kelly, L., Kerr, G., Drennan, J.: Avoidance of advertising in social networking sites: the teenage perspective. J. Interact. Advert. **10**(2), 16–27 (2010)
27. Smith, G.E., Berger, P.D.: The impact of direct marketing appeals on charitable marketing effectiveness. J. Acad. Mark. Sci. **24**(3), 219–231 (1996)
28. Bennett, R., Savani, S.: Predicting the accuracy of public perceptions of charity performance. J. Target. Meas. Anal. Mark. **11**(4), 326–342 (2003)
29. Schlüschen, A.: Celebrity endorsement in social media. In: Encyclopedia of E-Commerce Development, Implementation, and Management, pp. 1940–1956. IGI Global (2016)
30. Ellison, N.B., Vitak, J., Gray, R., Lampe, C.: Cultivating social resources on social network sites: Facebook relationship maintenance behaviors and their role in social capital processes. J. Comput.-Mediat. Commun. **19**(4), 855–870 (2014)
31. Ha, L., McCann, K.: An integrated model of advertising clutter in offline and online media. Int. J. Advert. **27**(4), 569–592 (2008)
32. Rodriguez, J.E.: Social media use in higher education: key areas to consider for educators (2011)
33. Kristofferson, K., White, K., Peloza, J.: The nature of slacktivism: how the social observability of an initial act of token support affects subsequent prosocial action. J. Consum. Res. **40**(6), 1149–1166 (2013)
34. Young, J.A.: Facebook, Twitter, and blogs: the adoption and utilization of social media in nonprofit human service organizations. Hum. Serv. Organ. Manag. Leadersh. Gov. **41**(1), 44–57 (2017)
35. Wukich, C., Khemka, A.: Social media adoption, message content, and reach: an examination of Red Cross and Red Crescent national societies. Int. J. Emerg. Manag. **13**(2), 89–116 (2017)
36. Bellucci, M., Manetti, G.: Facebook as a tool for supporting dialogic accounting? Evidence from large philanthropic foundations in the United States. Account. Audit. Account. J. **30**(4), 874–905 (2017)
37. Ure, C., Galpin, A., Cooper-Ryan, A.M., Condie, J.: Charities' use of Twitter: exploring social support for women living with and beyond breast cancer. Inf. Commun. Soc. 1–18 (2017). https://doi.org/10.1080/1369118X.2017.1402943
38. Ha, L.: Digital advertising clutter in an age of mobile media. In: Digital Advertising: Theory and Research, pp. 69–85. Routledge, New York (2017)
39. Bailey, A.A., Mishra, A., Tiamiyu, M.F.: Green advertising receptivity: an initial scale development process. J. Mark. Commun. **22**(3), 327–345 (2016)
40. Saxton, G.D., Waters, R.D.: What do stakeholders like on Facebook? Examining public reactions to nonprofit organizations' informational, promotional, and community-building messages. J. Public Relat. Res. **26**(3), 280–299 (2014)
41. Strauss, A., Corbin, J.M.: Basics of Qualitative Research: Grounded Theory Procedures and Techniques. Sage Publications Inc., Thousand Oaks (1990)

E-Banking and Competitive Intelligence

The Likelihood of Financial Inclusion in e-Banking: A BiProbit Sample-Selection Modeling Approach

Thabo Julian Gopane[(✉)]

University of Johannesburg, Johannesburg, South Africa
tjgopane@uj.ac.za

Abstract. There is a plethora of studies on financial exclusion of the poor, mostly in developing countries. A related but unanswered question is, whether the likelihood of e-banking inclusion and its determinants are similar for the banked and the unbanked. The distinction is important for both the corporate sector and policy makers to answer the question of whether the drivers of e-banking adoption are limited to technological progress. The objective of this paper is to model the likelihood of the banked in a traditional fiat money system (f-banking) to be e-banking included. The Bivariate Probit Sample Selection model is applied with a recent data set from the Kenya Financial Access Household Survey 2015. The results show that there is ninety two percent likelihood of the f-banked to be e-banked. By contrast, the results also show that the absolute financially excluded have seventy six percent probability of being e-banking included. Economic intuition supported by empirical analysis reveals that for an average financially excluded person, it is as a result of persevering over past hardship to be finally e-banking included. The results raise a call to policy makers that the easiness of the f-banked to enter the e-banking market may soon result in e-banking cost sky-rocketing to the detriment of the absolute financially excluded, who have so laboriously tested the e-banking market in the presence of uninsured and unhedged eminent risk.

Keywords: Financial inclusion · Financial exclusion · e-banking
f-banking · Sample selection · BiProbit

1 Introduction

The economic value of financial inclusion is compelling, and evident in the related literature reviewed by [1], as well as recent empirical studies such as [2]. A reliable and effective financial system is an important link in the economy to facilitate needed payment, savings, risk, and credit management services, to enable a value-chain of investment in productive activities such as entrepreneurship, taking advantage of emerging growth opportunities, and livelihood improvement, among others. If the above intuition makes sense, then the problem of financial inclusion has a connotation that the financial system is incomplete or manifests some flaws that call for viable corrective action. Further the benefits of financial inclusion in e-banking are persuasive and highlighted by others including, [3–5], but not without sceptics like, [6, p. 222].

© Springer Nature Switzerland AG 2018
M. A. Bach Tobji et al. (Eds.): ICDEc 2018, LNBIP 325, pp. 67–78, 2018.
https://doi.org/10.1007/978-3-319-97749-2_5

These authors protest that things like "...m-money systems in developing countries are not technically banking from either a financial or legal perspective: they do not provide interest on savings or facilitate access to credit from formal financial institutions, nor do they insure the value stored in the mobile account...". We are unconvinced of this rigid position in that, while this opinion may be persuasive as at 2012 it appears to be at risk of obsoleteness in time.

Kenya's mobile good story continues, with network connection standing at 6.3 million (for its market) an increase of approximately 8 million in a space of 12 months. With a population of about 47 million this translates to what the practitioners of mobile industry call SIM penetration. The purpose of this paper is to evaluate the likelihood of the adoption of e-banking by the banked, and then contrast this with the usual traditional absolute banking exclusions. For purpose of simplicity I will call the traditional brick and mortar banking that deals with fiat money f-banking (or f-money). In this sense when f-banking advances into e-money a scenario arises in which we can ask how many banks have adopted e-money, and how many have not. This intuition says we are dealing with the usual financial inclusion and exclusion question. Meaning, we ask the question: what is the likelihood of f-banking to be included into e-banking? Based on this explanation, the study will proceed, from now onwards, at par with prior advances in financial exclusion studies.

Methodologically I use an uncommon application (for financial inclusions studies) of Heckman's family of self-selection, the Bivariate Probit model. Prior academic researchers [2] and practitioners in the financial sector [7] have made all the necessary ground work on the fundamental questions. First, what has let to this sudden wave of active research in financial inclusion? Secondly how to measure, and therefore interpret financial inclusion in a more systematic way in intra- and international surveys? Regarding the first question, [8, p. 475] does well to summarize the salient points. After synthesizing the relevant debate the author signals the direction of current research, that: the financial sector development benefits the *don't-haves*, for the "...evidence suggests that 60% of the impact on the poorest 20% operates through aggregate growth while 40% operates through reducing inequality", to which they conclude: "The impact of this evidence has been to recently shift donor policy emphasis from a focus on providing financial services to the poor – in particular via microfinance to *the need* to provide 'Finance for All'". So the moral of the story is that, if financial sector development benefits the downtrodden, then it makes sense to prioritize studies for policy application of "financial inclusion" in the sector.

We now turn to what has become a standard on the proposed definition of financial inclusion namely, the use of financial services, as opposed to simply access to affiliation or membership of a financial product or institution [1, 2, 8]. The same definition is used in this paper. Related prior studies have made significant progress and their sentiment boils down to, among others, that yes the poor rural citizens are financially excluded, that this exclusion (or bad) is not necessarily different from other economic market failures, and most enlightening, mobile technology such as that of Kenyan M-Pesa has potential to make the needed positive impact [5, 9]. Observation regarding past studies is that mostly these papers tend to focus separately on the unbanked, and sometimes on the banked, and rarely a study combines both the bank and unbanked in the same paper, and within the same model. This is the gap addressed by the current paper. In so doing, this paper awakens the seldom considered econometric problem of self-selection. This problem is addressed in details under econometric modeling section. The remaining part of this paper continues as follows: Sect. 2 explains the rationales of e-money market and M-Pesa, Sect. 3 outlines the econometric model, Sect. 4 introduces the data set used in this paper, Sect. 5 gives a report of empirical results, Sect. 6 is discussion of empirical results, and Sect. 7 concludes the study.

2 The e-Money Market and the Kenyan M-Pesa

This paper is motivated by the growth and good work done by M-Pesa, among others, to integrate the poor unbanked into the financial sector. Nevertheless the question does arise, which is the subject of this paper that since electronic money has proved to be a good convenience to the poor, does it now mean the banked are now becoming excluded to the adoption of this fast-growing technology? By way of clarification, electronic money (or e-money) is also known by other names like, electronic currency (e-currency), e-cash, or digital currency, or mobile money (m-money), or mobile banking (m-banking). These phrases will be used interchangeably but contextually in this paper. The e-money alternative is different to fiat money (bank notes and coins). In the latter, money is physical, but both f-money and e-money are relatively similar in transactional motive or usage. The e-money usages include rapid and borderless transfer of value through pin-protected sms's, and store of value, where a balance is allowed to remain in an electronic device like cell phone, such as under the M-Pesa design.

The next question to answer is what makes e-money (as exemplified by M-Pesa) work. M-Pesa is known to be a first mover in mobile-money market. In the Kenyan language, the letter "M" stands for mobile, and the word, Pesa means money in Swahili language. So in English M-Pesa says m-money. We now turn to the question of what makes a product like M-Pesa work for the poor. Market failures have contributed to the state of financial exclusion. The rationales of adopting e-money alternative are well-known by practitioners and researchers in this field like, [6]. In particular, e-money is seen as a solution to the hardships of: limitation in ATM's and branch distributions in non-urban areas, cost of cash transfer particularly for remittances, application-qualifying barriers for bank accounts, as well as the cost of maintaining a bank account, among others. In the worst case scenarios, the unbanked and the rural poor of Africa seem to have a banking facility substitution of last resort, namely: To send cash by long distance taxi driver, bus driver, or other human intermediaries. Still this option comes with high inherent risk, which also points to e-money as a more viable option, even though it has its own set of risks. Nevertheless, not everyone is convinced about M-Pesa or at least how M-Pesa promote themselves and here is a complaint: "Although M-Pesa has been touted as "banking the unbanked," on average, M-Pesa users are wealthier, better educated, urban, and "already banked" .... Moreover, the data suggest that most of the transfers are occurring within urban areas [6].

Well, notwithstanding the critique, the authors do also acknowledge the manifested technological progress: "M-Pesa and other m-money systems have recently transitioned from a pure money transfer system into a payment platform that allows nongovernmental organizations, schools, hospitals, and firms to send and receive payments". In their paper, the authors actually justified their earlier cynicism with a table of numbers that appeared to support their case. The obvious limitation in this evidence is that the numbers referred to are actually absolute means. This paper is well positioned to evaluate the critique further: whether the banked are more likely to be included in e-banking than the unbanked.

3   Econometric Model

3.1   The Relevance of Self-selection Modeling

In order to study the determinants of the likelihood of e-banking inclusion, one needs to consider a population that consists of both the banked (subset1) and the unbanked (subset2). It is clear that based on these subsets, for an analyst to evaluate (a) the likelihood of e-banking inclusion, such an analyst must first identify (b) the approved bank account holders (here proxied by the banked). This means that we do not observe "a" unless we know "b". The style of econometric framework followed in this paper is similar to [10] which can be consulted for further theoretical background.

3.2   Model Estimation Equations

Outcome Model: This is the main set of equations of the study.

$$\text{Financial Exclusion:} \quad y_{1i}^* = x_i'\beta + \varepsilon_i, \quad where \quad \varepsilon_i \sim N(0,1) \tag{1a}$$

$$\text{such that,} \quad y_{1i} = 1\left(y_{1i}^* \geq 0\right), \quad and \quad P(y_{1i} = 1) = \Phi(x_i'\beta) \tag{1b}$$

$$\text{Marginal Effects:} \quad \theta_1 = \frac{\partial P(y_{1i} = 1)}{\partial x} = \varphi\left(x_i'\beta\right)\beta \tag{1c}$$

In Eq. (1a), y_{1i}^* is a latent variable measuring the underlying propensity for an individual i to be excluded. The subscript 1 indicates Eq. 1. From Eq. (1b), y_{1i} is a dichotomous variable indicating whether an individual i is classified as excluded, which is determined with $1\left(y_{1i}^* \geq 0\right)$. $x_i'\beta$ is an index function, x_i is a vector of factors that influence the likelihood of exclusion, β is a vector of coefficients to be estimated, and ε_i is, by assumption, a normally distributed disturbance term with a mean of zero, and a variance of 1. The probability of observing financial exclusion is given by a normal cumulative density function, $\Phi(.)$ in (1b). Equation (1c) serves to indicate that the probability of the outcome equation must be interpreted with reference to the marginal effects but not the, coefficients, β alone as in OLS.

Sample Selection Model: This equation controls for endogenous self-selection bias.

$$\text{Modeling f-banking: } \quad y_{2i}^* = z_i'\gamma + \mu_i, \quad where \quad \mu_i \sim N(0,1) \tag{2a}$$

$$\text{such that,} \quad y_{2i} = 1\left(y_{2i}^* \geq 0\right), \quad and \quad P(y_{2i} = 1) = \Phi\left(z_i'\gamma\right) \tag{2b}$$

$$\text{Marginal Effects:} \quad \theta_2 = \frac{\partial P(y_{2i} = 1)}{\partial z} = \varphi\left(z_i'\gamma\right)\gamma \tag{2c}$$

The set of Eqs. (2a, 2b, 2c) in 2 are interpreted analogous to the equations of (1). In Eq. (2a), y_{2i}^* is a latent variable measuring the underlying propensity for an individual i to be classified as banked. The subscript 2 indicates Eq. 2. From Eq. (2b), y_{2i} is a dichotomous variable indicating if an individual i is banked, which is decided on the basis of $1\left(y_{2i}^* \geq 0\right)$. $z_i'\gamma$ is the index function, z_i is a vector of factors that determine a random individual to be banked, γ is a vector of coefficients to be estimated, and μ_i is a normally distributed disturbance term assumed to have a mean of zero, and a variance of 1. The probability of observing a banked individual is given by a normal cumulative distribution function, $\Phi(.)$ in (2b).

Selection Assumption and Bivariate Normal Distribution: The moral of the story in Eqs. 1 and 2 is that, we only observe individuals who are approved bank account holders (the banked), and not all possible bankable individuals in Kenya. For this reason, the modeling process is designed to take this into consideration.

$$\text{Selectivity:} \quad Corr(\varepsilon_i, \mu_i) = \rho \quad and \quad \varepsilon_i \mu_i \sim N_2\left(0,0,1,\rho_{\varepsilon\mu}\right) \tag{3a}$$

$$\text{Conditional prob.:} \quad P(y_{i1} = 1 | y_{i2} = 1) = \Phi_2\left(x_i'\beta, \; z_i'\gamma\right)/\Phi\left(z_i'\gamma\right) \tag{3b}$$

From Eqs. (3a) and (3b) the subscript of 2 (on N and Φ) refers to bivariate normal distribution, and ρ is the correlation coefficient. If $\rho \neq 0$, the ε_i and μ_i are correlated. If $\rho = 0$, then the two error terms are uncorrelated, and the bivariate normal cumulative distribution function, Φ_2 in (3b) reduces to two univariate cumulative distribution functions. If $\rho = 1$, then the two equations are exactly the same. The log-likelihood in Eq. 4 is based on the theoretical predicted probabilities analyzed in Table 1, and is fitted through the Maximum Likelihood Estimation procedure outlined in (4).

$$LnL = \sum_{i=1}^{N} \left\{ \begin{array}{c} y_{i1}y_{2i}\ln[\Phi_2\left(x_i'\beta, \; z_i'\gamma, \rho\right)] + (1 - y_{i1})y_{2i}\ln[\Phi_2\left(-x_i'\beta, \; z_i'\gamma, -\rho\right)] \\ + (1 - y_{2i})\ln\left[1 - \Phi\left(z_i'\gamma\right)\right] \end{array} \right\} \tag{4}$$

4 Data Characteristics

In this paper we use FinAccess Household Survey 2015 that is collected by the Financial Sector Deepening Programme of Kenya FSD Kenya) supported by Central Bank of Kenya; (CBK); and Kenya National Bureau of Statistics [13], and published in

2016. The interviews were carried out for 8,665 individuals aged 16 and above. A total of 10,008 adults were interviewed on one-on-one basis guided by a Kish selection grid in 834 clusters over 13 sub-regional counties. The survey sampling methodology used by FSD Kenya is detailed in National Sample Survey and Evaluation Programme [11] designed by KBNS for national surveys. This data set was used previously in empirical research by [6, 8, 12], among others. In terms of variable design this study is closer to [8].

5   Empirical Results

The labels, C, D, and E in the first column of Table 1, refer to the terminal points of the tree diagram in Fig. 1. The observations in column II, and predicted probabilities in column III are related to Eqs. 1, 2, and 3 above. Column IV reports the average probabilities for the equations in column III, and they add up to unity.

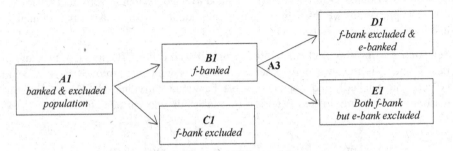

Fig. 1. Illustration of likelihood of e-banking given the f-banked

Table 1. Predicted probabilities (from Eqs. 1 and 2)

I	II	III	IV
From Fig. 1	Observation	Predicted probability	Average probability
C1	$y_{i2} = 0$	$P(y_{i2} = 0) = 1 - \Phi(z_i'\gamma)$	0.7969
D1	$y_{i1} = 1, y_{i2} = 1$	$P(y_{i1} = 1, y_{i2} = 1) = \Phi_2(x_i'\beta,\ z_i'\gamma, \rho)$	0.0235
E1	$y_{i1} = 0, y_{i2} = 1$	$P(y_{i1} = 0, y_{i2} = 1) = \Phi_2(-x_i'\beta,\ z_i'\gamma, -\rho)$	0.2696
These probabilities are part of the regression post-estimation results of Eqs. 1, 2, (5a), (5b) estimated using statistical application.			1

The main results of this study is presented through Eq. (5a) which gives a conditional probability (pcond1) of: (a) a banked individual adopting e-banking (or m-banking), given that the same individual is (b) banked. Equation (5a) below shows that the joint probability of "a" and "b" is 0.9198. This means that a banked person has a 91.98% of experiencing e-banking (or m-banking) financial inclusion.

$$P(y_{i1} = 1 | y_{i2} = 1) = \frac{\Phi_2(x_i'\beta, \ z_i'\gamma, \ \cdot\rho)}{\Phi(z_i'\gamma)} = 0.9198, \qquad p\_vlue = 0.000. \qquad (5a)$$

In contrast, terminal C1 of Fig. 1 (or row C1 of Table 1) shows that, the f-banking financial exclusion is approximately 80%. The paper by [8] reports an exclusion rate of around 70% (without controlling for sample selection) in their study for Kenya and Uganda. To recapitulate, we are ready to test [6]'s claim that the banked are taking-up m-banking more than the unbanked? Well the terminal C1 actually report the f-banking exclusion. In order to address [6] we need to consider Fig. 2 and compare conditional probabilities of terminal D2 with terminal D1 (of Fig. 1). Conditional probability for D1 is reported in Eq. (5a). Conditional probability for D2 is given in Eq. (5b), as follows:

$$(y_{i1} = 1 | y_{i2} = 0) = \frac{P(y_{i1} = 1, y_{i2} = 0)}{1 - \Phi(z_i'\gamma)} = 0.7571, \qquad p\_vlue = 0.000. \qquad (5b)$$

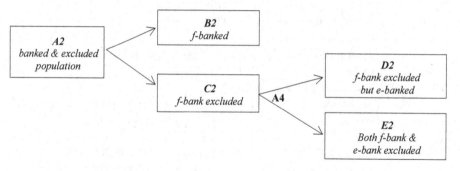

Fig. 2. Illustration of the likelihood of e-banking given the 'f-bank excluded'

So, the likelihood of an already f-banked excluded and now entering the m-banking system is 75.71%, which is indeed less than the adoption rate of the f-banked (reported in Eq. (5a) at 91.98%. Well, on the basis of these results [6], have a case. Further, given the hype around the M-Pesa's enlightening miracle, and the cautiousness of the f-banking system to lag-behind M-Pesa's brave innovation, one would have thought the reverse is the case. In fact while there are more clues in the individual variables in Table 2, overall the truth is, the poor people have a steep hill to climb even to access the less expensive M-Pesa service.

Now let us descend from high level intuition of overall results and zoom into the detailed regression output of Eqs. (1) and (2). We first look at the likelihood of f-banking (which is the sample selection equation) reported in Panel B of Table 2.

Table 2. BiProbit sample selection model

Panel A: Outcome equation results: likelihood of e-banking inclusion

Variable	Coefficient	Margins	P value
Wealth index (factor)	−0.3124	−0.0215	0.0080***
Rural money transfer risk	0.2051	0.0804	0.0000***
Age group (base = 16–18 yrs)			
18–25 yrs	1.5890	0.3023	0.0000***
26–35 yrs	1.5709	0.4503	0.0000***
36–45 yrs	1.7076	0.4560	0.0000***
46–55 yrs	1.1548	0.4082	0.0000***
>55 yrs	1.0978	0.3571	0.0000***
Lighting (base: firewood)			
Paraffin	0.5100	0.0332	0.3170
Electricity	0.7286	0.0204	0.5800
Financial literacy (base: low)			
Medium	0.1213	0.1842	0.0000***
High	0.5161	0.2644	0.0000***
Mobile owner (base: yes)	1.4303	0.6659	0.0000***
Constant	−2.2121		

Panel B: Sample selection results: likelihood of f-banking exclusion

Do you need bank account?			
No I don't	0.4734	0.1500	0.0000***
Unsure	0.0517	0.0050	0.9160
Age	0.0474	0.0057	0.0000***
Age square	−0.0004	−0.0592	0.0000***
Female (base: male)	−0.1850	−0.2213	0.0000***
Mobile owner (base: not own)	−0.8157	0.0110	0.0000***
Income Group (base: KSh0–100) in Kenyan KSh. *[KSh100 = USD1, approx]*			
KSh101–1500#	−0.4101	−0.0866	0.1860
KSh1501–3000	−0.2788	−0.0592	0.3670
KSh3001–7500	0.0320	0.0123	0.8510
KSh7501–15000	0.3966	0.1312	0.0470**
KSh15001–30000	0.7458	0.2609	0.0000***
KSh30001–50000	1.0712	0.3902	0.0000***
KSh50001–100000	1.1493	0.4234	0.0000***
KSh100001–200000	1.4309	0.5281	0.0000***
Over KSh200000	1.6918	0.6047	0.0000***
Urban (base: rural)	0.4719	0.1510	0.0000***
Language (base: English)			

(*continued*)

Table 2. (*continued*)

Panel B: Sample selection results: likelihood of f-banking exclusion

Swahili	−0.2871	−0.1034	0.0000***
Kikuyu	−0.1277	−0.0492	0.1380
Luo	−0.3665	−0.1212	0.0010***
Meru	−0.7355	−0.2239	0.0000***
Kisii	0.1752	0.0742	0.3650
Luhya	−6.1757	−0.0432	0.1174
Kalenjin	−0.3870	−0.1276	0.0010***
Kamba	−0.5150	−0.1679	0.0000***
Somali	−0.9385	−0.2582	0.0000***
Turkana	0.9993	0.4082	0.0000***
Masai	−0.5581	−0.1964	0.0280**
Embu	−0.2245	−0.1222	0.4990
Sub-region (base: Nairobi)			
Central	−0.1148	−0.0383	0.1850
Mombasa	−0.2225	−0.0657	0.0400**
Coast	−0.1923	−0.0564	0.0610*
Upper Eastern	−0.2116	−0.0667	0.0460**
Mid Eastern	0.1514	0.0588	0.0760*
Lower Eastern	−0.1080	−0.0359	0.3550
North Eastern	−0.7890	−0.1937	0.0000***
Nyanza	−0.2120	−0.0674	0.0280**
North Rift	−0.1652	−0.0561	0.1070
Central Rift	−0.1083	−0.0326	0.2420
South Rift	−0.0346	−0.0116	0.6960 -
Western	−0.0800	−0.0230	0.4550
Constant	−1.7836		
Post-estimation statistics			
/athrho	−0.5818		0.0000***
Rho	−0.5240		
Chi (1)	19.73		0.0000***

Legend: ***1% **5% *10%

In terms of Figs. 1 and 2, the results for Panel B relate to Probit sample-selection decisions at A1 and A2. The regression output shows that out of the 13 Kenyan sub-regions, 6 have insignificant margins meaning that there is no effect on the likelihood of f-banking inclusion. For the remaining 7, the 6 sub-regions have negative signs, meaning that if one is a resident of these areas then one has less chance of been f-banking included compared to the up market city of Nairobi (which is the base dummy). Only in sub-region 7, Mid Eastern, is there a positive coefficient meaning that its citizens have a better chance than Nairobi City dwellers to be f-banked. The next variable, ethnicity (proxied by languages), there are 4 insignificant coefficients judged by margins. For the remaining 8, only 2 (Kisii and Turkana) yield a better chance than English speakers (the base dummy) of been f-banked. Kisii is located in a favorable agricultural area of Kenya while Turkana is one of the poorest regions but second largest sub-region in terms of population size. This means that Turkana manifests a positive volume effect on f-banking likelihood. Further, the results show that males are more likely to be f-banked than females. Age has a positive effect on f-banking inclusion but this effect decreases with aging. Income less than Kenyan KSh3000 (equivalent of (USD30) have no effect on f-banking likelihood, but higher income brackets have a strong positive association with f-banking inclusion.

We now focus on the results for Panel A of Table 2. In the context of Figs. 1 and 2, Panel A corresponds to Probit decision outcome at A3 and A4. This regression output for Eq. (1) provides empirical results on the likelihood of e-banking inclusion. The results show that some household infrastructure like paraffin and electricity are irrelevant for e-banking inclusion propensity. People who are more financially literate (from medium to high) are more likely to adopt e-banking than those who do not understand banking. All ages above 18 years old have a positive likelihood of been e-banking included. Overall, the results for Panels A and B are consistent with the notion that hardships increase the likelihood of adopting e-money, while the well-offness increases the probability of f-banking inclusion. The results also show that Wealth index and Rural money transfer risk contribute positively and negatively, respectively to the likelihood of e-banking inclusion.

6 Discussion of Results

There is a wealth of empirical studies in financial exclusion of the poor [8, 12, 16, 18], and e-banking adoption by consumers [14, 17]. There are very few papers such as [14] that study both topics concurrently, but none that we are aware of that evaluate the two questions within the same model to study both the adoption its determinants. The need to study both banking inclusion and e-banking within the same model go beyond economic value-add, but econometric modeling necessity to control for self-selection bias as elaborated earlier in Sect. 3. This paper contrasts the likelihood of e-banking and its determinants for the banked and the unbanked. The results of the study in relation to e-banking likelihood show that the adoption rate by the banked (the financially included) is higher (at 92%) more than the financially excluded (at 75%). Prior study comparison shows f-banking likelihood of 80% at most [16], and e-banking adoption rate of around 73%, for example [17]. In contrast to current paper, these studies run separate regression for both f-banking and e-banking.

The f-banking results of this study are comparable with prior studies. Our findings show that the factors, male consumers, well-offness (high income bracket), education (higher financially literacy level), young to middle age, all increase the likelihood of financial inclusion [8, 14, 16]. Turning to e-banking, the results are still consistent with related research. For example, in this study we used age and age squared to show that e-banking adoption is positive but decreases at higher age levels. Similar results are reported by [15], who used Logistic Model with 483 survey respondents from Greece, but unlike current study, they used a dummy variable for different age brackets, and find that the age bracket, 56–65 is less likely to take-up embanking compared to 18–25. The same paper shows the educated (master's or PhD) adopt embanking more than primary and secondary school leavers which is consistent with result of the variable, *financial literacy* used in this study. Further, [17] from New Zealand used Logistic model with 529 survey data to evaluate e-banking adoption and found a negative but insignificant association. In this paper we used *wealth index* and found same negative sign but statistically significant.

Unlike e-banking, in absolute financial inclusion aging does not seem to be a limiting factor as observed in this study (Panel B, of Table 2) and a survey of 37 countries in Africa by [15]. Nevertheless, we do differ on the details with [15]'s overall conclusion that: "…mobile banking is driven by the same determinants than traditional banking in Africa. There is consequently no different pattern to explain the use of this alternative form of banking". Our study support the view that e-banking on the side of the banked is motivated by the benefit (or convenience) of technological progress such as mobile phones and internet [19], while e-banking by the financially excluded is driven by 'financial exclusion hardship'. Meaning that e-banking is seen by the financially-excluded as an alternative to f-banking.

7 Conclusion

The goal of this paper was to evaluate the conditional likelihood of a random individual to be e-banked, conditional upon been f-banked (for fiat money). Are the f-banked more likely to be e-banked than the complete financially excluded? We used BiProbit Sample Selection model along with national survey data set from Kenya to answer the question. The empirical results of this paper support the conclusion that the f-banked are more likely to be e-banked at ninety two percent compared to the absolute financially excluded who have a lesser e-banking likelihood of seventy five percent. The policy implication for the results is that policies or marketing strategies designed to encourage e-banking adoption should be aware that the banked and unbanked take-up rate differ overall and according to different groups such as gender, the rich, the educated, and geography.

References

1. World Bank: World Bank Policy Report: Finance for All? Policies and Pitfalls in Expanding Access (2008a). https://doi.org/10.1596/978-0-8213-7291-3
2. Demirguc-Kunt, A., Klapper, L.: Measuring financial inclusion: explaining variation in use of financial services across and within countries. Brook. Pap. Econ. Act. 279–321 (2013). https://doi.org/10.1353/eca.2013.0002
3. Burgess, R., Pande, R.: Do rural banks matter? Evidence from the Indian social banking experiment. Am. Econ. Rev. **95**(3), 780–795 (2005). https://doi.org/10.1257/0002828054201242

4. Levine, R.: Finance and growth: theory and evidence. In: Aghion, P., Durlauf, S. (eds.) Handbook of Economic Growth. Elsevier, Amsterdam (2005). https://doi.org/10.3386/w10766
5. Duncombe, R., Boateng, R.: Mobile phones and financial services in developing countries: a review of concepts, methods, issues, evidence and future research directions. Third World Q. 30(7), 1237–1258 (2009). https://doi.org/10.1080/01436590903134882
6. Aker, J., Mbiti, I.: Mobile phones and economic development in Africa. J. Econ. Perspect. 24(3), 207–232 (2010). https://doi.org/10.1257/jep.24.3.207
7. World Bank: Indicators of Financial Access – Household Levels Survey (2008b). http://siteresources.worldbank.org. Accessed 1 Jan 2017
8. Johnson, S., Nino-Zarazua, S.M.: Financial access and exclusion in Kenya and Uganda. J. Dev. Stud. 47(3), 475–496 (2011). https://doi.org/10.1080/00220388.2010.492857
9. Beck, T., Demirguc-Kunt, A., Peria, M.S.M.: Reaching out: access to and use of banking services across countries. J. Financ. Econ. 85(1), 234–266 (2007). https://doi.org/10.1016/j.jfineco.2006.07.002
10. Greene, W.H.: Econometric Analysis, 7th edn. Pearson, New York (2012)
11. NASSEP-V: National Sample Survey and Evaluation Programme, Kenya - Demographic and Health Survey, Kenya National Bureau of Statistics, Government of Kenya (2014)
12. Shem, A.O., Misati, R., Njoroge, L.: Factors driving usage of financial services from different financial access strands in Kenya. Sav. Dev. 36(1), 71–89 (2012)
13. FSD Kenya: Central Bank of Kenya, Kenya National Bureau of Statistics, FinAccess Household Survey 2015. Harvard Dataverse, V4 (2016)
14. Zins, A., Weill, L.: The determinants of financial inclusion in Africa. Rev. Dev. Financ. 6(1), 46–57 (2016). https://doi.org/10.1016/j.rdf.2016.05.001
15. Serener, B.: Statistical analysis of internet banking usage with logistic regression. Procedia Comput. Sci. 102, 648–653 (2016). https://doi.org/10.1016/j.procs.2016.09.456
16. Devlin, J.F.: J. Consum. Policy 28, 75 (2005). https://doi.org/10.1007/s10603-004-7313-y
17. Gan, C., Clemes, M., Limsombunchai, V., Weng, A.: A logit analysis of electronic banking in New Zealand. Int. J. Bank Mark. 24(6), 360–383 (2006). https://doi.org/10.1108/02652320610701717
18. Koku, P.S.: Financial exclusion of the poor: a literature review. Int. J. Bank Mark. 33(5), 654–668 (2015). https://doi.org/10.1108/IJBM-09-2014-0134
19. Berger, A.: The economic effects of technological progress: evidence from the banking industry. J. Money Credit Bank. 35(2), 141–176 (2003). https://doi.org/10.1353/mcb.2003.0009

Innovation, Banking Development and Governance

Jihene El Ouakdi[1]([⊠]), Dorra Guermazi[1], and Khira Alimi[2]

[1] Higher School of Digital Economy, Univ. Manouba, Manouba, Tunisia
jihene.elouakdi@gmail.com
[2] Higher Institute of Business Administration, Univ. Gafsa, Gafsa, Tunisia

Abstract. We investigate the influence of banking development on innovation, including firms that are dependent on external finance. We control, furthermore, the corporate governance impact. Using data from the listed French companies on the SBF 120, we find positive effect of banking development on innovation by financing R&D investments, including firms that are dependent on external finance. Further, when innovation is measured by new patents, the impact of banking development disappear. However, corporate governance seems to affect significantly innovation, including a positive effect of independent outside directors in the board.

Keywords: Financial development · R&D investment · Patents
Governance

1 Introduction

In recent years, the level of competition in several markets has increased because of globalization and liberalization. In order to remain competitive, it is imperative for firms to innovate (Solow 1957; Guan and Chen 2012; Guan and Yam 2015). Innovation is crucial for long-run competitiveness of firms. The innovation process, unlike conventional investment in tangible assets, involves a high probability of failure due to its dependence on unpredictable conditions and thus requires a particular type of financing. Banking development can affect positively the probability of process innovation, particularly for firms in sectors more dependent upon external finance, and where financial markets are not developed (Parisi et al. 2006; Benfratello et al. 2008; Ayyagari et al. 2011; Hsu et al. 2014). Internal factors can also impact innovation such corporate governance (Dong and Gou 2010; Becker-Blease 2011; Singh and Gaur 2013; Chakraborty et al. 2014; Guan and Yam 2015).

The purpose of this paper is to investigate the effect of banking development on innovation. We control, furthermore, the corporate governance impact. We consider also the effect of financial markets development and the dependence of the firm on external financing, besides some corporate variables. We are extending financial literature on innovation, which is not very abundant. Some papers have addressed the issue of the influence of banking development on innovation. Most of them focused on the influence of banking competition on innovation (Ayyagari et al. 2011; Cornaggia et al. 2015), and on the impact of banking deregulation (Jayaratne and Strahan 1996;

© Springer Nature Switzerland AG 2018
M. A. Bach Tobji et al. (Eds.): ICDEc 2018, LNBIP 325, pp. 79–94, 2018.
https://doi.org/10.1007/978-3-319-97749-2_6

Black and Straham 2002). Other authors studied the effects of the financial system development on innovation across countries (Hsu et al. 2014).

We propose to investigate the effect of banking development on innovation. To do so, we investigate the effect of proximity, credit market development, efficiency and banking performance. In addition, we include in our model the influence of corporate governance, the effect of the dependence on external financing, of the performance of the firm and the development of financial markets. This model would give more insight on exogenous and endogenous factors that are determinant of innovation.

We use data from the listed French companies on the SBF 120, from 2010 to 2015. The choice on this data set of French firms is interesting for several reasons. First, these firms belong to sectors in which innovation is a survival condition. R&D spending represents 2.25% of the GDP in 2016 leading to 16 200 patents. France is ranked third after the U.S. and Japan in the number of innovative firms and organizations. In addition, the French government is continuously taking measures in order to boost innovation and restructure corporate governance mechanisms (ex. Research Tax Credit). Second, the choice of the French context is motivated by the importance of the banking sector in financing the economy. According to the French Banking Federation, bank credits to firms has grown at the rate of 11.5% from 2010 to reach 871 billion euros at the end of 2015. This would allow us to isolate the role of banking development on innovation, given the limited role of financial markets. A better understanding of the determinants of innovation would give more insight about one of the important channels through which banking development affect economic growth.

The rest of the paper is organized as follows. Section 2 presents a literature review and the hypothesis. Section 3 defines the variables used in our model. Section 4 presents the data set. Section 5 presents and discuss regression results on Banking development and innovation. Section 6 presents and discuss regression results on Banking development, innovation and external-finance dependence while Sect. 7 concludes.

2   Literature Review and Fundamental Hypothesis

The probability of introducing an innovation depends on internal and external factors to the firm. The degree of development of the banking sector is one of the external variable that can influence the innovation output, for a given quantity of internal inputs (Benfratello et al. 2008; Bekaert et al. 2001, 2005; Di Bonaccorsi and Gabbi 2001a, b).

The empirical evidence on the effect of banking development on innovation is mixed. Some authors conclude for a positive effect (Benfratello et al. 2008; Ayyagari et al. 2011; Nanda and Nicholas 2011; Amore et al. 2013) and other papers confirm a negative effect (Atanassov et al. 2007; Hsu et al. 2014). According to the literature, banking development may lead to innovation at the firm level through two channels. The first channel is the ability of financial intermediaries to improve information collection and reduce screening and monitoring costs, with the resulting increase in efficiency of resource allocation, and then growth, initiated by Greenwood and Jovanovic (1990).

In this context, Benfratello et al. (2008) find that banking development, measured by geographical proximity may allow banks to be more effective on collecting information on borrowers, including their propensity to innovate. The decrease in information and monitoring costs has a beneficial effect on the cost and access to finance in the context of asymmetric information. According to Rice and Strahan (2010), such reduction in credit costs is likely to encourage innovative firms to ask for bank financing. They conclude that innovation is the main factor through which banking development affect economic growth.

The second channel through which banking development can influence innovation is banking competition. The entry of new banks may have an effect on the quality and innovative nature of the project undertaken. In this context, Ferraris and Minetti (2007) find that new banks are more appealing for high risk/high returns projects, because they are reluctant to liquidate projects prematurely (due to their low liquidation skills relative to incumbents). More recently, Cornaggia et al. (2015), based on a sample of U.S. listed corporations and private firms during the period of 1976 to 2006, argue that banking competition enables small, innovative firms to secure financing instead of being acquired by public corporations. According to Benfratello et al. (2008), there is no evidence on such an effect of banking competition on the availability and the cost of bank credit and therefore firm's innovation decision.

Degryse and Ongena (2005) find no evidence on the effect of banking agency concentration on innovation. However, they find that credit cost increase when the distance between the firm and competitor banks increase. This cost is supposed to decrease when the distance between the firm and the lending bank increase. This result can be consistent with the thesis of Harisson et al. (1999) which suppose that the lending banks' bargaining power increases when they are closer to the borrowing firms. Therefore, banking development, measured by bank proximity, could stimulate innovation through reducing credit costs.

Other papers conclude for a negative effect of banking development on innovation. Hsu et al. (2014), using a data set including 32 developed and emerging countries, find that development of credit market appears to discourage innovation in industries that are more dependent on external finance and that are more high-tech intensive. In this context, Rajan and Zingales (2001) suggest that, due to a lack of price signals, banks might continue financing firms even for projects with negative returns. Brown et al. (2012) argue that innovative firms often have unstable and limited internal cash flows to service debt, besides the fact that R&D usually creates intangible assets, which makes banks less likely to finance innovative projects. However, according to Hsu et al. (2014), equity market development has a positive effect on innovation.

As stated before, empirical evidence on the effect of banking development on innovation is mixed, and given the particularities of the French economy, we recall that, banking development may lead to innovation at the firm level through two channels, efficiency in resource allocation and banking competition.

Hypothesis 1: Banking development has a positive effect on innovation.

Some authors find that the positive effect of banking development is likely to matter for firms that are more dependent on external finance. In this context, Benfratello et al. (2008) find that banking development in the Italian market affects the probability of process innovation, particularly for firms in sectors that are dependent on external finance. As suggested in Rajan and Zingales (1998), the evolution of the banking sector will matter more, in general, for firms in industries that are more dependent upon external financing for technological reason. Another contribution form Ayyagari et al. (2011) confirm that financing from foreign banks is associated with higher level of innovation compared to financing from domestic bank, based on data across 47 developing economies.

However, Rajan and Zingales (1998) and more recently Hsu et al. (2014) argue that in case of dependence on external financing, the growth of the equity market affects innovation. As suggested by Brown et al. (2009), equity market investors share upside returns and there are no collateral requirements for equity financing. When additional equity is needed, equity financing would not increase a firm's probability of financial distress. In addition, as argued by Allen and Gale (1999); Hsu et al. (2014), the development of equity market allows valuable information about firm's investment opportunities because markets provide timely equilibrium security prices. Given the importance of bank financing in the French economy, our second hypothesis is:

Hypothesis 2: Banking development has a positive effect on innovation for firms that are dependent upon external financing.

3 Variables

In this paper, we investigate the effect of banking development on firm innovation and we control this effect by some corporate governance factors.

We measure firm innovation by its inputs and outputs. We measure innovation input by the natural logarithm of R&D investment (LNRD) (Benfratello et al. 2008; Aghion et al. 2013; Singh and Gaur 2013; Amore et al. 2013; Hsu et al. 2014). We measure innovation output by a dummy variable equal to 1 if R&D expenditures achieve to new patents (Benfratello et al. 2008; Guan and Zuo 2014; Guan and Yam 2015).

Banking development is measured by four variables commonly used in the literature. Bank proximity (ProxBan) is measured based on Degryse and Ongena (2005); Benfratello et al. (2008) researches. This variable is supposed to capture the effect of banking deregulation (Benfratello et al. 2008). Also, we think it is reasonable to still assume that proximity of banks matters in the French context, despite evolution in information and communication technology. According to some researches, financial constraints on firms increase with the distance between the bank and the firm (Carpentar and Peterson, 2002). In addition, distance is determinant in access to information on the firm and thus on the cost and flow of financing (Di Bonaccorsi and Gabbi 2001a, b). We measure proximity by the number of branches in the district of each firm of the sample. Following Rajan and Zingales (1998), we measure the development of the credit market (DevCred) by the ratio of credits provided by banks to private firms over GDP of the year. We also measure banking efficiency and banking performance respectively by the ratio of overall banking costs by total assets (Beck et al. 2010) and by return on assets (Melyon 2007).

In order to measure dependence on external finance, we use a proxy of the measure adopted by Rajan and Zingales (1998) given by the ratio of debts by total assets.

In our econometric framework that we present later, besides the main variables of interest, we control the effect of corporate governance on innovation, including ownership structure, characteristics of the board of directors and managerial characteristics. We also control for some firm characteristics, and for the growth of financial market as a complementary financing of innovation. We test for the effect on innovation of the presence of controlling shareholders (CalPre, CalDeu), the presence of institutional ownership (CalInst) and family ownership (CalFle). In this context, Ayyagari et al. (2011) find that innovative firms are characterized by concentrated ownership. McConnell and Wahal (2000); Eng and Shakell (2001) find that due to their skills and advantage in information collection, institutional shareholders are more likely to invest in innovative projects. A positive effect has also been found for family ownership (Claessens et al. 2002).

We also test the effect of the independence of the board of directors (Indca) and the influence of the fact that the manager has also the role of chairman of the board of directors (Cumul). Some Researchers suggest that the independence of the board of directors encourage valuable investment and thus R&D (Lennox 2005; Dong and Gou 2010). However, others argue that the board with inside members is more likely to take the best decisions in terms of innovation (Zahra and Stanton 1988). Ho and Wong (2001) found that cumulating the two roles of manager and chairman of the board can lead to conflicts, and thus negatively affects innovation.

We also investigate the effect of managerial compensation (RemFixe, RemVar), managerial shareholding (CalDirig), and incentive stock option plan (StockOpt). In this context, Dong and Gou (2010) suggest that the salary level is likely to increase managerial discretion, managers prefer to reduce the R&D investment to improve short-term financial performance and avoid the R&D risks. However, stock options are likely to reduce the manager's risk aversion (Coles et al. 2006; Lin et al. 2011), particularly with higher sensitivity of CEO compensation portfolio value to stock volatility (Chen and Zhang 2013).

In addition, we control for return on assets (ROA), firm growth opportunities (MB), and for the growth of financial market as a complementary financing of innovation (DevMarch). We finally, add a binary variable (a2013) in order to capture the effect of the governance on encouraging innovation, particularly the 2013 law on research and higher education. Some researchers find that policy intervention and R&D incentives have a positive effect on firm innovation, they can be designed in different forms such as tax credits (Czarnitzki et al. 2011; Cappelen et al. 2012).

4   Data

To give an empirical answer to our research question, we use two samples. The first sample represents innovation and concerns the French listed companies on the SBF 120. The second sample represents banking development and includes the main banks of the French financial system. Financial firm have been excluded from the first sample to have homogenous data. Our sample includes 95 french firms, covering the period

Table 1. Descriptive statistics, correlation and mean difference analysis

(a) : Descriptive Statistics

	RD	NbrPatent	Patent	ProxBan	DepFin	Calpre	CalDeu	CalIns	CalFle	Indca%	Cumul	RemFixe	RemVar	StockOpt	AgeDirig	CalDirig	ROA	MB
Mean.	384	234	-	1239	15.41	30.98	7.38	51.36	3.07	49.88	-	786 760	737 296	-	57	0.614	3.19	0.775
St. Dev.	753	779	-	1257	15.58	23.51	8.36	25.85	8.91	18.47	-	398 233	641 206	-	6	2.802	6.32	0.677
25%	103	0	-	188	14.38	25.58	5.20	51.40	0.20	50.00	-	750 000	655 621	-	57	0,03	3.28	0.553
Median	41	0	-	55	5.04	9.32	1.80	33.70	0.00	36.36	-	500 000	250 554	-	53	0,00	1,23	0.335
75%	384	117	-	2571	23.23	47.55	8.22	73.80	1,62	63,64	-	974 977	1 117 100	-	61	0,16	5,43	1,010
Freq.	-	-	248	-	-	-	-	-	-	-	342	-	-	150	-	-	-	-
(%)	-	-	43.51	-	-	-	-	-	-	-	60	-	-	26.32	-	-	-	-

(b) : Difference Mean Tests

		RD	NbrPatent	ProxBan	DepFin	Calpre	CalDeu	CalIns	CalFle	Indca	RemFixe	RemVar	AgeDirig	CalDirig	ROA	MB
RD	=0		132	776	0.1329	21.21	5.15	57.16	5.46	56.97	858 361	621 242	58	3.90***	2.10	1.0399
	=1		239	1260**	0.1553	31.75**	7.57*	51.20	2.94	49.55	783 475	742 619	57	0.45	3.23	0.7626
	t-test		0.2283	0.0299	0.4368	0.0134	0.0775	0.8706	0.9165	0.9752	0.8208	0.1776	0.8008	0.0000	0.1923	0.9783
Patent	=0	247		1176	0.1589	0.2977	0.0626	0.5295*	0.0446***	0.4783	775 878	737 283	56	0.9427***	0.0319	0.7661
	=1	561***		1319*	0.1480	0.3325**	0.0903***	0.4953	0.0124	0.5255**	737 314	800 889	57	0.1619	0.0316	0.7859
	t-test	0.0000		0.0893	0.4083	0.0384	0.0000	0.0582	0.0000	0.0012	0.4577	0.9995	0.6764	0.0004	0.9517	0.7281

(c) : Correlation Coefficients

	ProxBan	DepCred	EfficBan	PerfoBan	DepFin	Calpre	CalDeu	CalIns	CalFle	Indca	Cumul	RemFixe	RemVar	StockOpt	AgeDirig	CalDirig	ROA	MB	DevMarch
LNRD	0.0414	0.0153	-0.0366	-0.0047	-0.1427***	-0.0318	0.1455***	0.0076	0.0145	0.0749*	0.0501	0.3078***	0.1589***	0.1212***	0.0233	-0.1696***	0.0460	-0.1456***	0.0254
	(0.3246)	(0.7165)	(0.3833)	(0.9110)	(0.0006)	(0.4493)	(0.0005)	(0.8558)	(0.7305)	(0.0744)	(0.2324)	(0.0000)	(0.0001)	(0.0038)	(0.5794)	(0.0001)	(0.2726)	(0.0005)	(0.5456)
Patent	0.0565	-0.0167	-0.0148	0.0153	-0.0347	0.0685	0.1563***	-0.0626	-0.1798***	0.1266***	0.0953**	0.0312	0.0000	0.1184***	0.0175	-0.1426***	-0.0005	0.0146	0.0005
	(0.1785)	(0.6911)	(0.7250)	(0.7153)	(0.1028)	(0.1028)	(0.0002)	(0.1357)	(0.0000)	(0.0025)	(0.0228)	(0.4577)	(0.9995)	(0.0046)	(0.6764)	(0.0007)	(0.9906)	(0.7281)	(0.9900)

(a) and (b) concern specific variables of firms of our sample. (c) reports correlation coefficients of all dependent variables with independent variables of our model. RD refers to the amount (in millionof euro) of R&D investements. NbrPatent refers to the number of patents registered by the studied firms. Details about the remaining variables are given in appendix.
*, **, *** indicates that the coefficients are statistically significant, respectively at 1%, 5% et 10%. Number of observations = 570

from 2010 to 2015, giving a total of 570 observations. Data was collected from several sources. R&D spending and number of patents registered were collected from firms' reference documents and web pages. Data about banking development was collected from officiel web pages linked to the banking sector including Banque de France, Fédération Bancaire Française, the statistical web portal Statistica and the World Bank.

Table 1 presents the summary statistics on the key variables discussed in the previous section. Table 1a shows that 94.5% of the firms have invested in R&D, leading to the creation of 234 patents in average. However, only 43.5% of these firms have created patents. Banking proximity measured by the total number of banks (1239 bank branches) shows an important dispersion. As corporate governance is concerned, we report high concentration of capital mainly through institutional ownership (51.4%). We also note that 26.3% of firms CEO incentives are in forms of stock options with an average annual wage of 1 524 056 Euro.

Table 1b presents mean difference test when we split the sample in two parts: the first one including firms that have invested in R&D and the second firms that have registered patents. We perform a parametric mean difference test (*Student t*) on independent variables. Results show that firms having invested in R&D register more patents, benefit much more from bank proximity have more concentrated ownership and less managerial ownership. Table 1b also shows that firms having registered patents invest much more in R&D, which prove positive correlation between innovation input and output in the French context. These firms have also more bank branches in their region which suggest the importance of bank proximity in the innovation process. As noted for the first sample, these firms are characterized by concentrated ownership, lower institutional, familial and managerial ownership and higher independence of board members.

In Table 1c, we report no evidence on positive correlation between the two variables measuring innovation and banking development. However, we can see negative correlation between financial dependence and R&D investment. Innovation measured by its output (Patent) seems more correlated with corporate governance mechanisms then innovation measured by its input (LNRD).

5   Regression Results: Banking Development and Innovation

We consider a model with two equations, estimating innovation input (LNRD) and innovation output (Patent). We estimate the first equation by considering the presence of random effects in panel data. We conduct several tests, especially to insure the absence of heteroskedasticity, multicollinearity and omitted variables.

Results presented in the first row of Table 2 show no evidence on a significant effect of bank proximity on R&D investment. However, we can see that credit market development (DevCred), banking efficiency (EfficBan) and banking performance (PerfoBan) have positive and significant influence on innovation through financing R&D. In addition, results show that bank proximity is no longer determinant in access

Table 2. Banking development and innovation

	Independent variables	
	Equation 1	Equation 2
	LNRD	Patent
ProxBan	0.00009 (0.552)	0.00014 (0.716)
DevCred	**16.2306** (**0.013**)	−107.882 (0.169)
EfficBan	**−57.6552*** (**0.010**)	−238.428 (0.370)
PerfoBan	**43.3202** (**0.041**)	154.694 (0.637)
DepFin	−0.20535 (0.630)	0.35646 (0.865)
Calpre	0.00428 (0.993)	−5.08344 (0.116)
CalDeu	−1.71630 (0.327)	**−14.9670** (**0.014**)
CalIns	−0.13390 (0.749)	**−8.59731*** (**0.009**)
CalFle	−1.01224 (0.171)	−28.7112 (0.105)
Indca	−0.18148 (0.531)	**4.92415** (**0.036**)
Cumul	0.05649 (0.598)	0.74500 (0.332)
RemFixe	1.39^e-07 (0.310)	1.45^e-06 (0.129)
RemVar	-6.44^e-08 (0.360)	-4.07^e-07 (0.463)
StockOp	0.00213 (0.972)	0.50426 (0.479)
AgeDirig	**0.02385** (**0.012**)	0.03609 (0.443)
CalDirig	0.85790 (0.350)	**−193.798*** (**0.005**)
ROA	**1.34005** (**0.031**)	−0.63582 (0.931)
MB	0.03443 (0.702)	−0.28520 (0.544)
DevMarch	0.11575 (0.680)	1.12988 (0.724)

(*continued*)

Table 2. (*continued*)

	Independent variables	
	Equation 1	Equation 2
	LNRD	Patent
A2013	**0.13526***	−0.68821
	(0.085)	(0.510)
Cons.	−2.77627	45.3443
	(0.260)	(0.141)

This table reports regression resultsof innovation (measured by its input (LNRD) and output (Patent)), as a function of banking development (measured by proximity (ProxBan), credit market development (DevCred), banking efficiency (EfficBan) and performance (PerfoBan)). We control the effect of external finance dependence (DepFin), governance (measured by concentration and ownership structure (Calpre, CalDeu, CalIns, CalFle), board composition (Indca, Cumul), remuneration and some managerial characteristics (RemFixe, RemVar, StockOp, AgeDirig, CalDirig)), corporate performance (ROA) and firm growth opportunities (MB). We consider also the effect of the financial market development (DevMarch) and major government innovation incentives (A2013). Values between parentheses refer to P-value associated to each estimated coefficient.

***, **, *, indicates that the coefficients are statistically significant, respectively at 1%, 5% and 10%.

Number of observations = 570.

to financing. This result is in contradiction with Benfratelllo et al. (2008), which can be explained by the difference in the study period: 1992–2000 against 2010–2015. This last period, corresponding to our study, is characterized by the development of digital solutions replacing classical bank branches. In France, bank closing is growing at an annual average rate of 3% at the horizon of 2020[1].

Results presented in the first row of Table 2 show that R&D investment seem not to be affected by corporate governance variables, however it seems that the older the CEO is the more likely he invests in R&D. This result, in opposition with the entrenchment theory, is explained by the link between age and expertise, which makes manager more likely to take risky and valuable investment (Barker and Mueller 2002). Finally, it seems that corporate performance and government incentives positively influence innovation, given that firms have access to more funds to innovate (Cappelen et al. 2012).

We estimate the second equation of our model by a robust Probit regression taking into consideration the presence of random effects in panel data. The aim of this model is to capture the marginal effect of each independent variable on the probability to register new patents as a consequence of R&D investment. Results presented in the second row of Table 2 show that, banking development no longer influences innovation. In fact, banking development seems to affect innovation more in the upstream process (R&D investment) then in the downstream process (patents). However,

---

[1] De la Brosse. A, 2016, «Quel avenir pour les réseaux bancaires?», Revue Banque, 796.

innovation seems to be affected by corporate governance variables. In other terms, corporate governance is determinant for the transformation of R&D investment into registered patents. In this context, results show a negative and significant effect of ownership concentration, institutional ownership and managerial ownership. These types of ownerships seems to encourage corporate risk reduction and preference for short-term returns. This result is consistent with Ayyagari et al. (2007) who confirm that private firms whose controlling shareholder is a financial institution tend to be the least innovative.

Results of the second equation estimation also show that the independence of the board members positively influences the probability to innovate. According to Dong and Gou (2010), this effect is explained by the fact that independent outside directors are usually from the research and higher education field. Finally, when we focus on the innovation output, corporate performance and government incentives have no significant influence on innovation. These results prove that during the transformation process of innovation input in output, the impact of financing, internal (performance) or external (banking and government incentives) gives way to the influence of corporate governance.

6 Regression Results: Banking Development, Innovation and Financial Dependence

Several papers argue that the effect of banking development on innovation differs with the dependence of firms on external financing (Benfratello et al. 2008; Hsu et al. 2014). We present here the results of the second hypothesis' test: Banking development has a positive effect on innovation for firms that are dependent upon external financing. To do so, we estimate the two equations of our model taking into consideration the interaction between variables measuring banking development and variables measuring external-finance dependence. The same methodology and robustness tests are conducted.

Estimation results of the first equation in the second model are presented in the first row of Table 3. Results show that the same positive effect of credit market development, efficiency and banking performance on R&D investment is seen, yet becoming less significant. Bank proximity is also non-significant. However, financial market development positively influences R&D investments. This result confirms the financial role of banking development even when the firm dependant on external financing. We can see that external finance dependent firms are addressing the financial market to finance R&D investments. We also note again positive effect on innovation of the CEO age and the corporate performance.

The estimation results of the second equation, taking into consideration external-finance dependence, remain unchanged (second row of Table 3). The probability to register patents is much more influenced by corporate governance then by banking development. In the case of external-finance-dependent firms, concentrated, managerial, familial and institutional ownership seem to discourage significantly the innovation process (transforming innovation input in output). However, independence of board directors seems to positively affect the probability to register new patents.

Table 3. Banking development, innovation and external-finance dependence

	Independent variables	
	Equation 1	Equation 2
	LNRD	Patent
ProxBan × DepFin	0.00007	0.00049
	(0.790)	(0.568)
DevCred × DepFin	**1.05677***	−0.30530
	(0.084)	(0.930)
EfficBan × DepFin	**−138.340***	−402.920
	(0.054)	(0.130)
PerfoBan × DepFin	**328.118****	951.536
	(0.036)	(0.212)
Calpre	0.05560	−2.20180
	(0.914)	(0.278)
CalDeu	−1.72419	**−7.07265****
	(0.276)	**(0.028)**
CalIns	−0.09697	**−4.09895****
	(0.827)	**(0.044)**
CalFle	−1.02625	**−16.6625***
	(0.173)	**(0.052)**
Indca	−0.20558	**2.7846****
	(0.489)	**(0.035)**
Cumul	0.08510	0.42502
	(0.407)	(0.368)
RemFixe	1.43^e-07	6.08^e-07
	(0.294)	(0.346)
RemVar	-3.37^e-08	-1.53^e-07
	(0.616)	(0.726)
StockOp	−0.03131	0.27110
	(0.592)	(0.556)
AgeDirig	**0.02331*****	0.01263
	(0.009)	(0.689)
CalDirig	0.57169	**−106.291****
	(0.529)	**(0.013)**
ROA	**1.02259***	0.10513
	(0.074)	(0.981)
MB	0.01523	0.24733
	(0.858)	(0.473)
DevMarch	**0.44481****	−0.16281
	(0.049)	(0.934)

(*continued*)

Table 3. (*continued*)

	Independent variables	
	Equation 1	Equation 2
	LNRD	Patent
A2013	−0.01008	0.25173
	(0.832)	(0.628)
Cons.	**3.03587*****	0.99397
	(0.000)	(0.730)

This table reports regression results of variables measuring innovation ((LNRD, Patent), as a function of variables approximating the interaction between banking development and financial dependence (ProxBan × DepFin, DevCred × DepFin, EfficBan × DepFin, PerfoBan × DepFin). We control the impact of governance (measured by concentration and ownership structure (Calpre, CalDeu, CalIns, CalFle), board composition (Indca, Cumul), remuneration and some managerial characteristics (RemFixe, RemVar, StockOp, AgeDirig, CalDirig)) corporate performance (ROA) et firm growth opportunities (MB). We consider also the effect of the financial market development (DevMarch) and major government innovation incentives (A2013). Values between parentheses refer to P-value associated to each estimated coefficient.
***, **, *, indicates that the coefficients are statistically significant, respectively at 1%, 5% and 10%.
Number of observations = 570.

7   Conclusion

This paper studies empirically the impact on innovation of bank proximity, market credit development, efficiency and performance. We take also into consideration the impact of the financial market development, several corporate governance variables, external-finance dependence and corporate performance. We measure innovation by its input (R&D investment) and output (patents registered). Our sample includes 95 French listed companies on the SBF 120, covering the period from 2010 to 2015. According to the average difference test, firms having invested in R&D register more patents, benefit much more from bank proximity. This results is confirmed for firms having registered patents. Bivariate analysis of correlation coefficient do not find any significant correlation between the two variables measuring innovation and banking development. Results also show that innovation measured by its output is much more correlated with corporate governance mechanisms then innovation measured by its input.

Our multivariate analysis, coupled with individual effect identification, confirms partly these results. According to the test results, bank geographical proximity has no significant effect on innovation. However, it is shown that an efficient, performing banking sector that finance the economy through credits to firms seems to encourage firms to invest in R&D. This confirms that bank proximity is no longer determinant in access to financing.

R&D investment seem not to be affected by corporate governance variables such as ownership structure and board characteristics. However, R&D investment are positively influenced by corporate performance and government incentives.

When innovation is measured by the probability to register new patents, the significant effect of banking development totally disappears. However, a significant effect of corporate governance variables appears. These results prove that banking development seems to affect innovation more in the upstream (R&D investment) than in the downstream innovation process (patents).

When we estimate the two equation taking into consideration interaction between variables measuring banking development and external-finance dependence, our results confirm the effect of credit market development, efficiency and performance on R&D investment. This effect is still maintained in case of dependence upon external finance but becomes less significant. The results also show a significant positive effect of financial market development on R&D investment. The probability to register new patents remain dependent on corporate governance and not on banking development for firms that are dependent on external financing. In this case, concentrated, managerial, familial and institutional ownership seem to discourage significantly the innovation process. However, independence of board directors seems to positively affect the probability to register new patents.

Appendix. Variables Measures

Symbol	Variable	Measure	Tested hypothesis
Innovation			
LNRD	Innovation input	The natural logarithm of R&D expenditures	
Patent	Innovation output	Dummy variable equal to 1 if R&D expenditures achieve to new patents and 0 otherwise	
Banking development			
ProxBan	Bank proximity	The number of branches in the district of each firm of the sample	**H1**
DevCred	The credit market development	The ratio of credits provided by banks to firms over GDP (%)	**H1**
EfficBan	Banking efficiency	The ratio of overall banking costs by total assets (%)	**H1**
PerfoBan	Banking performance	The banking return on assets Ratio (%)	**H1**
External finzancial dependance			
DepFin	The debt ratio	The ratio of debts by total assets (%)	**H2**
Governance			

(*continued*)

(continued)

Symbol	Variable	Measure	Tested hypothesis
Ownership structure			
CalPre	The first majority shareholder	The percentage of capital held by the majority shareholder (%)	
CalDeu	The second majority shareholder	The percentage of capital held by the second majority shareholder (%)	
InvIns	Institutional ownership	The percentage of capital held by institutional shareholder (%)	
CalFle	Family ownership	The percentage of capital held by family shareholder (%)	
Board of directors: independance and duality			
Indca	Independance	The independent directors number to the total number of directors (%)	
Cumul	Duality	Dummy = 1 if the manager is the board chairman	
Managerial characteristic and compensation			
RemFixe	Fixed managerial compensation	Fixed salary (Thousand euro)	
RemVar	Variable managerial compensation	Variable salary (Thousand euro)	
StockOpt	Stock option plan	Dummy = 1 if the company offers managerial stock option plan	
CalDirig	Managerial ownership	The percentage of capital held by manager (%)	
AgeDirig	Manager age	The manager age during the year	
Other control variables			
MB	Growth opportunity	The market to book ratio	
ROA	Performance	The corporate return on assets Ratio (%)	
DevMarch	Equity market development	The equity market capitalisation to GDP (%)	

References

Aghion, P., Van John, R., Luigi, Z.: Innovation and institutional ownership. Am. Econ. Rev. **103** (1), 277–304 (2013)

Allen, F., Gale, D.: Diversity of opinion and financing of new technologies. J. Financ. Intermed. **8**, 68–89 (1999)

Alexandre, H., Paquerot, M.: Efficacité des structures de contrôle et enracinement des dirigeants: Une application du Boostrap. Finance Contrôle Stratégie 3(2), 5–29 (2000)

Amore, M.D., Schneider, C., Zaldokas, A.: Credit supply and corporate innovation. J. Financ. Econ. 109, 835–855 (2013)

Atanassov, J., Nanda, V., Seru, A.: Finance and innovation: the case of publicly listed firms, Working Paper, pp. 1–66 (2007)

Ayyagari, M., Demirgüç-Kunt, A., Maksimovic, V.: Firm innovation in emerging markets: the role of finance, governance, and competition. J. Financ. Quant. Anal. 46(6), 1545–1580 (2011)

Barker, V.L., Mueller, G.C.: CEO characteristics and firm R&D spending. Manag. Sci. 48(6), 782–801 (2002)

Becker-Blease, J.R.: Governance and innovation. J. Corp. Finance 17(4), 947–958 (2011)

Bekaert, G., Harvey, C.R., Lundblad, C.: Emerging equity markets and economic development. J. Dev. Econ. 66, 465–504 (2001)

Benfratello, L., Schiantarelli, F., Sembenelli, A.: Banks and innovation: microeconometric evidence on italian firms. J. Financ. Econ. 90, 197–217 (2008)

Bekaert, G., Harvey, C.R., Lundblad, C.: Does financial liberalization spur growth? J. Financ. Econ. 77, 3–55 (2005)

Black, S.E., Straham, P.E.: Entrepreneurship and bank credit availability. J. Finance 57(6), 2807–2833 (2002)

Di Bonaccorsi, E., Gobbi, G.: The effects of bank consolidation and market entry on small business lending. J. Bank. Finance 25(404), 2209–2237 (2001a)

Di Bonaccorsi, E., Gobbi, G.: The changing structure of local credit markets: are small businesses special? J. Bank. Finance 25(12), 2209–2237 (2001b)

Brown, J.R., Martinsson, G., Petersen, B.C.: Do financing constraints matter for R&D? Eur. Econ. Rev. 56, 1512–1529 (2012)

Cappelen, A., Raknerud, A., Rybalka, M.: The effects of R&D tax credits on patenting and innovations. Res. Policy 41, 334–345 (2012)

Carpenter, R.E., Peterson, B.C.: capital market imperfections, high-tech investment, and new equity financing. Econ. J. 112(477), 54–72 (2002)

Chakraborty, S., Kumar, P., Goyal, N., Ganguly, A., Mukherjee, A.: Towards a stratified learning approach to predict future citation counts. In: Digital Library, pp. 351–360 (2014)

Claessens, S., Djankov, S., Fan, J., Lang, L.: Disentangling the incentive and entrenchment effects of large shareholdings. J. Finance 57(6), 2741–2771 (2002)

Cornaggia, J., Mao, Y., Tian, X., Wolfe, B.: Does banking competition affect innovation? J. Financ. Econ. 115(1), 189–209 (2015)

Coles, J.L., Daniel, N.D., Naveen, L.: Managerial incentives and risk-taking. J. Financ. Econ. 79, 431–468 (2006)

Czarnitzki, D., Hottenrott, H., Thorwarth, S.: Industrial research versus development investment: the implications of financial constraints Cambridge. J. Econ. 35, 527–544 (2011)

Degryse, H., Ongena, S.: Distance, lending relationships, and competition. J. Finance 60, 231–266 (2005)

Dong, J., Gou, Y.N.: Corporate governance structure, managerial discretion, and the R&D investment in China. Int. Rev. Econ. Finance 19(2), 180–188 (2010)

Eng, L.L., Shackell, M.: The implications of long-term performance plans and institutional ownership for firms' R&D investments. J. Acc. 16, 117–139 (2001)

Ferraris, L., Minetti, R.: Foreign lenders and the real sector. J. Money Credit Bank. 39, 945–964 (2007)

Greenwood, J., Jovanovic, B.: Financial development growth, and the distribution of income. J. Polit. Econ. 98, 1076–1107 (1990)

Guan, J.C., Yam, R.C.: Effects of government financial incentives on firms' innovation performance in China: evidences from Beijing in the 1990s. Res. Policy **44**(1), 273–282 (2015)

Guan, J., Chen, K.: Modeling the relative efficiency of national innovation systems. Res. Policy **41**(1), 102–115 (2012)

Guan, J., Zuo, K.: A cross-country comparison of innovation efficiency. Scientometrics **100**(2), 541–575 (2014)

Hall, B.H., Lerner, J.: The financing of R&D and innovation. NBER Working Papers from National Bureau of Economic Research, Inc. (2010)

Ho, S., Wong, K.S.: A study of the relationship between corporate governance structures and the extent of voluntary disclosure7. J. Int. Acc. Audit. Tax. **10**(2), 139–156 (2001)

Hsu, P.H., Tian, X., Xu, Y.: Financial development and innovation: cross-country evidence. J. Financ. Econ. **112**, 116–135 (2014)

Jayaratne, J., Strahan, P.E.: The finance-growth nexus: evidence from bank branch deregulation the. Q. J. Econ. **111**(3), 639–670 (1996)

Lennox, C.: Management ownership and audit firm size. Contemp. Acc. Res. **22**(1), 205–222 (2005)

Lin, C., Lin, P., Song, F.M., Li, C.: Managerial incentives CEO characteristics and corporate innovation in China's private sector. J. comp. Econ. **39**(2), 179–190 (2011)

McConnell, J.J., Wahal, S.: Do institutional investors exacerbate managerial myopia? J. Corp. Finance **6**(3), 307–329 (2000)

Nanda, R., Nicholas, T.: Did bank distress stifle innovation during the great depression? J. Financ. Econ. **114**, 273–292 (2011)

Parisi, M., Schiantarelli, Sembenelli, A.: Productivity, innovation and R&D: micro evidence for Italy. Eur. Econ. Rev. **50**(8), 2037–2061 (2006)

Rajan, G., Zingales, L.: Financial systems, industrial structure, and growth. Oxf. Rev. Econ. Policy **17**, 467–482 (2001)

Rajan, R., Zingales, L.: Financial dependence and growth. Am. Econ. Rev. **88**, 559–586 (1998)

Rice, T., Strahan, P.: Does credit competition affect small-firm finance? J. Finance **65**, 861–889 (2010)

Singh, D.A., Gaur, A.S.: Governance structure, innovation and internationalization: evidence from India. J. Int. Manag. **19**(3), 300–309 (2013)

Solow, R.: Technical change and the aggregate production function. Rev. of Econ. Stat. **39**(3), 312–320 (1957)

Zahra, S.A., Stanton, W.: The implications of board of directors' composition on corporate strategy and performance. Int. J. Manag. **5**(2), 229–236 (1988)

Competitive Intelligence in the Start-Up Companies Belonging to the ICT Sector in Tunisia

Karima Dhaouadi[✉] and Fatma Turki

Higher Institute of Accounting and Business Administration, Manouba, Tunisia
dkarima76@yahoo.fr, Fatma_chichti@yahoo.fr

Abstract. The objective of this work is double. On the one hand, it aims at diagnosing the practices of environmental scanning in the start-up companies belonging to the ICT sector in Tunisia, and on the other hand, it aims at counting their real needs in information. Based on questionnaires and interviews, our results show that in spite of the awareness of the importance of competitive intelligence, the latter suffers from several cultural weaknesses (weak information sharing) and material weaknesses (financial and logistic). Our results, particularly demonstrate the pre-eminence of the informal sources of information collection and sharing and the urgent need for the technological scanning, the tenders' scanning the event scanning. The competitive intelligence remains a recent, poorly developed, and poorly structured, poorly formalized and poorly effective practice. It does not appear among the priorities of the young Tunisian entrepreneurs who grant it a little time.

Keywords: Competitive intelligence · Start-up · ICT sector
Contextual variables

1 Introduction

Nowadays, the companies operate in a complex environment. They are consequently obliged to innovate and to react quickly and wisely regarding the threats and to the environmental opportunities. However, this can only be realised through competitive intelligence.

The current economic environment is similarly characterized by the proliferation of the start-up companies in the field of new technologies. These young innovating companies have marked the years 2000 around the world. It is with the appearance of the first venture capital companies that the term «start-up» burst on the scene.

Consequently, the survival of a start-up depends on its capacity to adapt to the environmental evolution; which requires an excellent information control on the current environment and the future evolutions. Competitive intelligence makes it possible to the young companies to make judicious decisions and to choose a successful positioning on the market.

It is within this framework of competitive intelligence near the start-up companies that our work is situated. The objective of this work is double. On the one hand, it aims

© Springer Nature Switzerland AG 2018
M. A. Bach Tobji et al. (Eds.): ICDEc 2018, LNBIP 325, pp. 95–104, 2018.
https://doi.org/10.1007/978-3-319-97749-2_7

at diagnosing the practices of competitive intelligence of the start-up companies belonging to the ICT sector in Tunisia, and on the other hand, it aims at counting their real needs in information (types of information, formal and informal sources of information, types of the requested competitive intelligence as well as the sought periodicity...).

In order to meet our objectives, the present work will be divided into two parts: Theoretical and practical developments (methodology, the results of the investigation and discussion).

2 Competitive Intelligence and the Start-Up Companies: Theoretical Approaches

2.1 Definition of Competitive Intelligence

Various definitions of the concept of 'competitive intelligence' are employed by the authors according to their disciplinary belonging, and to the level of the analysis approached in treating this concept.

Cohen [4] proposes three phases of the evolution of the general concept of environmental monitoring. The first is the emergence phase ("scanning"), the second is the maturity phase (competitive intelligence) and the third is the consolidation phase (strategic and economic intelligence). The founding works date back to Aguilar [2] and Ansoff [3].

"Competitive Intelligence is the collective and proactive process, through which members of the company voluntarily track and use relevant information concerning their external environment and the changes possible to occur there" [9].

It is therefore about a formal continuous process of research, collection, treatment, and sharing of information useful for strategic management [14]. It integrates an informative and anticipatory function, allowing the detection of the threats and the opportunities of the environment. And, it rather adopts a proactive approach for strategic decision making.

2.2 The Process of Competitive Intelligence

The process of competitive intelligence comprises various stages aiming at transforming the raw information into useful ones for decision making. Although there is a variety of a description of the process of competitive intelligence, it seems that there is a consensus outlining five main stages [5].

Precondition: Raising awareness among the collaborators: This preliminary phase aims at informing the collaborators of the challenge process in order to evoke their support.

– *1st stage: Identification or the targeting of information needs:* It aims at defining the extent and the direction of the monitoring and at prioritizing the fields or the axes of competitive intelligence according to their importance for the company.

- *2nd stage: Information research and collection*: It allows the identification and the exploitation of the most relevant information sources in order to optimize information research [1].
- *3rd stage: Processing of the collected information*: It consists in trying to diagnose complete events starting from some perceived facts. There are no specific tools enabling data interpretation. The matrix SWOT[1], the model of five competitive strengths of Porter[2] and the BCG[3] matrix are examples of decision support tools facilitating the processing of the collected information.
- *4th stage: Memorizing information*: Memorizing is the operation which consists in retaining the raw and the processed information for a later use.
- *5th stage: Sharing of the synthesized information*: Lesca [10] defines the sharing as «the operation which consists in putting information and knowledge at the disposal of the potential users who are often the operational managers».

2.3 The Utility of Competitive Intelligence in the Development of the Start-Up Companies

A start-up is a young innovating company having a strong potential of development and requiring important investments in order to finance its fast growth. The objectives of the start-up are the following: to get known, to establish the loyalty of its customers, to enhance its brand image, to use new technology, to offer new products, to create new products and new markets [7].

Henceforth, competitive intelligence is more important than ever for the young innovating companies. The start-up need to release useful and relevant information in order to make good decisions and to anticipate the market needs. Information is a fundamental resource and competitive intelligence is a key weapon and a strategic lever for a young company which seeks the best positions [6].

3 Empirical Evidence in the Tunisian Start-Up Companies

3.1 Methodology

Positioning of the Research: Our research is exploratory and descriptive. It aims at identifying the opinions and the expectations of the young entrepreneurs in terms of competitive intelligence through a questionnaire and interviews near a sample of the studied population.

---

[1] SWOT matrix allows the identification of the strengths and the weaknesses of the company in the light of the opportunities and the threats of the external environment.

[2] The model is based on the study of 5 great strengths influencing the company: intensity of the intra-sectoral competition; the threat of new entrants; threat of the products and the substitutable services; the customers' and the suppliers' negotiation power.

[3] It's an analysis which identifies the DAS (Strategic Areas of Activity). The fundamental assumption of this method is that the company must optimally manage the cash flows generated by its activities. This method is founded on two main criteria: the growth rate of the market and the relative market share. The crossing of the two above mentioned criteria allows the construction of a matrix with four boxes named: Cash Cow, Dogs, Stars, and Question Marks (or Problem Child).

Sample: The target population in our investigation is all the start-up companies operating in the ICT sector and installed in the technological pole of "Elgazala" which is well known in Africa[4]. The total of 50 start-up companies, only 20 of them have answered our questionnaire (i.e. a return of 40%). This sampling method is based on the voluntarism of the respondents. It is a simple random sampling method. The abstention of the other start-up companies is explained by the lack of interest or quite simply time constraints. In order to further enrich our investigations, about ten semi-directive interviews have been carried out near young entrepreneurs.

Competitive Intelligence Measuring: We have adopted two types of competitive intelligence measurement: «direct and subjective» through the interviews conducted with certain start-up managers and «indirect and subjective» through the diffusion of a questionnaire on the practices of competitive intelligence. Our questionnaire is inspired from the work of the consulting cabinet "Kea & Partners" which has specialized in strategy. We have carried out a pre-test with three entrepreneurs in order to adjust and adapt the contents of the questionnaire to our context of study. The questionnaire contains two parts. The first part draws a diagnosis of the current practices of the start-up companies in terms of competitive intelligence, whereas the second part identifies its real needs.

In order to treat the collected data, we have used Excel and we have deployed simple statistical techniques based on the calculation of the percentage and the graphical representation in a diagram per sector.

3.2   Results: Diagnosis of the Existing

Use of Competitive Intelligence in the Start-Up Companies

Our investigations demonstrate that 45% of the interviewed start-up companies have an action plan in terms of competitive intelligence and 30% are in project development as it's demonstrated in the following figure. Among the 25% of the start-up who do not dispose an action plan, 40% do not know how to get involved, and 60% estimate that they do not have the necessary means to that end (Fig. 1).

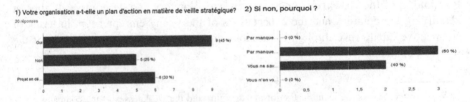

Fig. 1. Use of competitive intelligence

---

[4] Elgazala Technopark is the first techno pole in Tunisia. It was created in 1997; it was decided within the framework of the development strategy of the communication technologies sector. Its principal function is the accompaniment of the start-up during the launch phase and the coaching of the innovative projects leaders. Its main customers are the national and the international investors, the start-up, the SME, the large firms, the universities, the researchers and the research laboratories.

Satisfaction Regarding the Products of Competitive Intelligence

As it is demonstrated in the following diagram, the respondents, unanimously, express dissatisfaction regarding the products of competitive intelligence elaborated by their organizations. They estimate that the obtained information does not meet their real needs (Fig. 2).

15) Êtes-vous satisfait des documents de veille produits par votre organisation?

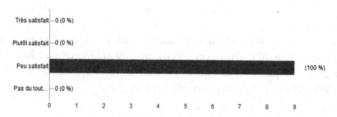

Fig. 2. The degree of satisfaction with competitive intelligence

The dissatisfaction of these young entrepreneurs is mainly explained by the following factors: lack of information sharing (65% of the respondents); weak commitment of the direction (55%); lack of human resources (40%), and the difficulty of data exploitation (30%) (Fig. 3).

7) Si vous rencontrez des difficultés lors de votre recherche d'informations et de vos pratiques de la veille, quelles sont à votre avis les raisons ?

20 réponses

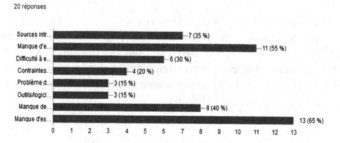

Fig. 3. Encountered difficulties

Awareness of the Importance of Competitive Intelligence

On the other hand, the majority of the respondents (80%) estimate that competitive intelligence is paramount for the decision-making process (Fig. 4).

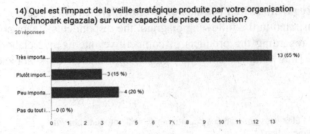

Fig. 4. Awareness of the importance of competitive intelligence

Usual Sources

Our interviews show that the most used sources are in order of importance, the following; relational networks (16 interviewed), quality standards and benchmarks (13), the thematic workshops (11), the social networks (10), the specialized press (9), the Web pages (8) and the patent pending platform (7) (Fig. 5).

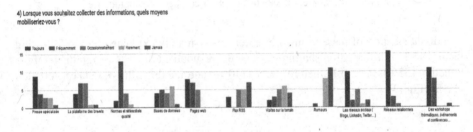

Fig. 5. Sources of information

The Dedicated Time for Competitive Awareness

According to our results and the following figure, 45% of the interviewed devote several hours per week, 40% devote only one hour per day, and 15% devote several hours per day. It seems that competitive intelligence does not occupy an important place in the agenda of the majority of the young entrepreneurs who are overwhelmed by the daily business management (Fig. 6).

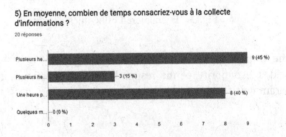

Fig. 6. The dedicated time for competitive awareness

3.3 Results: The Start-Up Companies Need Competitive Intelligence

The Main Reasons

The figure below show that the start-up need competitive intelligence for the following reasons; to identify the commercial opportunities, to systematically obtain news on a subject which they are interested in, to get opened to the international market, and to know the new technological trends in the world (Fig. 7).

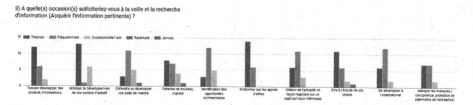

Fig. 7. Information needs

Favourite Supports

More than half of the start-up companies (55%) prefer the face to face to report the information, 50% prefer the e-mail with the information attached, 25% prefer the e-mail with the information in the message body, 25% via the telephone, and 10% prefer the paper file (Fig. 8).

Fig. 8. Favourite supports for information report and sharing

The most interesting supports of information sharing for the start-up are mainly the competitive intelligence newsletters (at a rate of 80%) and the thematic files (65%). Then, come the competitive intelligence alerts (35%) and the magazines (15%). In our interviews, the majority of the respondents find that face to face (the direct involved meeting) remains the surest and the most judicious means of information sharing.

Types of the Solicited Competitive Intelligence

To the question «Which types of competitive intelligence best meet your needs?», the usual, frequent and primary types of competitive intelligence are by order of importance: the technology scanning (17 respondents), the tenders' scanning (14 respondents), the event scanning (12 respondents), the commercial scanning (11 respondents) and the competitors' scanning (10 respondents). The types of competitive intelligence

which have an average importance and which were announced less than 10 guarantors
are in descending order: the patent scanning, the monitoring of the economic, legal and
societal environments (culture and lifestyle) (Fig. 9).

Fig. 9. Types of solicited competitive intelligence

Desired Frequency and Periodicity

Our results show that the majority of the start-up prefers less than a week old information (37.5%), while 25% prefer less than a month old information, finally 25%
prefer less than a day old information and 12.5% say that it depends on the type of the
considered competitive intelligence. A daily periodicity is required for the technological and event scanning, a weekly periodicity for the tenders' scanning and monthly
periodicity for the other types of scanning (Fig. 10).

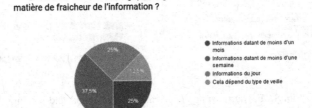

Fig. 10. Needs for fresh information

3.4   Summary and Recommendations

The key lessons drawn from our investigation are the following:

– Competitive intelligence is a secondary activity, but of growing interest. It constitutes a luxurious affair (and even ridiculed) in the agenda of the young entrepreneurs. Only a minority devotes daily time to it; however, there is the same
awareness of the competitive intelligence importance near the start-up companies.

- The start-up mainly suffers from the lack of skills in competitive intelligence and in material resources (financial and logistic), and from the disengagement of the entrepreneurs and from an adverse culture regarding information sharing and risk taking.
- The pre-eminence of the informal sources of information sharing. Although the start-up companies operate in the ICT sector, the basic and the archaic means prevail; it is a cultural feature where the relational value is dominant.
- The technological scanning is the most sought (it is normal since the start-up companies operate in the ICT sector). A daily and pressing need is displayed for the types of technological and event scanning. The societal and the economic intelligence are ranked last.

Our results meet the drawn conclusions in the previous works [8, 11–13, 15].

Based on these findings, we estimate that in order to improve the intelligence activity near the start-up companies, it would be necessary to grant a particular interest to the following axes:

- The implication and the support of the direction in implementing a formalized approach of competitive intelligence and to make the colleagues aware of the challenges of such practice.
- Improve the culture of teamwork in order to establish the routines of information sharing between the teammates and the training of specialists in competitive intelligence to obtain high quality services.
- Develop the technological and competitive intelligence tools: the tools of competitive intelligence are essential to produce an effective intelligence. "Technopark Elgazala" offers an excellent intelligence tool (*"Ami Enterprise Intelligence"*). Nevertheless, this tool is under-used and it is not at the disposal of the young entrepreneurs to help them elaborate their intelligence (culture of not sharing knowledge). In this context, we estimate that this tool must be more accessible in order to boost the activity of competitive intelligence near the start-up companies.
- Organize workshops and events on competitive intelligence: these means enable the entrepreneurs to broaden their professional networks and to update their knowledge. In the absence of the formal sources, the informal sources shall take hold, what may cause a problem of information reliability.

4 Conclusion

The present work aims at diagnosing the practices of competitive intelligence near the start-up companies belonging to the ICT sector in Tunisia while detecting their failures and their needs regarding competitive intelligence (types, periodicity, formal and informal sources and freshness).

The results of our exploratory investigation show that the majority of the start-up companies are aware of the importance of competitive intelligence in the piloting of a company. However, they are unhappy with their current practices in this regard. Competitive intelligence is a recent and little formalized activity. In most cases, there is no action plan of competitive intelligence. This is explained by the lack of material resources (financial and software: tools of data collection, processing, and diffusion).

Although the questioned start-up companies operate in the ICT sector, the most used tools for data collection and sharing remains the face to face and the informal relations. Moreover, it seems that the start-up companies pay special attention to the technological scanning, the tenders' scanning, and the event scanning.

Based on the interviews and the questionnaires, we estimate that competitive intelligence will be more judicious if the young entrepreneurs get more involved in this approach, and especially raising the awareness of their colleagues. They should set the example by granting more time in their daily time tables and by taking part in the workshops and the seminars. These young start-up companies have to cultivate a culture of information sharing and have to form certain frameworks in terms of competitive intelligence so that their services shall be efficient.

We suppose and hope that our investigation could make an assessment of the practices of competitive intelligence near the start-up companies belonging to the ICT sector in Tunisia while highlighting the effect of the study context.

References

1. AFNOR: Norme XPX 50-053: Prestations de veille et prestations de mise en place d'un système de veille, Paris, p. 5 (1998). ISSN 0335-3931
2. Aguilar, F.J.: Scanning the Business Environment. The Macmillan Company, New York (1967)
3. Ansoff, F.-I.: Managing strategic surprise by response to weak signals. Calif. Manag. Rev. **18**(2), 21–33 (1975)
4. Cohen, C.: Veille et intelligence stratégiques. Hermès Lavoisier, 286 p. (2004)
5. Dishman, P.-L., Calof, J.-L.: Competitive intelligence: a multi phasic precedent to marketing strategy. Eur. J. Mark. **42**(7/8), 766–785 (2008)
6. EPITA: La veille stratégique: Les yeux et les oreilles de votre entreprise? 10 p. Etude 3IE (2001)
7. Fridenson, P., Philip, S.: Reimagining Business History. JHU Press, Baltimore (2013)
8. Gretry, A., Brandt, C., Delcourt, C.: Bilan des Pratiques de Veille Stratégique au sein des PME Wallonnes. Revue Française du Marketing **241**, 73–87 (2013)
9. Lesca, H.: Veille stratégique: La méthode L.E.SCAnning, Editions EMS, 180 p. (2003)
10. Lesca, H.: Veille stratégique: Concepts et démarche de mise en place dans l'entreprise. Université de Grenoble (1997)
11. Lesca, N., Caron-Fasan, M.L.: Facteurs d'échec et d'abandon d'un projet de veille stratégique: retours d'expériences. Système d'Information et Management **13**(3), 17–42 (2008)
12. Miaux, J.F.: Mise en œuvre d'une activité de veille. Mémoire de Master Professionnel, Institut National des Techniques de la Documentation, France (2010)
13. Rouach, D.: La veille technologique et l'intelligence économique, Collection Que Sais-je? 4ème édition, Paris (2008)
14. Roulet, A., Bezençon, C., Madinier, H.: Évaluation de la performance et de l'impact de la veille, I2D. Information, Données & Documents **52**(3), 70–79 (2015)
15. Wright, S., Eid, E.R., Fleisher, C.S.: Competitive intelligence in practice: empirical evidence from the UK retail banking sector. J. Mark. Manag. **25**(9–10), 941–964 (2009)

Information System Technologies

Lightweight Cryptography for Resource-Constrained Devices: A Comparative Study and Rectangle Cryptanalysis

Tasnime Omrani[1(✉)], Rhouma Rhouma[1], and Layth Sliman[2]

[1] RISC Laboratory, ENIT, University of Tunis El-Manar, Tunis, Tunisia
tasnim.omrani@gmail.com
[2] EFREI Engineering Institute, Paris, France

Abstract. Several Lightweight cryptosystems were specially designed for constrained-devices. For this reason many papers have been comparing and assessing existing Lightweight cryptosystems. Our contribution; compared to those papers; is to analyse the recently and popular Lightweight cryptosystems using actual devices used in IoT context namely the Raspberry Pi 2 B and Arduino UNO. The evaluation is based on RAM and ROM consumption, speed performance by evaluating Encryption/Decryption time speed and clock cycle and security level. The results of this evaluation indicates the superiority of Speck in term of memory consumption, Rectangle in term of speed performance and Present in term of security level.

Keywords: Lightweight cryptosystem · IoT · Linear cryptanalysis
Speed performance · Memory consumption · Security

1 Introduction

Lightweight cryptography is used for resource-constrained devices. Indeed, these devices are used in Internet Of Things (IoT); which become implicated in many domains; in RFID tags, in wireless sensor networks, etc. These devices are limited in term of processing power and memory.

Constrained-devices are classified in three categories according to RFC-7228 [1]: Class-0 (C0), Class-1 (C1), and class-2 (C2). The Table 1 shows a comparison of these classes. The class-3 (C3) is added and define the devices that have no memory constraints but can still be constrained by a limited power/energy but also used in IoT context.

Giving the fact that the confidentiality of the exchanged data is essential and given the limitation of theses devices, the designed cryptosystems in constrained devices are different from conventional ciphers design such as AES [2] and DES [3]. Therefore, many researches are proposing several lightweight cryptosystems.

© Springer Nature Switzerland AG 2018
M. A. Bach Tobji et al. (Eds.): ICDEc 2018, LNBIP 325, pp. 107–118, 2018.
https://doi.org/10.1007/978-3-319-97749-2_8

Table 1. Classes of constrained devices

Name	RAM	ROM	Example (RAM/ROM)
Class-0	$\ll$10 KB	$\ll$100 KB	Arduino UNO (2 KB/32 KB)
Class-1	$\approx$10 KB	$\approx$100 KB	Crossbox TelosB (10 KB/48 KB)
Class-2	$\approx$50 KB	$\approx$250 KB	Arduino MK100 (32 KB/256 KB)
Class-3	$\gg$50 KB	$\gg$250 KB	Raspberry Pi 2 (1 GB,-)

The contributions of this work are the analysis of the recently and most popular lightweight cryptosystems in term of their memory requirements, and speed performance for the recently two different devices used in IoT context (Rapsberry and Arduino). The second contribution is the analysis of security level of each cryptosystem in term of confusion and diffusion levels defined by Claude Shannon and testing the feasibility of linear cryptanalysis on each one of them.

For this reason, the paper is organized as follows: We discuss the related work in Sect. 2 and we describe the lightweight cryptosystems analyzed in this paper. In Sect. 3, those presented lightweight ciphers are implemented on both Raspberry Pi 2 model B and Arduino UNO to measure the RAM and ROM consumption and also the speed performance. The constrained device "Arduino UNO" is characterized by 2 KB of RAM, 32 KB of ROM, a CPU equal to 16 MHz and the ATmega328P Microcontroller. And the IoT device named "Raspberry Pi model B" characterized by 1 GB RAM, a CPU equal to 900 MHz and the Debian GNU/Linux Operating System. In Sect. 4, the security level of each lightweight cryptosystem is evaluated according to the confusion and diffusion properties and the complexity of the linear cryptanalysis is tested. At the end of the paper, we finish by a conclusion and we describe our future works.

2   Related Work

Several papers have studied the performance of different lightweight cryptosystems.

Eisenbarth and Kumar [4] measure the RAM and ROM requirements and the required number of clock cycles for 8 different block encryption algorithms (DES, DESXL, Hight, Present, AES, IDEA, TEA, SEA) and all of them are implemented in 8-bit AVR microcontroller. The results show that Hight cryptosystem is the faster in term of encryption/decryption and IDEA represent the best cryptosystem in term of used memory.

Sumandeep and Supreet [5] evaluate the processing time, the correlation and the avalanche effect of three cryptosystems (AES, Leopard and Rectangle) in smart grid. The results show the rapidity of Rectangle compared to AES and Leapard which performs nearly 46 times faster than AES and 11 times faster than Leopard. However, in term of avalanche effect for data, Rectangle records the worst measurement result.

Alex and Leo [6] evaluate the performance (RAM, ROM and Clock cycle) of Chaskey, Simon, Lea, Rectangle, Spark, RC5-20, AES and Fantomas on three different microcontrollers (AVR (8-bit), MSP (16-bit) and ARM (32-bit)). This evaluation shows the dependence between the performance of the algorithm and the type of the used microcontroller. Indeed, the same algorithm A consumes less memory than B in a particular microcontroller and more memory in another microcontroller. In this paper, Simon records the best cryptosystem in term of the consumed RAM in all microcontrollers and the best cryptosystem in term of ROM quantity used in only AVR and ARM microcontroller. And Chaskey shows the minimum ROM consumed in MSP microcontroller and the minimum clock cycle.

Charalampos et al. [7] have implemented Hight, Present, PrintCipher, Katan-Katantan, Klein, Twine, Simon, Speck, Pride, Hummigbrid, Lblock, Mips and Piccolo and they have concluded the superiority of Speck in term of RAM, ROM and speed.

The following is a brief introduction of the used cryptosystems in this paper.

Simon: It consists of 10 variants with different block and key size. For instance Simon64/128 will employ 64-bit of data blocks and 128-bit keys. All Simon ciphers use Feistel structure. These ciphers are chosen to minimize the hardware implementation but they are not optimized for software implementation.

The generated Subkeys depend from each other and the key schedule function uses bitwise operations of circular shift and XOR because those operations can be easily implemented in hardware.

Speck: This cipher was designed to provide a high performance in software and hardware. It uses for that bitwise XOR, modular addition 2^n, left circular shift S^i by i bits and right circular shift S^{-j} by j bits.

Prince: This cipher uses 64-bit of data block size and 128-bit of key size and it follows a SPN structure on 11 rounds where each round is composed of an addition with a subkey, a substitution function using involutive Sbox 4×4, a Matrix-M based operations and addition with round constant. This cipher is characterized by the use of a perfectly symmetric structure where the five first rounds are the reverse of the last five rounds. The use of such involutive components and the round inversed characteristics makes the implementation of Prince works for encryption (transmitter) and decryption (receiver) in the same time.

Rectangle: This cipher uses a 64-bit block size and 64-bit or 128-bit key size. It is very flexible for hardware implementation. This is ensured by using bit-sliced design. The block is realized in the form of matrix with 4 rows and 16 columns of bits.

It uses SPN structure with 25 rounds containing a mixing with the sub-key, a substitution function using a parallel Sbox 4×4 for the 16 columns and finally a left rotation with 1 bit for row 1, 12 bits for row 2 and 13 bits for row 3.

LBlock: This cipher uses a 64-bit block size and 80-bit key size. It is based on a typical Feistel structure with 32 rounds. The Feistel function is composed of two operations: a substitution·operation that uses in parallel 8 different Sbox 4×4 and a permutation operation consisting of eight 4-bit permutations.

Present: This cipher uses 64-bit block size and 80-bit key size. And it follows a SPN structure on 31 rounds where each round is composed of a mixing with the round key using XOR operation, a substitution function using a 4×4 Sbox and a permutation function consisting of a bitwise operation. In 2012, this cipher was approved by ISO/IEC 29192-2 as a standard lightweight block cipher.

Pride: This cipher uses a 64-bit block size and 128-bit key size and it is a SPN on 20 rounds where each round is composed of an addition with subkey, a substitution function using an involutive Sbox 4×4 and a linear layer.

In this paper, we analyze and compare the most popular lightweight cryptosystems that we have just described in the previous paragraph. Compared to the existing papers, our paper provide a more detailed evaluation of security and performance levels on actual IoT-devices (Raspberry and Arduino) and also, we have only considered the most recent published lightweight ciphers in this study.

3   Performance Evaluation of Lightweight Ciphers

The used devices in IoT and in Wireless Sensor Networks (WSN) have considerable limitations in term of speed and memory. For this reason, we evaluated the performance of the existent Lightweight cryptosystems according to speed performance and memory consumption using Raspberry Pi model B and Arduino UNO for blocks of 64-bits.

Speed performance is evaluated by measuring the execution time and the number of clock cycles required for running the cryptosystem. The memory consumption can be evaluated by measuring RAM and ROM use to perform the encryption/decryption. In fact, the RAM is the space to hold temporary data and the ROM refers to the amount of memory used to store the code of the software implementation.

The presented results in Table 2 show that Prince requires a significant quantity of ROM to encrypt and decrypt a data using Raspberry. In contrast to Prince, Speck is the lightest among all cryptosystems.

Regarding the quantity of the consumed RAM, most consumed RAM for all those ciphers are equivalent except Simon that consumes more than the other cryptosystems by 12% in key setup.

Concerning the Arduino UNO, where the implementation results are depicted in Table 2. Speck is the lightest cryptosystem whereas Prince is the heaviest one. Given this fact, We can affirm that "Speck" is the most suitable cryptosystem for software implementation given its light structure and the reduced memory use.

In further analysis, we measured the RAM and ROM consumption (in KB) for each building block used by those cryptosystems when implemented in Raspberry and Arduino. The evaluation of the building blocks in term of consumed RAM is shown in Fig. 1. The ROM consumption is depicted in Fig. 2.

Table 2. Lightweight cryptosystems memory use on Raspberry and Arduino (KB)

Lightweight cryptosystems	Keyschedule				Encryption				Decryption			
	Raspberry		Arduino		Raspberry		Raspberry		Arduino		Raspberry	
	RAM	ROM	RAM	ROM	RAM	ROM	RAM	ROM	RAM	ROM	RAM	ROM
Present	0.297	1.368	0.203	2.629	0.293	1.485	0.201	2.277	0.293	1.532	0.201	2.285
Simon	0.340	1.091	0.230	1.643	0.293	1.181	0.186	1.678	0.293	1.532	0.186	1.678
Speck	0.297	1.126	0.189	1.609	0.293	1.060	0.186	1.543	0.293	1.060	0.186	1.543
Rectangle	0.297	2.122	0.213	1.779	0.293	1.688	0.186	1.654	0.293	1.704	0.186	1.662
Prince	0.301	1.138	0.193	1.489	0.293	4.411	0.311	2.469	0.293	4.411	0.311	2.471
Pride	0.305	0.873	0.178	1.357	0.293	3.755	0.264	1.896	0.293	3.888	0.264	1.9
LBlock	0.297	1.751	0.219	0.758	0.293	2.228	0.311	1.846	0.293	2.204	0.311	1.895

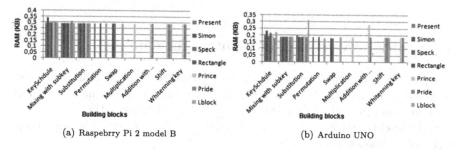

(a) Raspebrry Pi 2 model B   (b) Arduino UNO

Fig. 1. RAM consumption for the building blocks constituting the Lightweight Cryptosystems using Raspberry Pi 2 model B

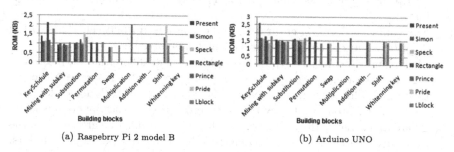

(a) Raspebrry Pi 2 model B   (b) Arduino UNO

Fig. 2. ROM consumption for the building blocks constituting the Lightweight cryptosystems using Arduino UNO

We have also measured the execution times and the number of clock cycle of key setup, encryption and decryption operations of the lightweight cryptosystems under study. The results of speed performance for Arduino UNO are shown in Table 3. We can see that Present represents the worst choice in software implementation which takes more than 220 times longer than Rectangle which can be evaluated as the fast cryptosystem among all the studied ones.

Table 3. Performance speed: execution times and number of clock cycle of lightweight cryptosystems in Arduino UNO

Lightweight cryptosystems	Keyschedule		Encryption		Decryption	
	Time (ms)	Clock cycle	Time (ms)	Clock cycle (ms)	Time	Clock cycle
Present	2.76	44 160	65.276	1 044 416	69.94	1 113 040
Simon	0.704	11 264	0.72	11 520	0.72	11 520
Speck	0.46	7 360	0.424	6 784	0.424	6 784
Rectangle	0.388	6 208	0.296	4 736	0.308	4 928
Prince	0.02	320	0.796	12 736	0.796	12 736
Pride	$\simeq$0	$\simeq$0	0.408	6 528	0.416	6 656
LBlock	0.67	9 430	0.320	5 120	0.320	5 120

4   Security Evaluation of Lightweight Ciphers

The security is the main goal of all cryptosystems. However, in lightweight context, the compromise between high security, performance speed and low memory consumption can lead to a security weakness. For this reason, the evaluation of security level is very important for any proposed cryptosystem. The basic properties of evaluation are as follows:

(a) The diffusion level: The diffusion level ensures that an inversion of an input bit (in the key or in the plain-text) will generate a 50% change in the output bits.

(b) The confusion level: it ensures that the relationship between the key, the plain-text and the cipher-text is as complex as possible.

(c) Linear and differential cryptanalysis: Linear and differential cryptanalysis are among the most common techniques used to attack symmetric cryptosystems. This leads us to estimate the complexity of each attack for various number of rounds. To say that a cryptosystem is resistant to linear and differential attacks, the complexity of those attacks must be greater than the exhaustive search effort that is equal to 2^{N_k}, where N_k is the key size in bits.

4.1   Confusion and Diffusion Level

To evaluate the confusion level of each Lightweight cipher considered in our paper, we use the Hamming distance [8] to quantify the difference between the plain-text (P) and the cipher-text (C). This quantity d_c is calculated using the following:

$$d_c = \sum_{i=1}^{b_z}(P_i \oplus C_i) \tag{1}$$

where b_z is the block size of the plain-text.

In our experiment, we repeat this evaluation 1000 times for different random plain-texts and we calculate the maximum, the minimum and the average values. The results are represented in Fig. 3 which shows that the cryptosystem "Present" is the best in term of confusion level with an average value of 50%. Also, we calculate the standard deviation (σ) of the sample of 1000 plain-texts using Eq. 2.

$$\sigma = \sqrt{\frac{\sum\limits_{i=0}^{100} |d_{c_i} - \bar{d}_c|^2}{1000}} \qquad (2)$$

where the d_{c_i} is the confusion level of the plain-text and $\bar{d}_c$ is the average of the 1000 confusion values founded for each plain-text. When the σ value is close to 0, the confusion values are compact (more the values are compact and the average value is close to 50%, the higher the level of confusion). The Table 4 shows the σ values of each lightweight cryptosystem and confirm that Present have the best confusion level. Similarly, to evaluate the diffusion level, we use the Hamming distance to quantify the difference between two cipher-text (C and C') which are the cipher-texts of two close plain-texts (P and P'), different in only one bit at position j (meaning $\sum\limits_i (P_i \oplus P'_i) = 1$).

This quantity d_d evaluating the diffusion level can be defined as:

$$\begin{cases} d_d = \sum\limits_{j=2}^{b_z} (\sum\limits_{i=1}^{b_z} (C_i \oplus C'_{i,j})) \\ C = E(P) \\ C' = E(P') \text{ and where } (P \oplus P') = 1 \end{cases}$$

We repeat this evaluation 1000 times for 1000 differential close plain-texts and we calculate the maximum, minimum and average values. The results represented in Fig. 3(b) show that the cryptosystem "Present" is the best in term of diffusion level which has as average value 50%. The standard deviation of diffusion measures are calculated and represented in Table 4. This evaluation confirms that Present represents the best cryptosystem in term of diffusion level.

Table 4. The standard deviation (σ) of confusion and diffusion levels

Lightweight cryptosystem	σ of confusion level	σ of diffusion level
Present	6.022	0.737
Simon	6.295	0.758
Speck	6.179	0.753
Rectangle	6.324	0.757
Prince	6.386	0.779
Prince	6.26	0.763
LBlock	6.326	0.773

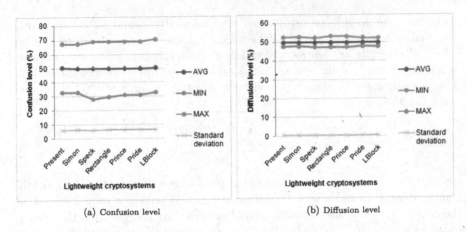

(a) Confusion level   (b) Diffusion level

Fig. 3. Evaluation of confusion and diffusion level for most recent lightweight ciphers.

4.2 Linear Cryptanalysis

The linear cryptanalysis [9] follows a known plain-text scenario. It consists on finding a linear approximation of the cryptosystem between plain-text, cipher-text and the secret key using the following equation:

$$\sum_u P_u \oplus \sum_v C_v = \sum_w K_w \tag{3}$$

where P_u is the uth bit of the plaintext $P = [P_1, P_2, ..., P_n]$, C_v is the vth bit of the ciphertext and K_w is the wth bit of the key.

The relation (3) holds between the input and the output crossing a linear building block with a probability equal to 1. However, for non-linear components like S-Boxes, it needs to be analyzed and tested. For this reason, we construct a linear approximation table of each S-Box used by each cipher by counting the number of times where Eq. (3) holds. The algorithm that can generate the approximation table is proposed in [10] and presented in Algorithm 1.

Data: n bit S-box
Result: linear approximation of S-box
$dist \leftarrow -2^{n-1}$
for $i=0$ to n **do**
    for $j = 0$ to n **do**
        $valuey \leftarrow 0, valuex \leftarrow valuex \oplus j \times i$
        for $k=0$ to n **do**
            $valuey \leftarrow 0, valuey \leftarrow valuey \oplus k \times Sbox[i]$
            if $valuesx = valuesy$ **then**
                | dist[i][k]++
            end
        end
    end
end
Algorithm 1. Generating the linear approximation table of an $n \times n$ S-Box

After constructing the linear approximation table of an S-Box, we have to iteratively construct the approximation of the cryptosystem by finding the highest probability relation between the input and the output for each pass of a non-linear component (S-Box) using its linear approximation table. The probability p of the approximation result is calculated using the Piling-Up Lemma defined as follows:

$$p = \frac{1}{2} + 2^{n-1} \prod_{i=1}^{n} (\epsilon_i) \tag{4}$$

where ϵ_i is the biais of this approximation which constitutes the variation from a random guess ($p_i = \frac{1}{2}$) and calculated by subtraction $\frac{1}{2}$ from the probability p_i of round i of the cryptosystem.

Finally, the data complexity of the linear attack is $O(\frac{1}{\epsilon^2})$ which constitutes approximately the needed number of known plain-text/cipher-text pairs to have a chance p guessing the right keys bits using a linear cryptanalysis. This probability is used to determinate if the cryptosystem resist the linear attack or not. In fact, when the data complexity of linear attack is greater than the data complexity of the naive brute force attack, the cryptosystem can resist the linear cryptanalysis.

In Table 5, we report previous results of the linear cryptanalysis complexity for some recent lightweight cryptosystems.

Table 5. Linear cryptanalysis complexity of most recent lightweight cryptosystems.

Cryptosystem (block size/key size)	Number of rounds (N_r) Full N_r/Attacker N_r	Complexity for Attacker N_r
Present 64/80	32/ < 28	2^{84} [11]
Simon 64/96	42/27	$2^{62.53}$ [12]
Speck 64/96	26/16	2^{63} [13]
Lblock 64/80	32/15	2^{66} [14]

During the analysis of lightweight cryptosystems, we have noticed that the cryptosystem "Rectangle" is the faster lightweight cryptosystem. For this reason, we have decided to test the robustness of Rectangle using linear cryptanalysis, and check if Rectangle can make a compromise between security and rapidity. In our paper, we tested the linear cryptanalysis on a lighter version of "Rectangle" with a rounds number equal to $N_r = 6$ given the high complexity of this attack.

First, we generate the linear approximation table of the non-linear component S-box used in Rectangle (see Table 6). The results of the approximation; using the algorithm 1; is depicted in Table 7:

We calculate next the linear approximation complexity by evaluating the bias ϵ_i in each round i as shown in Fig. 4. The Biais ϵ of the linear approximation of the whole cryptosystem Rectangle can be found using the Pilling-Up Lemma. Then the complexity of the linear attack C will be equal to $C = \frac{1}{\epsilon^2}$. In the same

Table 6. The S-box of Rectangle cryptosystem

i	0	1	2	3	4	5	6	7	8	9	A	B	C	D	E	F
S-box(i)	6	5	C	A	1	E	7	9	B	0	3	D	8	F	4	2

Table 7. Linear approximation table of Rectangle cryptosystem

	0	1	2	3	4	5	6	7	8	9	10	11	12	13	14	15
0	8	0	0	0	0	0	0	0	0	0	0	0	0	0	0	0
1	0	0	0	4	0	−4	0	0	2	−2	−2	−2	−2	−2	2	−2
2	0	0	0	0	0	0	4	4	0	0	4	−4	0	0	0	0
3	0	0	0	−4	4	0	0	0	−2	2	−2	−2	−2	−2	2	−2
4	0	0	0	0	0	0	−4	4	0	0	0	0	0	0	4	4
5	0	0	−4	0	0	−4	0	0	−2	2	−2	−2	2	2	−2	2
6	0	0	0	0	0	0	0	0	4	4	0	0	−4	4	0	0
7	0	0	−4	0	−4	0	0	0	−2	2	2	2	−2	−2	2	−2
8	0	0	0	−4	−2	−2	2	−2	0	−4	0	0	−2	2	2	2
9	0	0	0	0	−2	2	2	−2	2	2	−2	−2	4	0	4	0
10	0	0	0	−4	−2	−2	−2	2	4	0	0	0	2	−2	−2	−2
11	0	0	0	0	2	−2	2	−2	2	2	2	2	0	−4	0	4
12	0	4	0	0	−2	2	−2	−2	0	0	0	−4	−2	−2	−2	2
13	0	4	4	0	−2	−2	2	2	−2	2	−2	2	0	0	0	0
14	0	−4	0	0	−2	2	2	2	0	0	−4	0	−2	−2	−2	2
15	0	4	−4	0	2	2	2	2	2	−2	−2	2	0	0	0	0

figure, the calculus of every biais ϵ_i is depicted for each round i $(1 \leq i \leq 6)$. And the final biais is given using the following formula.

$$\epsilon = 2^{(N_r-1)} \prod_{i=1}^{N_r} (\epsilon_i) \tag{5}$$

This bias is equal to $\frac{1}{2^{39}}$ in Rectangle cryptosystem using 6 rounds (See Fig. 4). This bias is used to calculate the attack complexity of Rectangle cryptosystem which equal to $\frac{1}{\epsilon^2}$. From this latter, the linear attack complexity of Rectangle is equal to 2^{78} which is less than the exhaustive search effort that is equal to 2^{80}. This shows that for a reduced number of rounds equal to $N_r = 6$, Rectangle can be attacked using the linear cryptanalysis.

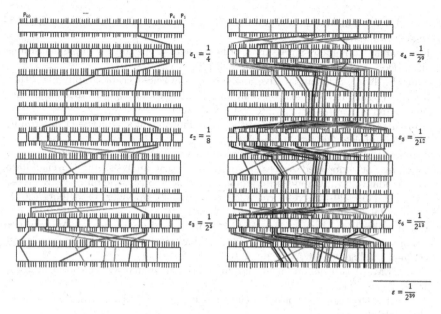

Fig. 4. Linear cryptanalysis of Rectangle with a reduced number of rounds equal to $N_r = 6$

5 Conclusion

In this paper we have analyzed some existing lightweight cryptosystems by evaluating their speed performance, memory consumption, and diffusion properties and their robustness against linear cryptanalysis. This evaluation indicates the superiority of Speck in term of memory consumption, Rectangle in term of speed performance and Present in term of security level. And confirm that there is a compromise between memory consumption, speed performance and high security level.

Given the existence of many lightweight cryptosystems specially designed for binary and text data, in our future works, we are interested in proposing a new lightweight cryptosystem specially designed for multimedia data. The proposition will take into accounts security exigence regarding linear and differential cryptanalysis as well as performance speed and memory consumption. This is to ensure its implementation in specially constrained devices frequently used in IoT and WSN environments.

References

1. Bormann, C., Ersue, M., Keranen, A.: Terminology for constrained-node networks. Technical report (2014)
2. Daemen, J., Rijmen, V.: The Design of Rijndael: AES-the Advanced Encryption Standard. Springer, Heidelberg (2013). https://doi.org/10.1007/978-3-662-04722-4

3. Data Encryption Standard. Data encryption standard. Federal Information Processing Standards Publication (1999)
4. Eisenbarth, T., Kumar, S.: A survey of lightweight-cryptography implementations. IEEE Des. Test Comput. **24**(6), 522–533 (2007)
5. Kaur, S., Kaur, S.: Comparative analysis of lightweight cryptography algorithms for smart grids. In: 2017 4th International Conference on Signal Processing, Computing and Control (ISPCC), pp. 564–567 (2017)
6. Biryukov, A., Perrin, L.P.: State of the art in lightweight symmetric cryptography. IACR Cryptology ePrint Archive (2017)
7. Manifavas, C., Hatzivasilis, G., Fysarakis, K., Rantos, K.: Lightweight cryptography for embedded systems – a comparative analysis. In: Garcia-Alfaro, J., Lioudakis, G., Cuppens-Boulahia, N., Foley, S., Fitzgerald, W.M. (eds.) DPM/SETOP -2013. LNCS, vol. 8247, pp. 333–349. Springer, Heidelberg (2014). https://doi.org/10.1007/978-3-642-54568-9_21
8. Hu, H., Zhang, L., Wu, J.: Hamming distance based approximate similarity text search algorithm. In: 2015 Seventh International Conference on Advanced Computational Intelligence (ICACI), pp. 1–6. IEEE (2015)
9. Heys, H.M.: A tutorial on linear and differential cryptanalysis. Cryptologia **26**(3), 189–221 (2002)
10. Jha, V.K.: Cryptanalysis of lightweight block ciphers. Ph.D. thesis, Aalto University, Helsinki (2011)
11. Bogdanov, A., et al.: PRESENT: an ultra-lightweight block cipher. In: Paillier, P., Verbauwhede, I. (eds.) CHES 2007. LNCS, vol. 4727, pp. 450–466. Springer, Heidelberg (2007). https://doi.org/10.1007/978-3-540-74735-2_31
12. Abdelraheem, M.A. et al.: Improved linear cryptanalysis of reduced-round simon. Cryptology ePrint Archive, Report 2014/681 (2014)
13. Ashur, T., Bodden, D.: Linear cryptanalysis of reduced-round speck. In: Proceedings of the 37th Symposium on Information Theory in the Benelux. Werkgemeenschap voor Informatie-en Communicatietheorie (2016)
14. Wu, W., Zhang, L.: LBlock: a lightweight block cipher. In: Lopez, J., Tsudik, G. (eds.) ACNS 2011. LNCS, vol. 6715, pp. 327–344. Springer, Heidelberg (2011). https://doi.org/10.1007/978-3-642-21554-4_19

An Improved CNN Steganalysis Architecture Based on "Catalyst Kernels" and Transfer Learning

Rabii El Beji, Marwa Saidi[✉], Houcemeddine Hermassi, and Rhouma Rhouma

Ecole Nationale d'Ingénieurs de Tunis, LR16ES07 Robotique, Informatique et Systèmes Complexes, Université de Tunis El Manar, BP. 37 Le Belvédère, 1002 Tunis, Tunisia
marwoua.saidi@gmail.com

Abstract. In recent years, the interest of using model architectures based on the Convolutional Neural Networks in steganalysis has been rapidly increasing. Regarding the success of deep learning in the field of imaging analysis. Previous approaches have focused on proposing complex architectures with large sizes of images rather than simple models. In this work, we propose a more adjustable flexible architecture with the use of small size images. The robustness of our method is based on using a set of High Pass Filters (HPF) to extract the residual noise on one hand and exploiting the concept of Transfer Learning ensuring the propagation of optimal weights on the other hand. Three state-of-the-art steganographic algorithms in the spatial domain: WOW, S-UNIWARD, and HUGO are used to evaluate the effectiveness of our classification method. Our proposed technique shows an accelerated convergence for the low payloads and provides a better detection accuracy for the high payloads with a classification accuracy rate crossing 96%.

Keywords: Steganalysis · Convolutional Neural Networks
Deep learning · Binary classification · High-Pass Filter (HPF)
Transfer learning

1 Introduction

Steganography is the art of hiding secret data through various multimedia supports such as videos, audio files, network packets and last but not least digital images. In the state-of-art literature, various embedding approaches have been proposed, one of the major methods which has been well introduced and used is embedding data through slight alteration of pixels values specifically embedding within the LSBs which referred to the spatial domain embedding. Other methods, in the frequency domain, were based on modifying the DCT coefficients instead of manipulating pixels values which seemed to be more efficient in terms of embedding capacity. The highly undetectable steganographic schemes tend to embed the secret data in the regions with complex content, called as well rich

© Springer Nature Switzerland AG 2018
M. A. Bach Tobji et al. (Eds.): ICDEc 2018, LNBIP 325, pp. 119–128, 2018.
https://doi.org/10.1007/978-3-319-97749-2_9

or textured regions where the embedding artifacts are less detectable. Recently recognized approaches aims to be adaptive to the texture of the image, contrary to previous uniform techniques of embedding. Some of adaptive approaches in the spatial domain, we can include HUGO [1], WOW [2] and S-UNIWARD [3].

As a countermeasure to Steganography, the Steganalysis aims mainly to detect the very existence of potential secret messages statistically within the content of the images and decide a given object is a cover or a stego object. Nowadays, with the enormous evolution of hardware (GPUs) serving to minimize the calculus complexity, techniques of telescopic learning machines such as the Support Vector Machine (SVM), the Ensemble Classifier (EC) or the Deep Learning models such as the Convolutional Neural Networks (CNN or ConvNet) have been introduced and applied within a steganalysis context. The properties of such tools showed an efficient performance in terms of data classification.

Recently, various CNN architectures [5–7,10] have been developed for binary classification. These architectures have been inspired initially from the work of *Qian et al.* [4].

To accelerate the convergence of a given CNN model for a staganographic scheme in the JPEG domain, *Chen et al.* [10] proposed four specific filters fixed in the first layer of their CNN architecture. These filters act as "catalyst kernels" (activator in chemical reactions) for the following layers and accelerate network convergence by ensuring accurate classification between stego and cover images.

Inspired by this latest work, we have exploited the efficiency of these catalyst kernels through a fairly simple though efficient CNN architecture. In this paper, we have proposed a new approach based on the combination of kernels catalyst and transfer learning to ensure rapid convergence for low payloads by weights propagation.

The rest of this paper is organized as follows. In Sect. 2 we outline the details of our proposed method. Experimental results and discussions are presented in Sect. 3. Evaluation results of the proposed architecture are presented in Sect. 4. Conclusion is drawn in Sect. 5.

2   Model Description

The methods based on CNN combine the traditional handcraft feature extraction as well as the classification phase. Thus, it improved the classification results through exploiting a back-propagation mechanism.

Typically CNN complex models, which use huge dataset, large image sizes, multi-layers architecture and several neurons, are implemented on a very high-performance GPUs to accelerate network convergence and minimize the training time as much as possible.

Our idea was to build up a model with a minimum calculation cost so that we can do the training on low performing CPUs. To this aim, we reduce the size of the dataset.

Then we outline the design of our CNN network architecture, shown in Fig. 1, with three convolution layers for preprocessing and feature learning and three dense layers for the binary classification.

The preprocessing layer consists of four un-trainable neurons. Then, the second and the third convolutional layers are formed respectively by 5 and 10 neurons. Each neuron has a kernel size of 5 × 5 with a stride equal to 2 during the convolution process. A Batch Normalization layer is applied before each non-linear activation function to normalize the weak stego noise and improve the network convergence. The LeaKyReLU function is applied for all activation layers.

Finally, the classification layer consists of 2 fully connected-layer and a softmax layer. Each fully connected layer composed of 200 filters to prepare flatted data to the softmax layer. The softmax layer is a classifier consisting of two kernels, each one gives as an output the probabilities of each class (cover or stego).

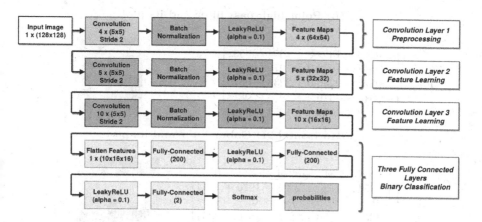

Fig. 1. The proposed CNN model architecture.

2.1   Preprocessing Layer

For the preprocessing layer, we fixed the 4 neurons of the convolution layer with specific filters. These filters shown in Fig. 2 are used together in the work of *Chen et al.* [10], as "catalyst kernels".

The first 5 × 5 size F_{KV} filter, was exploited in the Spatial Rich Model (SRM) [8] feature extractor, and later in one of the first CNN steganalysis detectors [4] as well as other models [7,9]. Fundamentally, this filter presented a pre-processing phase of the input data. Due to its sign-changing symmetric checkerboard pattern, It conceal the correlated components while largely preserving the high frequencies of the treated signal.

F_P filter is introduced as a high-pass filter selected to complement F_{KV}. The F_H and F_V are two second-order horizontal and vertical Gabor filters (1), with $\psi = \pi/2$, $\sigma = 1$, $\theta = 0$ and $\theta = \pi/2$, respectively. These two filters are added within the pre-treatment step due the fact that F_{KV} and F_P are not directional.

$$F_{KV} = \frac{1}{12} \begin{bmatrix} -1 & +2 & -2 & +2 & -1 \\ +2 & -6 & +8 & -6 & +2 \\ -2 & +8 & -12 & +8 & -2 \\ +2 & -6 & +8 & -6 & +2 \\ -1 & +2 & -2 & +2 & -1 \end{bmatrix}$$

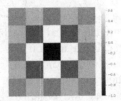

(a) **KV filter and its plot.**

$$F_P = \frac{1}{261} \begin{bmatrix} 0 & 0 & +5.2 & 0 & 0 \\ 0 & +23.4 & +36.4 & +23.4 & 0 \\ +5.2 & +36.4 & -261 & +36.4 & +5.2 \\ 0 & +23.4 & +36.4 & +23.4 & 0 \\ 0 & 0 & +5.2 & 0 & 0 \end{bmatrix}$$

(b) **Point high-pass filter and its plot.**

$$F_H = \begin{bmatrix} +.0562 & -.1354 & 0 & +.1354 & -.0562 \\ +.0818 & -.1970 & 0 & +.1970 & -.0818 \\ +.0926 & -.2233 & 0 & +.2233 & -.0926 \\ +.0818 & -.1970 & 0 & +.1970 & -.0818 \\ +.0562 & -.1354 & 0 & +.1354 & -.0562 \end{bmatrix}$$

(c) **Horizontal 2D Gabor filter and its plot.**

$$F_V = \begin{bmatrix} -.0562 & -.0818 & -.0926 & -.0818 & -.0562 \\ +.1354 & +.1970 & +.2233 & +.1970 & +.1354 \\ 0 & 0 & 0 & 0 & 0 \\ -.1354 & -.1970 & -.2233 & -.1970 & -.1354 \\ +.0562 & +.0818 & +.0926 & +.0818 & +.0562 \end{bmatrix}$$

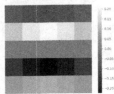

(d) **Vertical 2D Gabor filter and its plot.**

Fig. 2. Four square (5×5) kernels fixed in the first convolutional layer for preprocessing.

$$g(x, y; \lambda, \theta, \psi, \sigma, \gamma) = \exp\left(-\frac{x'^2 + \gamma^2 y'^2}{2\sigma^2}\right) \cos\left(2\pi \frac{x'}{\lambda} + \psi\right) \qquad (1)$$

where $x' = x\cos\theta + y\sin\theta$, $y' = -x\sin\theta + y\cos\theta$.

Basically, The catalyst kernels are beneficial in terms of increasing the SNR between the cover and the stego objects. They also act as regularizers to reduce the feature space dimensionality, thus helping facilitating the convergence of the network.

2.2   Feature Maps Computation

After obtaining the feature maps, each network layer will process these features in 3 layer in three steps: convolution, batch normalization and non-linear activation.

CNN's convolutional layers are characterized by an input map I, a bank of filters K and biases b. In the case of images, we could have as input an image with a height parameter denoted by H, width denoted by W and $C = 3$ channels (red, blue and green) such that $I \in \mathbb{R}^{H \times W \times C}$. Subsequently for a bank of D filters we have $K \in \mathbb{R}^{k_1 \times k_2 \times C \times D}$ and biases $b \in \mathbb{R}^D$. The output from this convolution procedure is given as follows:

$$(I * K)_{ij} = \sum_{m=0}^{k_1-1} \sum_{n=0}^{k_2-1} \sum_{c=1}^{C} K_{m,n,c} \cdot I_{i+m,j+n,c} + b \qquad (2)$$

In our case the input image is grayscale, as shown in Fig. (??) i.e single channel $C = 1$. The Eq. (2) will be transformed to:

$$(I * K)_{ij} = \sum_{m=0}^{k_1-1} \sum_{n=0}^{k_2-1} K_{m,n} \cdot I_{i+m,j+n} + b \qquad (3)$$

The Batch Normalization [11] step is applied right before each non-linear activation layer to normalize the feature map to zero-mean and unit-variance, and thus help the gradient descend back-propagation algorithm to avoid being trapped in local minima. It serves mainly the speed of the learning phase and improves the detection accuracy. *LeakyReLU* Fig. 3 (for Leaky Rectified Linear Units) is performed as an activation function at the end of each convolutional layer. The use of *LeakyReLU* helps us avoid expensive exponentials operations by *tanh* function for example and other problems like vanishing gradient problem by *sigmoid* or dying neurons by the simple *ReLU* function.

$$f(x) = \begin{cases} 0.1 \times x & \text{for } x < 0 \\ x & \text{for } x \geqslant 0 \end{cases}$$

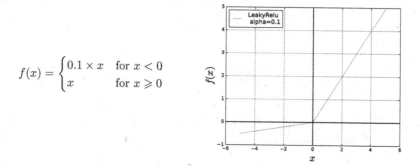

Fig. 3. *LeakyReLU* activation function (left) and its plot (right).

2.3 Classification and Optimization

The classification part of our network consists of a sequence of Three Dense layers, which are densely connected (also called fully connected) neural layers. The first two layers include 200 neurons (per each). every neuron kernel is followed by **LeakyReLU** activation function (shown in Fig. 3).

The Third (and last) layer is a 2-way softmax layer, which means it will return an array of 2 probability scores (sum-ming to 1). Each score presents the probability of classification. In other words, the probability that a given input object belongs class1 (cover) or class2 (stego).

The fundamental trick in deep learning is to use the classification error between the real and the predicted class computed by a loss function (binary cross entropy in our case) in each iteration as a feedback signal to adjust the weight value gradually, in a direction presenting a lower loss rate.

Such adjustment is given through an optimizer, which is implemented fundamentally basing on what we call the back-propagation algorithm. We use RMSProp (for Root Mean Square Propagation) optimizer [12] with their default parameters.

2.4 Leaning from Scratch and Transfer Learning

For the highest payload (1 bpp in our case), we trained our network from scratch for 100 epoch to improve the detection accuracy and minimize the loss value as much as possible. The Fig. 4 shows the training model accuracy ans loss from scratch using WOW algorithm for stego embedding. This model cross 96% of detection accuracy after 100 epoch of training.

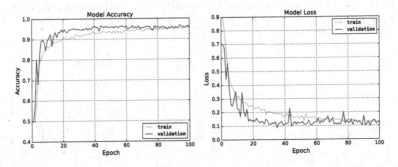

Fig. 4. Training model accuracy (right) and loss (left) during 100 epoch using WOW algorithm with high payload (1.0 bpp).

As shown in Fig. (5(a)), it is impossible to ensure a convergence with our model using learning from scratch with low payload such as 0.7 bpp, 0.5 bpp or 0.3 bpp. Thus, we choose to exploit the best weights of convolutional layers obtained by training on high payloads first, then we adjust these weights as an initialization to the training of our new dataset with lower payloads. This concept is called transfer learning and it is widely used in deep learning to minimize training time and ensure a rapid convergence of networks towards the best accuracy. Transfer learning gives better results in similar problems. As the figure Fig. (5(b)) shows, the convergence of accuracy and loss becomes more stable and closer to logic. As the detection accuracy of training and validation remains stable, we limited the training process to 10 epoch.

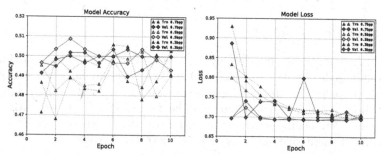

(a) Training model accuracy (right) and loss (left) without transfer learning.

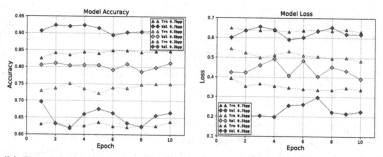

(b) Training model accuracy (right) and loss (left) with transfer learning.

Fig. 5. Difference between training with and without transfer learning using WOW algorithm with various payloads: 0.7 (blue curves), 0.5 (red curves) and 0.3 (green curves) bpp. (Color figure online)

3   Experimental Setup

3.1   Dataset

The used dataset is a part of the BOSSbase v1.01 [13] which contain 10,000 cover images of size 512×512. We just take the first 2400 images and resized to 128×128. Out of the 2400 pairs of images, 400 pairs (cover,stego) were split and left for testing to verify the performance of the proposed model; the rest of pairs were used in the training set. To train each CNN as a base learner, 1700 out of the 2000 training data are randomly shuffled at the beginning of each epoch, then the left 300 pairs were used for the validation. A mini-batch of 16 images (8 cover/stego pairs) was fed as in input for each iteration.

3.2 Software Platform

Training of the CNNs is performed on a Keras API using TensorFlow as backend. The implementation of the algorithms was performed on a computer CPU Intel Core $i3 - 2370M$, $2.40\,$GHz $\times$ 4, with Ubuntu 14.04 LTS.

4 Model Performance

For the test, We choose three highly undetectable stenographic algorithms in the spatial domain: WOW, S-UNIWARD, and HUGO. Similarly to the training phase, we prepared for the testing process different datasets with 1 bpp, 0.7 bpp, 0.5 bpp and 0.3 bpp payloads. In the following Table 1, we outline the classification accuracy measurement as well as the detection error obtained after the training of these different algorithms for several payloads.

Table 1. Model evaluation.

	S-UNIWARD				WOW				HUGO			
Payload (bpp)	1.0	0.7	0.5	0.3	1.0	0.7	0.5	0.3	1.0	0.7	0.5	0.3
Accuracy	0.96	0.93	0.88	0.73	0.96	0.92	0.83	0.67	0.96	0.91	0.84	0.69
P_E	0.04	0.07	0.12	0.27	0.04	0.08	0.17	0.33	0.04	0.09	0.16	0.31

We notice that in Fig. 6 our method shows an efficient performance, in terms of classification, against S-UNIWARD algorithm for small payloads. The curve of WOW has the weakest detection almost for all payloads comparing to other approaches' curves.

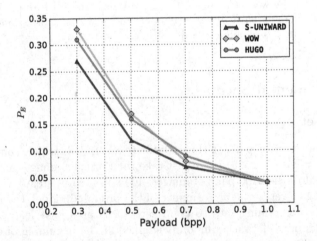

Fig. 6. Detection errors of the proposed classifier for the 3 state-of-the-art steganographic schemes (S-UNIWARD, WOW, HUGO) as a function of the embedded payload.

5   Conclusion

In this paper, on the one hand, we combined the robustness of the catalyst kernels to extract the residual noises in the aim of improving the difference between the cover and the stego images and on the other hand we exploited the technique of transfer learning which reduces the time of the convergence of our network specifically for small payloads. Provided experimental results show an interesting and a competitive performance, which can be the starting point of our future works intending mainly the establishment of accurate classification rates, not only for small sized images with small payloads, but for higher dimensions of the used input data.

References

1. Pevný, T., Filler, T., Bas, P.: Using high-dimensional image models to perform highly undetectable steganography. In: Böhme, R., Fong, P.W.L., Safavi-Naini, R. (eds.) IH 2010. LNCS, vol. 6387, pp. 161–177. Springer, Heidelberg (2010). https://doi.org/10.1007/978-3-642-16435-4_13
2. Holub, V., Fridrich, J.: Designing steganographic distortion using directional filters. In: 2012 IEEE International Workshop on Information Forensics and Security (WIFS), pp. 234–239. IEEE (2012)
3. Holub, V., Fridrich, J., Denemark, T.: Universal distortion function for steganography in an arbitrary domain. EURASIP J. Inf. Secur. **2014**(1), 1 (2014)
4. Qian, Y., Dong, J., Wang, W., Tan, T.: Deep learning for steganalysis via convolutional neural networks. In: Media Watermarking, Security, and Forensics, vol. 9409, p. 94090J (2015)
5. Couchot, J.-F., Couturier, R., Salomon, M.: Improving blind steganalysis in spatial domain using a criterion to choose the appropriate steganalyzer between CNN and SRM+EC. In: De Capitani di Vimercati, S., Martinelli, F. (eds.) SEC 2017. IAICT, vol. 502, pp. 327–340. Springer, Cham (2017). https://doi.org/10.1007/978-3-319-58469-0_22
6. Pibre, L., Pasquet, J., Ienco, D., Chaumont, M.: Deep learning is a good steganalysis tool when embedding key is reused for different images, even if there is a cover sourcemismatch. Electron. Imaging **2016**(8), 1–11 (2016)
7. Xu, G., Wu, H.-Z., Shi, Y.Q.: Ensemble of CNNs for steganalysis: an empirical study. In: Proceedings of the 4th ACM Workshop on Information Hiding and Multimedia Security, pp. 103–107. ACM (2016)
8. Fridrich, J., Kodovsky, J.: Rich models for steganalysis of digital images. IEEE Trans. Inf. Forensics Secur. **7**(3), 868–882 (2012)
9. Xu, G., Han-Zhou, W., Shi, Y.-Q.: Structural design of convolutional neural networks for steganalysis. IEEE Sig. Process. Lett. **23**(5), 708–712 (2016)
10. Chen, M., Sedighi, V., Boroumand, M., Fridrich, J.: JPEG-phase-aware convolutional neural network for steganalysis of JPEG images. In: Proceedings of the 5th ACM Workshop on Information Hiding and Multimedia Security, pp. 75–84. ACM (2017)
11. Ioffe, S., Szegedy, C.: Batch normalization: accelerating deep network training by reducing internal covariate shift. In: International Conference on Machine Learning, pp. 448–456 (2015)

12. Tieleman, T., Hinton, G.: Divide the gradient by a running average of its recent magnitude. COURSERA: Neural networks for machine learning. Technical report. https://zh.coursera.org/learn/neuralnetworks/lecture/YQHki/rmsprop-divide-the-gradient-by-a-running-average-of-its-recent-magnitude. Accessed 21 Apr 2017
13. Bas, P., Filler, T., Pevný, T.: Break our steganographic system: the ins and outs of organizing BOSS. In: Filler, T., Pevný, T., Craver, S., Ker, A. (eds.) IH 2011. LNCS, vol. 6958, pp. 59–70. Springer, Heidelberg (2011). https://doi.org/10.1007/978-3-642-24178-9_5

DAPER Joint Learning from Partially Structured Graph Databases

Marwa El Abri[1,2(✉)], Philippe Leray[2], and Nadia Essoussi[1]

[1] LARODEC Laboratory ISG, Université de Tunis, Tunis, Tunisia
nadia.essoussi@isg.rnu.tn
[2] LS2N UMR CNRS 6004, DUKe research group, University of Nantes, Nantes, France
marwa.el-abri@etu.univ-nantes.fr, philippe.leray@univ-nantes.fr

Abstract. In this paper, we are interested in learning specific probabilistic relational models, named Directed Acyclic Probabilistic Entity Relationship (DAPER) models, from partially structured databases. Algorithms for such a learning task already exist for structured data coming from a relational database. They have been also extended to partially structured data stored in a graph database where the Entity Relationship (ER) schema is first identified from data, and then the DAPER dependency structure is learnt for this specific ER schema. We propose in this work a joint learning from partially structured graph databases where we want to learn at the same time the ER schema and the probabilistic dependencies. The Markov Logic Network (MLN) formalism is an efficient solution for this task. We show with an illustrative example that MLN structure learning can effectively learn both parts of the DAPER model in one single task, with a comparative precision, but with a very high complexity.

Keywords: Probabilistic relational model
Directed Acyclic Probabilistic Entity Relationship Model
Markov Logic Network · Graph database · Partially structured data
Structure learning

1 Introduction

Statistical Relational Learning (SRL) [1,2] combines the descriptive power of relational modeling with the flexibility of statistical learning to develop models and learning algorithms capable of representing complex relationships among entities in uncertain domains. Several models emerged, with Probabilistic Relational Models such as Direct Acyclic Probabilistic Entity Relationship models (DAPER) [3] or Relational Bayesian Networks (RBN) [4,5], but also frameworks such as Markov Logic Networks (MLN) [6], ProbLog [7] or Bayesian Logic Programs (BLP) [8] where the relational information is described using First-Order Logic.

© Springer Nature Switzerland AG 2018
M. A. Bach Tobji et al. (Eds.): ICDEc 2018, LNBIP 325, pp. 129–138, 2018.
https://doi.org/10.1007/978-3-319-97749-2_10

In this paper, we are interested in learning DAPER models from partially structured databases. Algorithms for such a learning task already exist for structured data coming from a relational database [9–14]. It has been also extended to partially structured data stored in a graph database [15] where the Entity Relationship (ER) schema is first identified from data, and then the DAPER dependency structure is learnt for this specific ER schema.

We propose in this work a joint learning from partially structured graph databases, where we want to learn at the same time the ER schema and the probabilistic dependencies. The MLN formalism is an efficient solution for this task. The ER schema and the set of probabilistic dependencies of the models are described in the same logical way, and dedicated structure learning algorithm could be able to retrieve both information at the same time. The logical formulas used by MLN formalism can also manage exceptions, i.e. data which are not coherent with an underlying structured model, as we have to deal with when working with partially structured data.

This paper is organized as follows. Section 2 is dedicated to define the DAPER model and the MLN formalism. Section 3 describes how a DAPER can be expressed with Markov Logical framework. In Sect. 4, we describe our proposed method. A detailed illustrative example is presented in Sect. 5. Some conclusions and future works are drawn in Sect. 6.

2   Background

Direct Acyclic Probabilistic Entity Relationship models (DAPER) [3] and Markov Logic Networks (MLN) [6] are Probabilistic Relational Models that can be learnt from uncertain and relational information. We briefly present both models in the section before describing how they can be related in the next section.

2.1   DAPER Model

A DAPER [3] is a probabilistic extension of Bayesian network [16] based on the representation of Entity-Relationship (ER) model defined by [17]. DAPER model is composed by a set of entity classes $\mathcal{E}$, relationship classes $\mathcal{R}$ and attribute classes $\mathcal{A}(X)$ (with $X \in (\mathcal{E} \cup \mathcal{R})$) where all attributes $\mathcal{A}(X)$ are random variables that can depend on each other. Generally, the probabilistic dependency structure is graphically defined by a set of parents $pa(X.A)$ for each attribute object $X.A$, associated to a local distribution corresponding to this set of variables. In [18], these local distributions are defined for each attribute $X.A \in \mathcal{A}(\mathcal{E} \cup \mathcal{R})$ by the conditional probability distribution denoted $P(X.A|pa(X.A))$. Fig. 1 shows an example of a DAPER model for the university domain where a student's grade for one course depends both on the student's intelligence and on the difficulty of the course. In Fig. 1, the probabilistic dependencies between attributes are represented by red solid arcs.

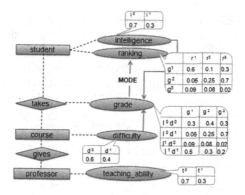

Fig. 1. Example of a DAPER model (inspired from [5]). (Color figure online)

Parents $pa(X.A)$ of a given attribute can be defined by using paths (also named slot chains) in the ER model [5,9] or more general constraints [3]. Formally, a slot chain is a set of slots $\rho_1, \rho_2, ..., \rho_n$ where ρ is a (inverse) reference slot which relates objects of a class $X \in (\mathcal{E} \cup \mathcal{R})$ to objects of a class Y. $takes.student$ is the student associated to the corresponding registration. $student.student^{-1}$ is an inverse reference slot corresponding to all the registrations of a given student. As an example of slot chain, $student.student^{-1}.course$ will correspond to all the courses taken by a particular student.

Another important concept in DAPER is the notion of aggregator that comes into play when there is dependency between the objects that have one-to-many or many-to-many relations. In Fig. 1, $student.ranking$ depends on $student.student^{-1}.grade$. As a student can take more than one course, $student.ranking$ will depend on grades of more than one $takes$ object and this number will not be the same for all students. So, in order to get a summary of such dependencies, aggregators (such as MODE or MIN) are introduced.

The structure learning task for DAPER models aims at identifying the probabilistic dependencies between attributes (and the corresponding conditional probability distributions) given an ER model and its instantiation. DAPER models are used to be learnt from relational database for which the Entity Relationship (ER) schema is already defined and the data are well structured. Thus, all existing structure learning approaches are based on this ER schema for learning the set of probabilistic dependencies from structured data [9–14]. [15] proposed to learn both the ER schema and the set of probabilistic dependencies from partially structured databases where the ER schema is not a priori defined. In this paper, we aim to learn both ER schema and the graph dependencies at the same time from partially structured data.

2.2 Markov Logic Networks

When DAPER can be seen as relational extensions of Bayesian networks, Markov Logic Networks (MLN) [6,19] are probabilistic relational models that generalize both full first-order logic and Markov networks. Formally, a Markov Logic Network is defined as a set of pairs (F_i, φ_i), where F_i is a formula in first-order logic and φ_i is a weight associated with this formula.

As an example, let us consider a university domain with four predicates $Smart(x), Easy(y), Take(x,y)$ and $Grade(x,y,val)$. Equation 1 shows a possible (and very simple) MLN composed of one formula for this domain.

$$F : \forall x,y \quad Grade(x,y,val) \implies Smart(x) \wedge Easy(y) \wedge Take(x,y) \qquad (1)$$

Some algorithms have been proposed for MLN structure learning, i.e. identifying the set of formulas, or more usually their clausal form, and the corresponding weights, from data [19–21].

3 Expressing a DAPER in Markov Logic

Based on [22], we describe in this section how to define a DAPER in the Markov Logic framework. We first define $predicates_\mathcal{E}$, the set of predicates corresponding to the set of entity classes $\mathcal{E}$ of the ER schema, where each entity class E will correspond to a $predicate_E(object)$ describing if this object belongs to this class. In the same way, we define $predicates_\mathcal{R}$, the set of binary predicates corresponding to the set of $\mathcal{R}$ in the ER schema, where each relationship class R corresponds to a $predicate_R(object1, object2)$. We finally define $predicates\_\mathcal{A}$ which are divided into two classes $predicates\_\mathcal{A}(\mathcal{E})$ and $predicates\_\mathcal{A}(\mathcal{R})$. Each $predicate_A(object, value)$ corresponds to an attribute class $A \in \mathcal{A}(\mathcal{E})$ where the first argument is the entity class to which this attribute is associated and the second one is a value for this attribute. Each $predicate_A(object1, object2, value)$ corresponds to an attribute class $A \in \mathcal{A}(\mathcal{R})$ with the first two arguments are the entities involved in the corresponding relationship class.

In the MLN formalism, we also have to declare that a separate weight must be learned for each formula obtained by grounding that variable to one of its values. Finally, some prior knowledge can be added. For instance, in our case, each object belongs to a unique class.

Let us illustrate these steps by considering the DAPER described in Fig. 1. The corresponding MLN will contain the knowledge base described in Table 1 which defines the set of predicates and the prior knowledge.

After defining all these concepts, we can now define the ER schema as a set of clauses $\mathcal{F}_{ER}$, one for each relationship, $f_{ER} : predicate_R \Rightarrow predicate_{E1} \wedge predicate_{E2}$ when the relationship R is defined for entities $E1 \times E2$. With perfectly structured data, these formulas are certain.

Equation 2 shows us the exact formulas corresponding to the ER schema defined in Fig. 1.

$$takes(s,c) \Rightarrow student(s) \wedge course(c)$$
$$gives(p,c) \Rightarrow professor(p) \wedge course(c) \qquad (2)$$

We can finally describe the probabilistic dependencies of the DAPER with a set of formulas $\mathcal{F}_{PD}$. Each formula is defined with one head which is related to

Table 1. Knowledge base corresponding to the DAPER described in Fig. 1.

Predicates ER	Predicates attributes	Prior knowledge
student(s)	s_intelligence(s,ival!)	student(x) ⇔ !course(x)
course(c)	s_ranking(s,rval!)	student(x) ⇔ !professor(x)
professor(p)	c_difficulty(c,dval!)	course(x) ⇔! professor(x)
takes(s,c)	p_teaching_ability(p,taval!)	
gives(p,c)	t_grade(s,c,gval!)	

one predicate attribute (and a specific value) and whose body involves the values of the parents of this attribute (as defined in the DAPER dependency structure) and the logical description of the slot chain between this attribute and its parents. For instance, in the DAPER described in Fig. 1, parents of *takes.grade* are *takes.student.intelligence* and *takes.course.difficulty*. The logical description of this dependency involves 12 formulas (as the total number of values in the conditional probability distribution) with the pattern described in Eq. 3.

$$takes\_grade(x, y, valG) \Rightarrow student(x) \wedge s\_intelligence(x, valI)$$
$$\wedge \ course(y) \wedge c\_difficulty(y, valD) \quad (3)$$

4   DAPER Joint Learning Using MLN Framework

We propose in this work a joint DAPER learning from partially structured graph databases, where we want to learn at the same time the ER schema and the probabilistic dependencies by using Markov Logic Network formalism. As described in Sect. 3, both parts of the model (ER schema and probabilistic dependencies) can be described in the same logical way in Markov logic framework. MLN structure learning algorithm could then be able to retrieve simultaneously both information.

4.1   DAPER Joint Learning

In order to learn a DAPER from partially structure data, we propose to learn first an MLN from the same database, and then to extract (1) the ER schema and (2) the set of probabilistic by extracting the associated formulas in the MLN.

Identification of the ER Schema. The first format of formulas we are looking for is the set of formulas $\mathcal{F}_{ER}$ that describe the ER schema, as described in Sect. 3, $f_{ER} : predicate_R \Rightarrow predicate_{E1} \wedge predicate_{E2}$, or in a clausal form $\neg R \vee E_1 \vee E_2$.

As we are dealing with partially structured data, several formulas can be extracted for the same relationship. We propose to consider only the strongest f_{ER} in term of weight (in normalized absolute value) as the relevant relationship. We then apply a user-defined threshold $\lambda_{er} \in [0, 1]$ to identify our ER schema.

Identification of the Probabilistic Dependencies. The second format of clauses we are looking for is the set of formulas $\mathcal{F}_{PD}$ that correspond to the probabilistic dependencies. f_{PD}: predicate$_Y$ $\Rightarrow$ K_1.predicate$_{X1}$ $\wedge, \ldots, \wedge$ K_n.predicate$_{Xn}$. As mentioned in the Eq. 3, a probabilistic dependency between one random variable and its parents can generate several logical formulas, one for each possible configuration of the variables. We then propose to extract such a dependency only when the average of the normalized absolute values of the weights $avg\varphi$ of the corresponding compatible f_{PD} is greater than another user-defined threshold $\lambda_{pd} \in [0,1]$.

As the formulas are described in their clausal form, it's not always possible to identify the direction of the dependency, as defined in DAPER framework, nor the possible aggregation function. Only the slot chains between variables can be retrieved from the formulas. We then summarize our dependency graph with an undirected graph where the nodes are the attributes, the edges are the probabilistic dependencies discovered, labelled with their associated slot chains.

4.2 Evaluation Process

Several metrics have been proposed to evaluate DAPER structure learning algorithms. Concerning the ER schema, as described in [15], we use a Hamming distance (RSHD_ER) between the graphs describing the original ER schema and the learnt one in order to evaluate the quality of this step. The task concerning the probabilistic dependencies is more complex. We cannot use directly existing metrics described for instance in [14,23] to compare the original probabilistic directed model and the undirected one obtained in the Sect. 4.1. Thus, we propose to use a weighted Hamming distance between the undirected counterpart of the original model and the one created from the logic formulas of the MLN (RSHD_PD). [14] proposed a same idea for directed models, with a weight for a given edge defined as the similarity between the slot chains associated to this edge in both models. This computation does not take into account the starting class of the slot chain, which leads to overestimating the error when comparing an empty slot chain to a non empty one. We propose here to simply add this starting class in the similarity computation in order to solve this problem.

5   Illustrative Example

In this section, we introduce an illustrative example detailing all the steps of our approach.

5.1   Experimental Protocol

We have used the sampling process defined by [24] to first generate a theoretical DAPER with 2 entity classes and 1 relationship class, 8 attributes (2 or 3 per class) and 7 probabilistic dependencies with slot chain length between 0 and 2)

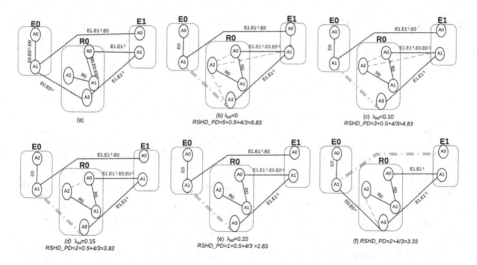

Fig. 2. Undirected dependency structure (a) of the theoretical DAPER, (b,c,d,e) extracted from the MLN with various thresholds λ_{pd} and (f) from the concurrent solution proposed in [15], with RSHD_PD between these models and (a). Information in solid lines correspond to true discovered edges compared with model (a). Information in dashed lines and double dash-dot lines correspond respectively to additional and missing edges.

and then to sample a relational database instance from this DAPER, with 3000 instances.

As performed in [15], this relational database is transformed into a graph databases. Some "exceptions" (with respect to the relational schema) have been added by transforming some existing relationship signatures by another ones not conform with the underlying ER model. The final graph database is finally containing partially structured data where we control the percentage of exceptions (30% in the following experiments). This partially structured graph database is also converted into a knowledge database with 7681 ground predicates.

We used two different approaches to learn our DAPER model. The first one consists in using an MLN learning algorithm from the given knowledge base (Beam search from Alchemy software[1], with the following parameters: Maximum predicates per clause = 6, Penalization of weighted pseudo-likelihood = 0.1) and then extract the ER schema and the undirected dependency structure as described in Sect. 4.1. The second approach consists in using the method proposed by [15] where the ER schema and the dependency structure are learnt separately from the graph database, with an identification threshold $\lambda = .5$ for ER identification and a maximum possible slot chain length $k_{max} = 2$ for the dependency structure identification. Experiments have been carried out on a dedicated PC with Intel(R) Core(TM)i7-4600M CPU 2.7 GHz, 64 bits architecture, 8 Gb RAM memory and under Windows 7.

---

[1] https://alchemy.cs.washington.edu/.

5.2   Results and Evaluation

Once the MLN is learnt from the previous database, we automatically extract the following formulas.

$$\varphi = 4.707 : relationshipclass0 \Rightarrow entityclass2 \wedge entityclass1 \qquad (4)$$

$$\varphi = 0.334 : relationshipclass0 \Rightarrow entityclass1 \wedge entityclass2$$

The first formula with the higher weight corresponds to the original ER schema, when the one with the lower weight corresponds to the exceptions present in our partially structured database. When applying a threshold $\lambda_{er} = 0.5$ to extract the ER schema from the formulas, we are able to perfectly identify it, so RSHD_ER $= 0$ in this experiment. We also extract 66 clauses $\mathcal{F}_{\mathcal{PD}}$ corresponding to probabilistic dependencies that are converted into an undirected structure.

Figure 2(a) provides the undirected dependency structure of the theoretical DAPER. Figure 2(b) to (d) respectively provide the structure derived from the MLN formulas with a threshold $\lambda_{pd} = 0, 0.10, 0.15$ and 0.20. As we can see the solution we propose here is able to perfectly retrieve the underlying ER schema and to identify the dependency structure with an increasing quality when λ_{pd} increases and an optimal RSHD_PD $= 2.83$.

The result of the concurrent algorithm is described in Fig. 2(f). It also perfectly retrieves the underlying ER schema and identifies the dependency structure with RSHD_PD $= 3.33$. Also, we have compared both approaches in term of running time. We have spent more than 10 h by using our MLN learning based algorithm, but only 2 min from the initial concurrent method.

6   Conclusion and Future Works

In this paper, we were interested in learning Directed Acyclic Probabilistic Entity Relationship (DAPER) models, from partially structured databases. We proposed here a joint learning from partially structured graph databases, where we simultaneously learn the ER schema and the probabilistic dependencies. The Markov Logic Network formalism appeared as an efficient solution for this task. We show with an illustrative example that MLN structure learning can effectively identify both part of the DAPER model in one single task, with a comparative precision, but with a very higher complexity. MLN semantics, and more specifically formulas described in clausal form, also restrict ourself by only identify undirected dependency structures, whereas DAPER are directed probabilistic models. In an opposite way, the logical formulas used by MLN to describe both the ER schema and the probabilistic dependencies can manage exceptions, i.e. data which are not coherent with an underlying structured model, which is not possible with the DAPER framework.

As our objective is obtaining an efficient probabilistic framework dealing with partially structured graph databases, we are now interested by improving this work into several directions. We are currently working on more complete experiments to test this method with all datasets used in [15] to consolidate our results. Since MLN structure learning algorithms seem to suffer from complexity issues, we are also interested by other probabilistic and relational frameworks derived from Logic such as ProbLog models [7]. If we can confirm that DAPER structure learning is really less complex than its MLN/ProbLog counterparts, a last perspective would be to improve MLN/ProbLog structure learning by first learning a more restrictive by less complex DAPER model.

References

1. Taskar, B., Abbeel, P., Wong, M.-F., Koller, D.: Relational Markov networks. In: Getoor, L., Taskar, B. (eds.) Introduction to Statistical Relational Learning. MIT Press, Cambridge (2007)
2. Neville, J., Jensen, D.: Relational dependency networks. In: Getoor, L., Taskar, B. (eds.) Introduction to Statistical Relational Learning (2005)
3. Heckerman, D., Meek, M.: Probabilistic entity-relationship models, PRMs, and plate models. In: ICML, pp. 55–60 (2004)
4. Koller, D., Pfeffer, A.: Probabilistic frame-based systems. In: AAAI/IAAI, pp. 580–587 (1998)
5. Getoor, L.: Learning statistical models from relational data. Ph.D. dissertation, Stanford (2001)
6. Richardson, M., Domingos, P.: Markov logic networks. Mach. Learn. 62(1–2), 107–136 (2006)
7. Raedt, L., Kimmig, A., Toivonen, H.: ProbLog: a probabilistic prolog and its application in link discovery. In: Veloso, M.M. (ed.) IJCAI, pp. 2462–2467 (2007)
8. Kersting, K., Raedt, L.: Bayesian Logic Programming: Theory and Tool. MIT Press, Cambridge (2007). (Chapter 10)
9. Friedman, N., Getoor, L., Koller, D., Pfeffer, A.: Learning probabilistic relational models. In: IJCAI, pp. 1300–1309 (1999)
10. Ettouzi, N., Leray, P., Messaoud, M.B.: An exact approach to learning probabilistic relational model. In: PGM, pp. 171–182 (2016)
11. Maier, M., Marazopoulou, K., Jensen, D.: Reasoning about independence in probabilistic models of relational data. In: CoRR, abs/1302.4381 (2013)
12. Lee, S., Honavar, V.: On learning causal models from relational data. In: AAAI, pp. 3263–3270 (2016)
13. Li, X.-L., He, X.-D.: A hybrid particle swarm optimization method for structure learning of probabilistic relational models. Inf. Sci. 283, 258–266 (2014). New Trend of Computational Intelligence in Human-Robot
14. Ben Ishak, M.: Probabilistic relational models: learning and evaluation. Ph.D. dissertation, Université de Nantes, Université de Tunis, June 2015
15. El Abri, M., Leray, P., Essoussi, N.: Daper learning from (partially structured) graph database. In: IEEE AICCSA (2017)
16. Pearl, J.: Probabilistic Reasoning in Intelligent Systems: Networks of Plausible Inference. Morgan Kaufmann Publishers Inc., San Francisco (1988)
17. Chen, P.-S.: The entity-relationship model: toward a unified view of data. ACM Trans. Database Syst. 1(1), 9–36 (1976)
18. Kaelin, F., Precup, D.: A study of approximate inference in probabilistic relational models. JMLR.org 13, 315–330 (2010)

19. Kok, S., Domingos, P.: Learning structure of Markov logic networks. In: ICML, 441–448 (2005)
20. Domingos, P., Kok, S.: Learning Markov logic networks structure via hypergraph lifting. In: ICML, pp. 505–512. ACM (2009)
21. Kok, S., Domingos, P.: Learning Markov logic networks using structural motifs. In: ICML, pp. 551–558 (2010)
22. Domingos, P., Richardson, M.: Markov logic: a unifying framework for statistical relational learning. In: Proceeding of the ICML-2004 Workshop on Statistical Relational Learning and Its Connections to Other Fields, pp. 49–54 (2004)
23. Maier, M., Marazopoulou, K., Arbour, D., Jensen, D.: A sound and complete algorithm for learning causal models from relational data. In: CoRR, abs/1309.6843 (2013)
24. Ben Ishak, M., Leray, P., Ben Amor, N.: Probabilistic relational model benchmark generation. Intell. Data Anal. **20**, 615–635 (2016)

An Adverse Drug Events Ontology Population from Text Using a Multi-class SVM Based Approach

Ons Jabnoun$^{(\boxtimes)}$, Hadhemi Achour, and Kaouther Nouira

Universite' de Tunis, ISGT, LR99ES04 BESTMOD, 2000 Le Bardo, Tunisia
jabnoun.ons@gmail.com, hadhemi_achour@yahoo.fr,
kaouther.nouira@planet.tn

Abstract. In recent years, semantic web technologies and ontologies in particular, are being increasingly used in various e-Health systems and applications. However, issues related to automatically constructing, populating and enriching such ontologies are still outstanding. In this paper, we propose an automatic Adverse Drug Events (ADE) ontology population approach so called ADETermino. The proposed approach is based on Information Extraction methods and mainly aims to extract new concept instances and relationships from textual drug leaflets. It combines a Named-Entity Recognition (NER) system using lexical resources and a machine learning method using a multi-class Support Vector Machine (SVM) classifier for relations detection. Experiments were performed using 102 cardiac drug leaflets corresponding to 5706 input vectors. The results show the performance of our approach with an F-score of 89%.

Keywords: ADE ontology · Ontology population · Information extraction
Text mining · Machine learning · Natural Language Processing

1 Introduction

The Adverse Drug Event (ADE) is an undesirable and harmful drug reaction, it happens during a taking of drug with recommended dose in a preventive, diagnostic or therapeutic purpose [1]. According to Handler et al. in [1], every ADE extends the duration of hospitalization to 2.2 days. That's why they recommended the use of clinical event monitoring systems. Such systems will improve the health care service quality and reduce the cost up to $760,000 per year and by hospital.

Unfortunately, the systems, which were developed in the literature, have deficiencies. In fact, the health domain contains an important volume of information (information relative to patients, therapy, drugs, surgical operations, administration, etc.) collected from heterogeneous data sources. The absence of a high-level data structuring, causes a problem of data extraction and analysis [2].

To address this problem, ADE Ontologies have been proposed by Nouira and Nakhla in [2, 3]. Their aim was to organize and to structure information related to the ADE specific to respectively, diabetes and cardiac diseases.

© Springer Nature Switzerland AG 2018
M. A. Bach Tobji et al. (Eds.): ICDEc 2018, LNBIP 325, pp. 139–150, 2018.
https://doi.org/10.1007/978-3-319-97749-2_11

When ontologies are used in such systems, the issues of automatically construction, populating and enriching these ontologies arise and present nontrivial tasks to perform. These issues fall indeed, under the ontology learning field [4], which is concerned with knowledge and information extraction (new concepts, relations and instances) from various data sources that can often be unstructured such as natural language text documents.

In relation with ADE ontologies in particular, various textual sources can be used for the construction, enrichment and population of these ontologies. However, the big amount of information about adverse events, especially in full and unstructured text, presents a big challenge for automatically extracting the required ontological elements (concepts, relations, instances, etc.) to build and maintain ADE ontologies.

In this work, we propose to populate an ADE ontology by implementing an approach of information extraction from textual drugs' leaflets. The instances of concepts to be extracted are essentially, drugs, classes of drugs, diseases and classes of diseases. The relationships to be extracted are essentially prohibited or warning relationships linking the instances of these concepts. For this purpose, the proposed approach combines the use of linguistic resources (specialized lexica) for the concept entities recognition with a machine learning method for the detection of relations between these entities.

The remainder of this paper is structured as follows. In Sect. 2, we present the global context of our research by introducing the e-health system in which the aimed ADE ontology is intended to be used. In Sect. 3, we propose a literature review of previous work related to both concept and relation extraction from medical documents. Section 4, is dedicated to the proposed approach for populating our ADE Ontology where we present the textual dataset, from which the needed information is extracted and describe the used concept extraction system and the proposed Support Vector Machine (SVM) based model for detecting relationships between concepts. An evaluation of the proposed approach is given in Sect. 5. Results of the conducted experiments are indeed discussed and a brief error analysis is presented.

2   Research Context

The present work is part of a research project which aims to propose an e-health system to improve the quality of health services and to decrease the cost of health care. Such system so called "Adverse Drug Events Prevention System" (ADEPS), warns the medical staff against ADEs. ADEPS allows not only to reduce the number of ADEs but also to have a unique medical record for every citizen since birth. In fact, the system is connected to a platform that collects electronic medical records and ADEs. Such platform will be installed in a cloud server. This will allow doctors to access patients' electronic medical records and ADE database anywhere via a web-based portal. ADEPS allows entering prescriber order automatically. Based on the data in the patient electronic medical record, the system alerts doctors when it detects a possibility of ADE such as interactions or contraindications.

This database stores all information that we need to detect ADEs, e.g. dosage according to age, indications, contraindications, interactions, symptoms in case of

ADE, etc. However, such knowledge is characterized by an unstructured and important volume of data which explains the use of ontological representation.

At a first stage, ADE ontology dealing with cardiac diseases was designed manually [3]. It was mapped to database using OntoMapDB module [5]. Knowing that ADEs evolve over time, an ontology population module, so called ADETermino, is proposed in this paper. Every time when ADETermino module detects new ADEs, OntoMapDB module maps the new portion of ontology in the ADE database. This work presents the approach used by ADETermino for automatically populating the ontology, which is based on a Named-Entity Recognition (NER) system for recognizing concept instances and a multi-class SVM classifier for relations detection.

3   Related Work

Several works have been interested in extracting information from textual data in the medical field, in order to construct ontologies. Among these works, we can mention those who are interested in the extraction of concepts such as Torii et al. [6], who proposed a machine learning based method adapting the BioTagger-GM dictionary matching and Conditional random fields (CRF) as a baseline tagger for concept extraction from different clinical documents. Concepts to extract are of three types: problem, treatment and test. The tagger, when trained on multiple sources, achieved an F-Score of 0.890. Doan and Xu [7] proposed a method to extract drug-related entities (Dosage, Mode, Frequency, Reason, etc.) from hospital discharge summaries. They used an SVM-based NER system and reported an F-score reaching 90.05% with an evaluation on manually annotated data from the 2009 i2b2[1] challenge and based on 10-fold cross validation.

As to the works that have dealt with relation detection, we can cite Minard et al. [8] and Rink et al. [9] who proposed both in 2011 methods to identify relations between entities like treatment, test and problem, existing in medical reports, by using a multi-class classification based on SVM. They obtained respectively an F-Score of 0.709 and 0.736. Roller and Stevenson [10] proposed in 2014 an approach for relation extraction using distant supervision on a large knowledge base called the Unified Medical Language System (UMLS) containing information about several medical concepts and relations between them. The highest score was achieved by the first experiment with an F-Score of 53. Sahu et al. [11] proposed in 2016 a framework using convolutional neural network to extract relations between clinical entities existing in clinical texts. The framework was tested on 2010 i2b2 clinical relation extraction challenge dataset, achieving an F-Score of 0.71.

Other contributions combined concept and relation extraction methods, in order to populate medical ontologies. Aramaki et al. [12] for instance, proposed a method to extract adverse drug events and effects from clinical records including two steps: Term identification (drug and symptom expressions) using CRF and Relation identification

---

[1] i2b2 (Informatics for Integrating Biology and the Bedside) is *an NIH-funded National Center for Biomedical Computing (NCBC) based at Partners Healthcare System in Boston* [7].

where the system identifies the type of the adverse effect related to each recognized drug using a Pattern-Based Method (PTN) as well as SVM with Radial Basis Function kernel. The evaluation using 10-fold validation achieved for both PTN and SVM, F-Score values below 0.65.

Regarding the population of ADE ontologies in particular, several approaches have been proposed such as the solution proposed by Gurulingappa et al. [13] which is the adaptation of a machine learning-based system to identify the relations between drugs and adverse effects in MEDLINE case reports using an ontology-driven and manually annotated clinical text. They used ProMiner, a dictionary-based named entity recognition system employing DrugBank and MedDRA dictionaries to identify the drugs and conditions. For the Relation extraction, they employed a Java Simple Relation Extraction model. This approach achieved an F-Score of 0.87. Kang et al. [14] proposed a knowledge-based system in order to extract relations that exist between drugs and its different adverse effects from biomedical text. The ADE corpus was made of medical case reports abstracts collected from Pubmed. The system consists of two main tasks: the identification of the drug names and the adverse effects using a dictionary-based recognition system then a rule-based Natural Language Processing module and the relation extraction that identifies the potential relation between concepts using the UMLS Metathesaurus and the UMLS Semantic Network as a knowledge base. They have obtained an F-Score of 0.5. In addition, Wang et al. [15] proposed a method that automatically extracts specific causality relationships between specific ADE and a specific drug from PubMed abstracts. First, they developed a drug-ADE classification method to detect neutropenia which was the target adverse event based on a pre-selected set of drugs and then they extended this method to apply it for other adverse events.

As we can see, and regarding works related to ADE ontologies in particular, most of them used clinical texts (mainly clinical records, clinical discharge summaries and medical reports) as a data source for information extraction. As for relation extraction, F-Scores vary between 0.5 to 0.87 and this is may be explained by the nature of the used textual contents that may include incomplete sentences, abbreviations and acronyms, thus making the task more challenging [11].

In this work we propose to explore another type of textual data for the extraction of useful information for ADE ontologies construction. Indeed, we propose to treat drug leaflets accompanying systematically any medicinal marketed product, which contain detailed instructions about each drug and thus constitute, a rich source of information. They are usually structured into short and ordered sections (product description, side effects, contra-indications, etc.).

4   Proposed Approach for ADE Ontology Population from Text

As mentioned above, we focus in this work on the analysis of textual drug leaflets, in order to extract useful information for building our ADE ontology. Our main purpose is indeed, to detect relationships that prohibit the use of a drug with another drug, another class of medication, a disease or a class of diseases.

In order to extract a corpus of drug instructions for our proposed approach, we resort to the French public drug database[2] which is implemented by the National French Agency for the Safety of Medicines and Health Products and the National Union of Health Insurance, under the confirmation of the French Ministry of Social Affairs and Health. This database allows the general public and healthcare scientists the ability to access data and referenced documents on drugs.   ,

In this work, we only focused on the drug instructions related to the cardiology domain. Indeed, the project in which this work is carried out concerns this field. In order to automatically build a corpus of textual drug notices, we have implemented a system to extract each cardiology drug notice from html pages and transform them to text files.

Our main purpose is to explore these textual instructions in order to contribute to the ADE ontology population by adding and linking new instances of concepts. Full-text written in natural language is however, an unstructured source of information that makes the task of identifying new concepts and relations, a very challenging task. In this work, we propose an information extraction system that is able to automatically extract from textual drug instructions, new concept instances, as well as new relation instances between these concepts.

4.1   Concept Extraction

This process consists in automatically recognizing the different concept instances existing in the medical instructions. For this purpose, we propose a Named Entity Recognition system that recognizes the needed entities for our ADE ontology which are related to drugs and diseases, by using a set of lexical lists written in French as a previously established knowledge base.

The entities of interest are drug names, drug classes, diseases and disease classes. The proposed NER system, as described by the example in Fig. 1, aims to annotate the input text (drug instructions), by assigning to the recognized entities, their appropriate tag indicating the type of each entity. Thus, it performs an automatic tagging of the text provided in the drug instructions using the different tags that are defined in Table 1.

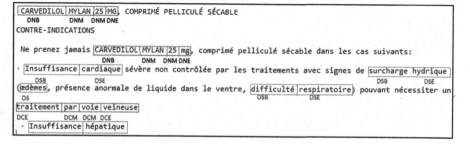

Fig. 1. Illustration of the recognition task

---

[2] Available on: http://base-donnees-publique.medicaments.gouv.fr/.

Table 1. Different concept tags

Drug tags		Drug classes tags	
DN	*Drug name in one word*	DC	*Drug class in one word*
DNB	*Beginning word in a drug name*	DCB	*Beginning word in a drug class*
DNM	*Word in the middle of a drug name*	DCM	*Word in the middle of a drug class*
DNE	*Ending word of a drug name*	DCE	*Ending word of a drug class*
Disease tags		Disease classes tags	
DS	*Disease name in one word*	DSC	*Disease class in one word*
DSB	*Beginning word in a disease name*	DSCB	*Beginning word in a disease class*
DSM	*Word in the middle of a disease name*	DSCM	*Word in the middle of a disease class*
DSE	*Ending word of a disease name*	DSCE	*Ending word of a disease class*

The tagging process is described in Fig. 2 in which:

- w_i: i^{th} word existing in the drug instructions.
- t_i: the corresponding tag to $w_{i,}$ t_i belongs to the tags defined in Table 1.
- **DNL, DSL, DCL, DSCL**: represent our knowledge base (DNL: Drug Names lexica, DSL: Disease Names lexica, DCL: Drug Classes lexica, DCL: Disease Classes lexica).

This Tagging process (Fig. 2) consists in two main steps:

- Step 1: Tokenization. This step provides a better structure for the system to tag each word separately. In order to split the text into a list of words known as tokens, we developed a specific tokenizer.
- Step 2: Concept Recognition. This step consists of recognizing the different instances mentioned in the text by comparing each token with the four corresponding word lists. The system also marks the beginning, the middle and the end of each type of instance.

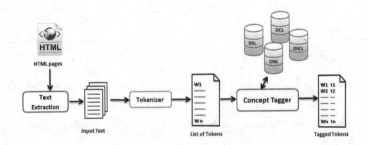

Fig. 2. Concept extraction process

4.2   Relation Extraction

Problem Definition. As explained previously, our purpose is to populate the ADE ontology with new instances of concepts and the relations that can exist between these different entities. After identifying the different concept instances that may exist in the drug instructions, we need now to define the relations that can exist between these concepts instances.

We have a set of texts. Each text is a set of drug instructions relating to a drug where we can extract two different types of relations:

1. *Warning*: A cautionary advice to not use a drug in conjunction with a specific other entity.
2. *Prohibition*: A strict forbidding to not use drug in conjunction with a specific other entity.

For more precision, and to cover the various possible cases that may be encountered, we have decided to assign for each type of entity a respective type of relation. Accordingly, the different relations that we aim to extract are defined in Table 2.

Table 2. Relation types

Prohibition		Warning	
P1	*Prohibition if disease*	W1	*Warning if disease*
P2	*Prohibition if disease class*	W2	*Warning if disease class*
P3	*Prohibition when drug*	W3	*Warning when drug*
P4	*Prohibition when drug class*	W4	*Warning when drug class*

However, and in order to extract more precise and non-erroneous results, we propose to consider an additional type of relations that takes into account if there are specific conditions to the prohibition or the warning. For example in the following statement:

« *Ne prenez jamais CARVEDILOL MYLAN 25 mg, com- primé pelliculé sécable dans les cas suivants: · Insuffisance cardiaque sévère non contrôlée par les traitements avec signes de surcharge hydrique (oedèmes, présence anormale de liquide dans le ventre, difficulté respiratoire) pouvant nécessiter un traitement par voie veineuse.* »

The prohibition of taking the drug "*CARVEDILOL MYLAN 25 mg*" with the disease "*Insuffisance cardiaque sévère*" (severe heart failure), is actually a conditioned prohibition and a not systematic.

Thus, the following additional conditioned relations are considered by our proposed relation extraction system:

– CP1: Conditioned Prohibition if disease
– CP2: Conditioned Prohibition if disease class
– CP3: Conditioned Prohibition with drug
– CP4: Conditioned Prohibition with drug class

- CW1: Conditioned Warning if disease
- CW2: Conditioned Warning if disease class
- CW3: Conditioned Warning with drug
- CW4: Conditioned Warning with drug class.

Finally, we should mention that we consider a special type of relations which is the NULL relation, when two entities are extracted from the same text and none of the prefixed relationships exist between these two entities.

The problem of extracting relations consists therefore in automatically determining, from each considered drug use leaflet (textual instructions), the type of the relationship existing between this drug and each of the recognized entities in the text. We consider thus, this problem as a multi-class classification problem with a total of 17 classes, and propose a machine learning approach based on (SVMs) [16]. SVMs have indeed, been proved as providing a robust method to avoid overfitting and have been successfully used in many classification applications.

An (SVM) is a supervised classification algorithm that separates training data by a separating hyperplane. That means, given labeled training data, the algorithm gives as an output an optimal hyperplane that splits the data into two categories if it's the case of a binary classification or into different categories if it's a multi-class case. The model, given as an SVM's output, assigns new examples to the corresponding categories. In the multi-class case, SVM tries to transform the multi-class problem into multiple binary classification problems.

ADE Relation Representation. In order to automatically discover the different relations previously described, we have decided to detect the potential relations by pair of entities. Each potential interaction with a Drug D can be represented by four type of pairs: (D, Drug i), (D, Drug Class j), (D, Disease k) and (D, disease class e) where:

- Drug i: each one of the drugs mentioned in the instructions.
- Drug Class j: each one of the drugs classes mentioned in the instructions.
- Disease k: each one of the diseases mentioned in the instructions.
- Disease class e: each one of the diseases classes mentioned in the instructions.

In order to detect the different pairs that represent all the potential relations that may exist between entities in each window in the text and to increase the performance of our approach, we decided to adopt dynamic sliding windows.

Proposed Features for the SVM Classifier. In order to assign the corresponding labels, the SVM classifier uses a set of features that describe each window or space comprising a pair of entities and thus, potentially stating a relation between these two entities. The proposed features used for the classification system are defined as follows:

- Feature 1: Window Position. This feature indicates the position of the current window in the notice.
- Feature 2: Second Entity Type. A relation connects a pair of entities. The first entity is the concerned drug in the notice and the second entity can be a drug, a disease, a drug class or a disease class. This feature defines the type of the second entity.

- Feature 3: Indicator Type. This feature indicates the type of the relation indicator (warning indicator vs prohibition indicator).
- Feature 4: Distance. Distance is the number of words between the second entity and the relation indicator. The distance can be negative if the second entity comes before the relation indicator. Knowing that we have 20 words per each mobile window, the maximum value that can the distance have is 20.
- Feature 5: Presence of Exceptions. This feature indicates if there is an exception indicator (words such as "*sauf*" (except), "*certains*" (some)) among the four words in the left of the second entity.

5 Experiments and Results

5.1 Concept Extraction Results

In order to evaluate our NER System based of dictionary lookup previously described, we randomly took a sample from our main corpus (20271 tokens). The performance was measured by the usually-used F-score as well as the precision and recall measures. F-Score is the harmonic average of precision and recall.

Table 3 shows the respective results for each type of tag. As we can notice, our system achieved, on average for all types of tags, a global F-Score of 92%, where the best tagged concept is the drug names achieving an F-Score of 95%.

Table 3. The evaluation results of the NER system

Tags	Tokens	Precision	Recall	F1-score
Drug name	112	0.972	0.923	0.945
Disease	200	0.887	0.853	0.882
Drug class	168	0.924	0.893	0.897
Disease class	31	0.907	0.887	0.895
All tags	**511**	**0.956**	**0.895**	**0.9247**

5.2 Relation Extraction Results

As we said before, we applied the multi-class SVM that is trained using the tool Scikit-learn[3] [17]. The corpus prepared for testing our approach, is made up of 102 cardiac drug textual notices (drug use leaflets) corresponding to 5706 pairs of entities (SVM vectors) that were manually labeled by the type of the corresponding relation between them. The model evaluation is performed using a k-cross validation method with k value equal to 4.

---

[3] http://scikit-learn.org/stable/.

In order to measure the impact of the selected features on the performance of the SVM classifier, we propose a series of experiments using different features combinations. The obtained evaluation results are given in Table 4.

Table 4. Overall evaluation results

Tags	Precision	Recall	F1-score	Accuracy
Base	0.362	0.592	0.445	0.592
F2+F3	0.735	0.787	0.752	0.785
F1+F2+F3	**0.830**	**0.897**	**0.860**	**0.895**
F1+F2+F3+F4	0.830	0.887	0.857	0.889
F1+F2+F3+F4+F5	0.827	0.867	0.837	0.865

From the above Table 4, we can notice that the best results are given by the third experimentation that involves the three features F1, F2 and F3 which are the position of the mobile window, the 2nd entity type and the relation indicator type, for which the system reaches an accuracy of 89% with an F-Score of 86%.

These results show that learning the relations only with the base (second entity type) gives lower performance achieving an accuracy of 60% with an F-Score of 45% and it is necessary to add other features to the model to enhance its performance. In addition, adding the Feature F4 which is the distance between the second entity and the indicator does not influence the performance of the model. However, when adding the Feature F5 (exceptions), there is a slight decrease by 3% of the F-Score. This is attributed to the fact that words from our list of exception indicators, may be present in text expressing a relation between entities, but do not always relate to the concerned relation.

Regarding the Concept Extraction, we notice that some of the entities have not been detected. This is mainly due to the absence of these entities in the used knowledge base that have been established for the NER system. In addition, in some cases, the same entity can be expressed in different forms (plural, singular, a synonym, etc.) in the training corpus.

As for misclassified relations, the main difficulties causing these errors can be summarized as follows:

- The same relation can be expressed in several different ways in the text so that it becomes difficult to systematically recognize the exact type of the relation.
- In some cases, the relation between two entities is expressed in such a way that, it is hard to be classified even by a human intervention and needs an expert verification to decide if it is a systematic relation or it is a conditioned relation.
- The relation indicator can be mentioned before or after the second entity, which can change the value of distance (negative or positive) and thus prevent the classifier from predicting the right relation.

6   Conclusion

In this work, we deal with ADE ontology population based on an Information Extraction approach from textual drug leaflets. In fact, this approach is based on two main steps: The identification of the different types of ADE entities (drug, disease, drug class, disease class) using a knowledge-based NER system.

The second step is the relation extraction task that after identifying the different instances in the text uses a multi-class Support Vector Machine classifier, in order to identify the different kinds of relations (warning, prohibition) between these instances. This classifier is built using a prepared training corpus and uses a proposed set of features.

In order to evaluate the proposed approach, we have performed a set of different experiments by testing different combinations of features and calculating different measures to evaluate the impact of each feature on the model. The training set was made of cardiac related drug instructions organized by pairs of entities. For a better evaluation of the performance of our model, we used the 4-fold Cross Validation method.

We consider that the obtained results reaching an accuracy of 89% and an F-Score of 86% are encouraging and using a multi-class SVM approach for the considered kind of medical textual resources proved to be promising for the extraction of the aimed relations.

It would however, be interesting to evaluate our approach, considering additional medical specialties to give an additional population for the ADE ontology. We propose also to experiment with other machine learning methods such as Neural Networks in order to make a comparative study of their performance in the context of ADE relation extraction. Regarding the NER system, we suggest to improve the proposed approach by introducing a language analysis component into our system that can reduce errors due to natural language ambiguities, such as the non-recognition of plural forms, term or expression synonyms that are not found in our dictionary database.

References

1. Handler, S.M., et al.: A systematic review of the performance characteristics of clinical event monitor signals used to detect adverse drug events in the hospital setting. J. Am. Med. Inform. Assoc. **14**(4), 451–458 (2007)
2. Nakhla, Z., Nouira, K.: Development of ontology for the representation of adverse drug events of diabetes disease. Int. J. Comput. Appl. **42**, 10–16 (2012)
3. Nouira, K., Nakhla, Z.: Ontology-based cardiac adverse drug event problem prevention. In: 2013 International Conference on Computer Applications Technology (ICCAT), pp. 1–6, January 2013
4. Drumond, L., Girardi, R.: A survey of ontology learning procedures. In: WONTO, vol. 427, pp. 1–13 (2008)
5. Nakhla, Z., Nouira, K.: Automatically building database from biomedical ontology. In: International Work-Conference on Bioinformatics and Biomedical Engineering, pp. 1403–1411 (2014)

6. Torii, M., Wagholikar, K., Liu, H.: Using machine learning for concept extraction on clinical documents from multiple data sources. J. Am. Med. Inform. Assoc. **18**(5), 580–587 (2011)
7. Doan, S., Xu, H.: Recognizing medication related entities in hospital discharge summaries using support vector machine. In: Proceedings of the 23rd International Conference on Computational Linguistics: Posters, pp. 259–266. Association for Computational Linguistics, August 2010
8. Minard, A.L., Ligozat, A.L., Grau, B.: Multi-class SVM for relation extraction from clinical reports. In: RANLP, pp. 604–609, September 2011
9. Rink, B., Harabagiu, S., Roberts, K.: Automatic extraction of relations between medical concepts in clinical texts. J. Am. Med. Inform. Assoc. **18**(5), 594–600 (2011)
10. Roller, R., Stevenson, M.: Applying UMLS for distantly supervised relation detection. In: Proceedings of the 5th International Workshop on Health Text Mining and Information Analysis (Louhi)@ EACL, pp. 80–84, April 2014
11. Sahu, S.K., Anand, A., Oruganty, K., Gattu, M.: Relation extraction from clinical texts using domain invariant convolutional neural network. In: ACL BioNLP 2016 Workshop (2016)
12. Aramaki, E., et al.: Extraction of adverse drug effects from clinical records. Stud. Health Technol. Inform **160**(Pt 1), 739–743 (2010)
13. Gurulingappa, H., Mateen-Rajput, A., Toldo, L.: Extraction of potential adverse drug events from medical case reports. J. Biomed. Semant. **3**(1), 15 (2012)
14. Kang, N., Singh, B., Bui, C., Afzal, Z., van Mulligen, E.M., Kors, J.A.: Knowledge-based extraction of adverse drug events from biomedical text. BMC Bioinform. **15**(1), 1 (2014)
15. Wang, W., Haerian, K., Salmasian, H., Harpaz, R., Chase, H., Friedman, C.: A drug-adverse event extraction algorithm to support pharmacovigilance knowledge mining from PubMed citations. In: AMIA Annual Symposium Proceedings, vol. 2011, pp. 1464–1470, October 2011
16. Vapnik, V.N., Vapnik, V.: Statistical Learning Theory, vol. 1. Wiley, New York (1998)
17. Pedregosa, F., et al.: Scikit-learn: machine learning in Python. JMLR **12**, 2825–2830 (2011)

E-Learning, E-Government and E-Health

E-Learning Effectiveness: A Survey in Two Tunisian Higher Education Establishments Using an Educational Platform

Rabeb Mbarek(✉)

Nabeul, Tunisia

Abstract. This work seeks to identify the determinants of e-learning effectiveness. We have measured this effectiveness through three individual variables which are motivation, self effectiveness and anxiety towards technology. The objective is to make it possible to the various concerned actors to better understand the factors influencing e-learning effectiveness. Therefore, the research question is formulated as follow: What are the factors contributing to e-learning effectiveness?

The empirical validation of the model has been carried out through a sample of 350 learners registered in two Tunisian establishments. The empirical validation is ensured by factor analyses and structural equations models. Based on these analyses, we could partially validate the effect of motivation, and computer anxiety on the learners' reaction. Moreover, we were able to check the important effect of motivation on learning.

Keywords: E-learning effectiveness · Meta-analysis · Self effectiveness
Feedback · Learning · Structural equation

1 Introduction

Since the end of the 70s, there exists a recurring interest concerning the application of information and communication technologies (ICT) in teaching and e-learning (Bronfman 2003; Audet 2012; Cottier and Lanéelle 2016). The opportunities of information technologies quickly develop and multiply, which supports the introduction of a new spirit adapted to build a culture of information sharing. These changes supported the emergence of new learning forms such "e-learning". Thereby, "e-learning" is at the heart of the projects aiming at renewing the learning mechanisms. E-learning effectiveness concerns two main research currents namely: educational sciences and information systems (Houze and Meisonnier 2005; Ben Romdhane 2013).

Through a conducted meta-analysis, we have explored the literature which allowed us to investigate the effectiveness determinants of e-learning. This theoretical review has enabled us to release three individual factors which are; motivation, self effectiveness, and anxiety towards technology and one situational factor: feedback.

Starting from these premises, the object of this research is to evaluate the effect of these factors on e-learning effectiveness in a context of university course.

M. A. Bach Tobji et al. (Eds.): ICDEc 2018, LNBIP 325, pp. 153–164, 2018.
https://doi.org/10.1007/978-3-319-97749-2_12

The research question which we want to answer is the following: **What are the factors contributing to e-learning effectiveness?**

Considering the nature of our research, **the positivist positioning is the most adapted, because it enables us to explain the causal links between these factors on the one hand, and on e-learning, on the other hand.** Thereby, we have adopted an exploratory quantitative approach followed by a confirmatory analysis in order to test the hypothesized links of our conceptual model.

In order to collect these data we have chosen to develop an e-learning platform "aad-Tunisia. Com". This platform has facilitated to us the experimentation control as far as we could ensure the system management and control.

2 Theoretical Framework of the Research

E-learning is one of the adapted technologies intending to replace or complete the traditional teaching approaches. This practice is characterized by certain characteristics as far as it implements new teaching approaches. Thereby, "E-learning" is presented as an educational device through any electronic media (Tastle et al. 2005). Consequently, learners acquire knowledge through the individual use of digital media: computers, Cd-ROMs, Internet, Intranet, wireless technologies, etc. (Homan and Macpherson 2005; Imamoglu 2007).

Several research has studied the suitable factors for the effectiveness of a teaching platform by learners (Houze and Meizonnier 2005; Fenouillet and Déro 2006; Wang et al. 2007; Lim et al. 2007a, b; Lee and Lee 2008). These researches stipulate that measuring e-learning effectiveness is a great question, the extent of which was circumscribed in many studies by using the traditional learning like standard (Ben Zammel et al. 2016).

The learning effectiveness, translates the study of the variables which seem to influence its results at various levels: before, during and after (Alvarez et al. 2004). Thereby, multiple effectiveness measurements of e-learning were used. Wang et al. (2007) have proposed a "multi-criterion" model of evaluation of e-learning effectiveness, which comprises six dimensions, namely: The quality of the system, the quality of the information, the quality of the service, the use of the system, the user satisfaction, and the system advantages. As for Lee and Lee (2008), they have worked out a measurement model of e-learning effectiveness. Through this model, the authors have shown that effectiveness is determined by the learner's satisfaction.

3 The Theoretical Framework and the Development of the Research Model

Our research focuses on two variables' categories; including four independent variables (anxiety towards technology; motivation, self effectiveness, and feedback) and a dependent variable (e-learning), which we will clarify in the following.

A. Influence relationships between the individual and the situational determinants

(1) The feedback effect on motivation: The social cognitive theory considers that feedback plays a considerable role in the self-regulation of motivation. Within this framework, the feedback seems to have an effect on the effort direction, the energy development, the learner's challenge to carry out his learning. Within this framework, Zimmermann (2000) suggests that the feedback influences motivation. Indeed, the author considers that the feedback can help the learners to develop their desires, their efforts and their perseverance to achieve their learning. Several researches have shown that the feedback influences the motivational process (Zimmermann 2000). Furthermore, feedback exerts a positive effect on the learner's desire to follow or to repeat the learning experience.

Indeed, more the learner receives the feedback, more he develops efforts to easily achieve a learning behaviour, and more he will have a belief in his capacities to succeed a learning experience (Zimmermann 2000).

Within the framework of our research, we think that the feedback constitutes a considerable determinant of e-learning motivation. Consequently, we base ourselves on the literature review and the social cognitive theory to put forth the following hypothesis:

H1: The positive feedback influences positively, and more significantly the learners' motivation than the negative feedback.

(2) The effect of computer self effectiveness on motivation: The social cognitive theory considers that the learners' self effectiveness plays a fundamental role in the self-regulation of motivation. As for, Bandura (1998), he stipulates that self effectiveness influences the effort level, the perseverance and the choice of the activities. Within this framework, Zimmermann (2000) suggests that the self effectiveness has shown a convergent validity through influencing the key indices of motivation such as the choice of the activities, the level of the effort and the emotional reactions. By referring to the meta-analyzes carried out by Multon et al. (1991), the self effectiveness seems to have a considerable effect on the motivation in terms of effort and perseverance. Several researches have shown that self effectiveness influences the motivational processes (Zimmermann 2000).

Thereby, Zimmermann (2000) has concluded that self effectiveness is positively related to the effort exerted by the learner for the achievement of his learning. Indeed, more the learner believes in his capacities, more he will easily ensure a difficult task (Bandura 1998). Consequently, more the learner believes in his capacities to succeed the learning, more he will have a desire to make an effort to complete this learning experience. Thereafter, he will be motivated to learn.

The results of the literature review and the social cognitive theory lead us to study the effect of self effectiveness on the learners' motivation.

Thereby, we formulate the following hypothesis:

H2: Computer self-effectiveness positively influences the learners' motivation.

(3) The effect of computer self-effectiveness on technology anxiety: While referring to the social cognitive theory, Bandura (1998) considers that the learners who believe to have capacities to control the execution of their learning can influence their emotional states, such as frustration, fear, anxiety, and stress, as well as

motivation and the learning results. In addition, the more the learner feels anxious, frustrated, threatened, stressed, the more he will have negative cognitive representations which can lead him to depression. Still, Bandura (1998) adds that the learners who have beliefs and convictions in their capacity to make a successful future action develop positive scenarios for their performance, whereas the learners who doubt their self effectiveness develop negative scenarios, which lead them to fail their learning experience.

Many researchers have studied the effect of self effectiveness on the learners' emotional reactions (Compeau and Higgins 1995; Chou 2001). Indeed, Chou (2001) has noted that the more the learner believes in his capacity to suitably conduct an action, the less he feels anxious and frustrated. In addition, self effectiveness regulates the learners' anxiety through the control which it exerts on the person's thinking process (Ozer and Bandura 1990). Self effectiveness influences the threat perception as well as their cognitive treatment (Bandura 1998).

Bandura (1998) considers that the social support plays a central role in stress reduction and learning frustration. The author adds that the learners' self effectiveness reduces the anxiety through the support provided by the modalities of conduct which transform a non secure environment into a secure one.

The results of the literature review and the social cognitive theory lead us to study the effect of self effectiveness on the learners' motivation.

Thereby, we will test the following hypothesis:

H3: Computer self-effectiveness positively influences technology anxiety.

B. Influence relationships between the individual determinants and e-Learning

(1) Motivation: Motivation can be defined as the desire, the will, the energy, the effort, the direction to acquire the learning contents, and to realize the objectives (Meyer and Becker 2004; Guillemet 2014b). In what follows, we apprehend the influence of motivation on the learner's reaction, on the one hand, and on the learning, on the other hand.

Many researchers have established that motivation significantly and positively influences the learning results (Noe and Schmitt 1986; Noe 1986; Baldwin and Ford 1988; Warr and Bunce 1995; Colquitt and Lepine 2000; Ainley et al. 2002). Within this framework, more the learner is motivated to follow the learning contents, more he will positively influence the results of this learning experience (Facteau et al. 1995; Noe and Wilk 1993; Guillemet 2014b).

We can, therefore, advance the following hypothesis:

H4: The learner motivation positively influences the learning process.

(2) Technology anxiety: Anxiety is considered by the literature as a negative emotional state, more precisely, a fear which appears when a person is confronted with an undesirable situation. Similarly, computer anxiety refers to a general feeling of nervousness, fear, anxiety, stress anticipating the negative results related to the actions related to the computer (Chang 2005).

Former researches have succeeded in showing the relation of negative influence which exists between technology anxiety and the learning (Warr and Bunce 1995;

Brosman 1998; Chou 2001; Cybinski and Selvanathan 2005). Indeed, more the learner is frustrated, stressed, nervous, and anxious; the less he will ensure reflection and attention to acquire new knowledge and competences. Consequently, more the learner expresses a raised anxiety, more he will be embarrassed and disturbed to accomplish a learning experience.

Thereby, anxiety proves to be one of the most important psychological features of the social cognitive theory which has integrated researches on learning effectiveness (Fig. 1).

Thus, the anxious learners must show negative perceptions regarding the acquisition of new knowledge and skills from the learning experience compared to the less anxious learners (Sitzmann et al. 2008). Thereby, we can advance the following hypothesis:

H5: The technology anxiety of the learner negatively influences his e-learning effectiveness.

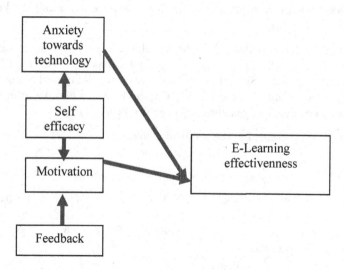

Fig. 1. Conceptual model

C. Research Methodology

The study was conducted in an online course setting spanning 16 week in 2016. Thought the 16 weeks, learners in computer architecture used to access course material and interact with a system content, classmates and tutors.

At the end of the period, a survey instrument was administered to 350 learners participated in this study.

Our sample is composed of 260 learners aged less than 20 years, 51 learners aged between 20 and 29 years, 38 learners aged between 30 and 39 years, and one learner aged between 40 and 49 years. Moreover, the learners constitute a sample mainly composed of men (301).

(1) Questionnaire Development: The questionnaire of the present research has been elaborated in view of operationalizing the previously defined concepts and measuring the explicit relations in the theoretical model.

Thereby, for each variable of the model, we have assigned items drawn from researches into information system and in educational sciences. Consequently, these items have been adapted to the Tunisian context. All the items were measured using five point likert- type scale with anchors from "Strongly disagree" to "Strongly agree". The average necessary time to fill out the questionnaire is between 15 and 20 min. Within this framework, the questionnaire is given to learners in two stages. The first stage «T1» before starting the learning experience where the learners were asked to present socio-demographic information and the second part of the questionnaire is communicated at the end of the experience in the second stage «T2». The questionnaire was firstly submitted to a pre-test in order to appreciate the validity of its contents and to check the comprehension of the questions. For that we have carried out a first experience near 105 learners, including 60 belonging to the *Higher Institute of Technological Studies Nabeul*, and 45 from the *Espace des Langues Vivantes et Informatique of Nabeul*.

(2) Methods of Data Analysis: In order to validate the constructs, we have carried out a confirmatory factor analysis; a principal component analysis (PCA) with varimax rotation under SPSS 16.0 and a convergent validity analysis under Amos 20.0. We have calculated the coefficient Cronbach' Alpha in order to make sure of the internal coherence of our research variables (Table 1).

The results are presented in the following table:

Table 1. Syntheses of the factor analyses

Variables	Analyses schales	PCA	Fiability	Validity
		Variance explained in %	Cranbach's L > 0.6	P of validation > 0.5
Motivation	Motivation	67.598	0.878	0.597
Individual effectiveness	Computer individual effectiveness	75.651	0.891	0.676
Anxiety towards technology	Anxiety towards technology	65.659	0.824	0.545
Feedback	Positive feedback	51.483	0.827	0.598
	Negative feedback	67.026	0.908	
Learning	Personal learning	20.915	0.936	0.619
	Course value	18.275	0.878	
	Course content	16.401	0.824	
	Behavioural learning	15.783	0.824	

C. The results of the empirical research

We have elaborated the statistical analyses of the two partial models through the confirmatory factor analysis. We have thereafter explained the results of the various structural models in order to answer the research question (Fig. 2).

(1) Test of the first partial model:

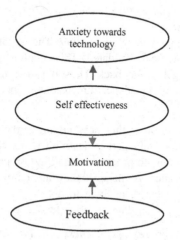

Fig. 2. The structural model relative to the links between e-learning determinants

(2) Test of the second partial model: This stage is based on the established links between the e-learning determinants (motivation and technology anxiety), and learning dimensions (course values, course contents, personal training and behavioural training). We have used the second data collection (n = 350) and we have applied the method of structural equations to the structural model below (Fig. 3).

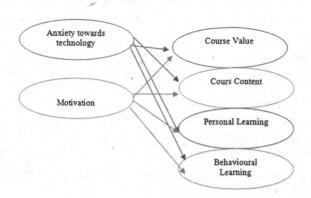

Fig. 3. The structural model relative to the links relating the e-learning determinants, and the learning dimensions

The results of the confirmatory factor analysis relative to the second structural model are acceptable and show the good quality of the model adjustment. Indeed, the values of the GFI (*The goodness-of-fit statistic*) and the AGFI (*the adjusted goodness-of-fit statistic*) approach the suitable standards; this gives us the opportunity to conclude the adjustment from the model to the data. Our model joins the parsimony standards since the Chi-squared has a satisfactory value (1,750) which is lower than 3.

D. Results Discussion

(1) Discussion of the results relative to the causal links between the determinants of e-learning effectiveness:

(1-1) Feedback effect on learners' motivation: The hypothesis relative to feedback effect on motivation has been validated. This relation is more significant for the positive than for the negative feedback. Thus, the structural link is significant in the positive direction for the two feedback dimensions, respectively (t = 6,447 > 5,886, with p = 0,000).

Our result joins the direction of the social cognitive theory which considers that a positive feedback is an interesting part of learning motivation as receiving a correct responses can motivate learners to progress in learning program. Furthermore, positive feedback lead learners to success the task they are enrolled in than receiving bad responses and errors. For instance, positive feedback reinforce student effort, energy and enhance learning progression than negative feedback (Wood and Bandura 1989).

(1-2) Effect of computer self-effectiveness on the learner's motivation: The hypothesis relative to the effect of computer self-effectiveness on motivation has been validated. Indeed, the hypothesis stipulates that the relations between self effectiveness, on the one hand, and the learning motivation, on the other hand present a positive and a significant structural link (t = 3,853, p = 0.000).

In addition, motivation seems to be influenced by computer self-effectiveness. This result coincides with the direction suggested by the social cognitive theory which considers that self effectiveness exerts a significant effect on motivation (Wood and Bandura 1989). Within this framework, learners can show more effort, energy and will to learn when they believe in their capacities and their aptitudes to follow an online managed course.

(1-3) Effect of computer self-effectiveness on computer anxiety: The hypothesis relative to the effect of computer self-effectiveness on computer anxiety has been accepted. Indeed, we have found significant results as for the influence of computer self-effectiveness on computer anxiety. Computer self-effectiveness seems to have a significant linear link with computer anxiety (T = 2,803, p = 0,000). This result confirms the former results (Chou 2001). This can be explained by the fact that learners associate their fear and frustration when they use new technologies and their aptitudes and capacities to use IT.

More the learner's beliefs increase with respect to their capacities to use new technologies more their fears and anxieties decrease.

(2) Discussion of the results of the learning background and e-learning

(2-1) The motivational effect on learning: concerning the relation between motivation and learning, the obtained result has been validated. This relation is significant for the course value, the course contents, the personal learning, and the behavioural learning. To date, the structural link is significant for the four dimensions (t = 5,480,   p = 0,000;   T = 5,439,   p = 0,000;   T = 6.423,   p = 0,000; T = 6,666, p = 0,000).

This confirms the results of several researches in the field (Noe 1986; Colquitt and Lepine 2000; Tai 2006).

Indeed, motivation leads to improve and enhance effort spent by the learners to achieve goals related to learning. Therefore, motivation effects positively learners ability to perform learning program.

(2-2) The effect of computer anxiety on learning: The hypothesis relative to the effect of computer anxiety on learning has been rejected. Indeed, computer anxiety seems to have significant linear links with the course value, the course contents, the personal learning, and the behavioural learning (t = 3,692, p = 0,000; t = 6,353, p = 0,000; t = 7,875, p = 0,000; T = 4,093, p = 0,000).

Therefore, we mention that computer anxiety positively influences the learning. In other words, the learner's fear and frustration encourage him to learn. This result contradicts the results found by several researchers such as Chou (2001), and Brosman (1998). In addition, the authors have shown that fear and frustration negatively influence the learning. Finally, learning achievement are more likely to be positive when learners experienced anxiety and frustration. The findings demonstrate the importance of considering learners anxieties as part of their e-learning performance.

4 Conclusion

Throughout this research, we have tried to apprehend e-learning effectiveness for the learners as well as its principal determinants. A literature review has enabled us to determine the explanatory factors of e-learning effectiveness. In the light of this theoretical approach, we have proposed a conceptual model integrating the explanatory factors of e-learning effectiveness and its measurements.

In order to test the model we have developed an e-learning platform to enable us to collect the data following an e-learning experience over a period of 16 weeks. Our theoretical and empirical results highlight the contributions and the limits, which we are going to mention hereafter.

These choices have been carried out while respecting the results of the literature review. In addition, the empirical results have confirmed the existence of these dimensions.

Our research offers a better understanding of the factors influencing learning effectiveness. While referring to our meta-analysis, the majority of the researchers were interested in the direct influence of these factors, through learning.

Indeed, our concern is to support a learning experience to be effective in order to minimize the failure rate and thereafter the rejection of this new learning technique.

With this intention, preliminary actions must be taken by the organizations while acting on the determinants of e-learning effectiveness.

In other words, it would be interesting to act on motivation and to find a favourable learning environment in order to reduce the feeling of fear which can invade the learner.

Thereby, so that the learners shall be motivated to follow an online managed course, the leaders must give importance to the technological infrastructure which must be satisfactory (clear, convivial, and easy to use). Indeed, the e-learning system must be clear, comprehensible and convivial.

Thereafter, the leaders must look after the improvement of the learners' beliefs and aptitudes regarding the use of new technologies of e-learning. This can be realized through implementing an awareness service. This service will make it possible to reveal the importance, the facility, the user-friendliness of the learning platform to the learners, on the one hand, and to assist them in the first learning sessions, on the other hand.

Similarly, the organization must grant special attention to the learner–tutor communication, in order to inform the learners by their progression levels in the learning. In this respect, the organization must guarantee the quality of the online learner–tutor communication.

References

Ainley, M., Hidi, S., Berndorff, D.: Interest, learning, and the psychological processes that mediate their relationship. J. Educ. Psychol. **94**, 545–561 (2002)

Alvarez, K., Salas, E., Garofan, C.M.: An integrated model of training evaluation and effectiveness. Hum. Resour. Dev. Rev. **3**(4), 385–416 (2004)

Audet, L.: Regards sur l'évolution de la formation à distance au Canada francophone. Distances et savoirs **9**(3), 313–330 (2012)

Baldwin, T.T., Ford, J.K.: Transfer of training: a review and directions for future research. Pers. Psychol. **41**(1), 63–105 (1988)

Bandura, A.: Personal and collaborative efficacy in human adaptation and change. Adv. psychol. Sci. **1**, 52–71 (1998)

Ben Zammel, I., Chichti, F., Gharbi, J.E.: Comment favoriser le transfert d'apprentissage dans l'organisation par le biais de l'utilisation du e-learning? Réflexion à partir du contexte tunisien, @GRH, vol. 3, no. 20, pp. 81–101 (2016)

Ben Romdhane, E.: La question de l'acceptation des outils de e-learning par les apprenants: quels dimensions et déterminants en milieu universitaire tunisien? Revue internationale des technologies en pédagogie universitaire **10**(1), 45–57 (2013)

Bronfmam, S.V.: Facteurs de succès dans la mise en place d'un projet e-learning: une recherche action. In: Conférence de L'AIM, Grenoble (2003)

Brosman, M.J.: The impact of computer anxiety and self-efficacy upon performance. J. Comput. Assist. Learn. **14**, 223–234 (1998)

Chang, S.E.: Computer anxiety and perception of task complexity in learning programming – related skills. Comput. Hum. Behav. **21**, 713–728 (2005)

Chou, H.W.: Effects of training method and computer anxiety on learning performance and self efficacy. Comput. Hum. Behav. **17**, 51–69 (2001)

Colquitt, J.A., Lepine, J.A.: Toward an integrative theory of training motivation: a Meta-analytic path analysis of 20 years of research. J. Appl. Psychol. **85**(5), 678–707 (2000)

Compeau, D.R., Higgins, C.A.: Computer self-efficacy: development of a measure and initial test. MIS Q. **19**(2), 189–211 (1995)

Cottier, P., Laneelle, X.: Enseignement et formation en régime numérique: nouveaux rythmes, nouvelles temporalités? Distances et médiations des savoirs **16**, 1–26 (2016)

Cybinski, P., Selvanathan, S.: Learning experience and learning effectiveness in undergraduate statistics: modelling performance in traditional and flexible learning environments. Decis. Sci. J. Innov. Educ. **3**(2), 251–271 (2005)

Facteau, J.D., Dobbins, G.H., Russell, J.E.A., Ladd, R.T., Kudisch, J.D.: The influence of general perceptions of the training environment on pre-training motivation and perceived training transfer. J. Manag. **21**, 1–25 (1995)

Fenouillet, F., Dero, M.: Le e-learning est il efficace? Une analyse de la literature anglo-saxonnes. Savoirs **12**, 87–100 (2006)

Guillemet, P.: Les étudiants préfèrent Facebook. Distance et médiations des savoirs **6** (2014b). https://doi.org/10.4000/dms.762

Homan, G., Macpherson, A.: E-learning in the corporate university. J. Eur. Ind. Train. **29**(1), 75–90 (2005)

Houze, E., Meissonier, R.: Performance du e-learning: de l'amélioration des résultats de l'apprenant à la prise en compte des enjeux institutionnels. Systèmes d'Information et Manag. **10**(4), 1–26 (2005)

Imamoglu, Z.S.: An empirical analysis concerning the user acceptance of e-learning. J. Am. Acad. Bus. Camb. **11**(1), 132–137 (2007)

Lee, J.K., Lee, W.K.: The relationship of e-learner's self-regulatory efficacy and perception of e-learning environmental quality. Comput. Hum. Behav. **24**, 32–47 (2008)

Lim, H., Lee, S.G., Nam, K.: Validating e-learning affecting training effectiveness. Int. J. Inf. Manag. **27**, 22–35 (2007a)

Lim, J., Kim, M., Chen, S.S., Ryder, C.E.: An empirical investigation of student achievement and satisfaction in different learning environments. J. Instr. Psychol. **35**(2), 113–119 (2007b)

Meyer, J.P., Becker, T.E.: Employee commitment and motivation: a conceptual analysis and integrative model. J. Appl. Psychol. **89**(6), 991–1007 (2004)

Multon, K.D., Brown, S.D., Lent, R.W.: Relation of self-efficacy beliefs to academic outcomes: a meta-analytic investigation. J. Couns. Psychol. **18**, 30–38 (1991)

Noe, R.A.: Trainees' attributes and attitudes: neglected influences on training effectiveness. Acad. Manag. Rev. **11**(4), 736–749 (1986)

Noe, R.A., Schmitt, N.: The influence of trainee attitudes on training effectiveness: that of a model. Pers. Psychol. **39**, 497–523 (1986)

Noe, R.A., Wilk, S.L.: Investigation of the factors that influence employees' participation in development activities. J. Appl. Psychol. **78**(2), 291–302 (1993)

Ozer, E.M., Bandura, A.: Mechanisms governing empowerment effects: a self-efficacy analysis. J. Pers. Soc. Psychol. **58**, 472–486 (1990)

Sitzmann, T., Brown, K.G., Caper, W.J., Ely, K., Zimmerma, R.D.: A review and meta – analysis of nomological network of trainee reactions. J. Appl. Psychol. **93**(2), 280–295 (2008)

Tai, W.T.: Effects of training framing, general self-efficacy and training motivation on trainees' training effectiveness. Pers. Rev. **35**(1), 51–65 (2006)

Tastle, W.J., White, B.A., Shackleton, P.: E-learning in higher education: the challenge, effort, and return on investment. Int. J. E-learn. **4**(2), 241–251 (2005)

Wang, Y., Wang, H., Shee, D.Y.: Measuring e-learning systems success in an organizational context: scale development and validation. Comput. Hum. Behav. **23**, 1792–1808 (2007)

Warr, P., Bunce, D.: Trainee characteristics and the outcomes of open learning. Pers. Psychol. **48** (2), 347–375 (1995)

Wood, R., Bandura, A.: Social cognitive theory of organizational management. Acad. Manag. Rev. **14**(3), 361–384 (1989)

Zimmerman, J.B.: Self-efficacy: an essential motive to learn. Contemp. Educ. Psychol. **25**, 82–91 (2000)

Determinants of E-Learning Effectiveness: The Case of Tunisian Virtual School of Post Office

Ibticem Ben Zammel[1], Tharwa Najar[2], and Afef Belghith[1(✉)]

[1] Manouba University, Manouba, Tunisia
ibticembenzammel@gmail.com,
afef.belghith@iscae.rnu.tn
[2] Gafsa University, Gafsa, Tunisia
th.najar@laposte.net

Abstract. Individuals update their knowledge and integrate new one within their professional behavior by training. The literature review revealed a set of variables which affect the acquisition and the realization of skills and knowledge by learners of the virtual school of the post office. In the research, the effectiveness of e-learning experience refers to the realization of learning. Based on the Kirkpatrick's model, we admit the effect of learner reflexivity, the e-learning system quality and the motivation to learn on the effectiveness of learning on line. The work focuses on these factors and their conceptual and empirical relation with the acquisition and the realization of skills via e-learning. Building on the same perspective, we propose a theoretical model for the purpose to discuss the following question; what are the determinants of the acquisition and realization of learning?

Keywords: E-learning effectiveness · Learning realization
Reflexivity of learner · Motivation to learn · E-learning system quality

1 Introduction

Several works focused on factors inherent to the effectiveness of e-learning (Ben Zammel et al. 2016; Zhang et al. 2005; Wang et al. 2007; Lim et al. 2007; Lee and Lee 2008). These researchers stipulate that measuring e-learning effectiveness is an important issue which is confined in numerous studies by calling the concept of traditional learning. Multiple measures of e-learning effectiveness appeared. Wang et al. (2007) proposed a "multicriterion" model of e-learning effectiveness assessment containing the six dimensions of the quality of the system, the quality of the information, the quality of the service, the use of the system, the satisfaction of the user and the advantages of the system. Moreover, Lee and Lee (2008) constructed a model that measures the effectiveness of e-learning and demonstrated -within this model- that the effectiveness is related to the learner satisfaction.

The said authors attempted to extract variables which affect e-learning effectiveness. However, a great debate concerned the determination of assorted dimensions of this kind's learning effectiveness. Several authors based on the works of Kirkpatrick (1959, 1960) had estimated the effectiveness of training (Noe 1986; Gilibert and Gillet 2010).

M. A. Bach Tobji et al. (Eds.): ICDEc 2018, LNBIP 325, pp. 165–172, 2018.
https://doi.org/10.1007/978-3-319-97749-2_13

How to estimate an electronic learning? This question outlines the main objective of the research and guides us throughout this work. We aim obviously to extract factors that could enhance the realization of learning by employees.

Our purpose is to measure the e-learning system effectiveness in the virtual school of the Tunisian post office. We are thus going to lead a questionnaire-based investigation supported by interviews with professionals who have already attended an on-line course.

2   Theoretical Model

E-Learning Effectiveness: Based on a number of papers realized during the period between 1950 and 1960, Kirkpatrick proposed a model of evaluation of training effectiveness regarding to four levels: the reaction, the learning, the behavior and the results. The first three levels concern the trainee: the first level concerns the satisfaction of the trainee or what the trainee appreciated the second, the acquired knowledge or what he knows and learned, the third concerns the changes occurred in the realization of the tasks or what changed in his behavior. And the last level of external impact to the trainee or what the training brings to the organization. In the present research, we are focusing on the second level which concerns the acquisition of learning. Our attention to this level is quite relevant since it brings sounds in the field of management of information. In fact, the acquisition of learning or the objective of the implementing of e-learning tools is the acquisition of new knowledge and know-how by employees.

E-Learning Effectiveness Determinants: Lee and Lee (2008) stipulated that the effectiveness of training is affected by several constructs, which are; the quality of service, the quality of the information, the received utility and the ease of the received use. Also, Lim et al. (2007), tried to refine the determinants of the effectiveness of e-learning which are: the motivation, the individual effectiveness, the contents of the training, the meeting face to face, and the ease of use. In the present research, we are concerned about the motivation to learn, the reflexivity of learner and the e-learning system quality.

The Motivation to Electronic Learning: Several authors tried to study the effect of factors inherent to personality of the trainees on the effectiveness of learning. The concept of motivation is the most cited in this issue. This concept appears almost within major papers treating whether the classic or on-line training. The motivation to learn becomes one of the most important individual studied characteristics susceptible to influence the realization of the learning (Guerrero and Majesty 1999; Noe 1986; Tracey et al. 2001; Warr and Bunce 1995). This kind of motivation influences consequently the success of learning process. However, in a process of electronic learning, besides the motivation to the course, the learner must be also motivated to learn via the electronic device.

Based on this theoretical analysis, we claim the following hypothesis (H1): The motivation to learn affects positively the e-learning effectiveness.

The Reflexivity of Learner: The learner, as every actor, controls reflectively his action. The reflexivity is not only the capacity of the actor to understand what he is doing while he's doing and of why he is doing it (discursive consciousness), but it is also assorted to all that the actor knows how and all that he knows in a tacit manner (practical consciousness), as well as his capacity to make a continuous assessment of the action done and thus a control of the " flow of the daily conducts" and diverse contexts of the social activity (Giddens 1984). So, the reflexivity is the skill which reveals from the discursive consciousness, the practical consciousness (who does not express himself directly in a discursive way) and of the continuous reflexive control of the action. *"The demarcation line between discursive consciousness and practical consciousness is fluctuating and permeable, both on the scale of the individual experience of every agent as in that of the comparison between various actors committed in diverse contexts of social life"* (Giddens 1984, p. 52).

From these analyses, we can advance the following hypothesis (H2): *The reflexivity of the learner influences positively the e-learning effectiveness.*

E-Learning System Quality: Contrary to the traditional learning, the implementation of e-learning system requires technological resources (Ben Zammel et al. 2016). The effectiveness of e-learning is determined, then, by the technological aspect since that this system is based on the use of Web technologies. Various studies show that the technologies have positive effects on learning (Cavanaugh 2001; Cavanaugh et al. 2004; Waxman et al. 2003). Nevertheless, these technologies can cause frustrations and reject problems with certain learners (Maor and Volet 2007).

In addition, some authors, as Ho (2009), Ho and Kuo (2010) Ho et al. (2010) recommend a training session on computer to the learners a before e-learning experience.

From these analyses, we expose the following hypothesis (H3): *The e-learning system quality affects positively the e-learning effectiveness.*

Based on cited analysis, we assign that the effectiveness of e-learning (the realization of learning) depends on the motivation of employee to learn through the system, of its reflexivity and the technological system quality used. At this level, we advance the theoretical model of the present research;

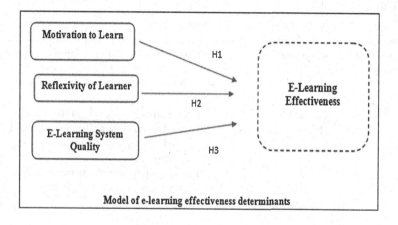

Model of e-learning effectiveness determinants

3 Empirical Evidences

Presentation of the Site: The virtual training school the Tunisian Post office works with a platform called "waheeb". It is a system of creation, management and distribution of trilingual course (Arab, French and English).

"Waheeb" offers a LCS (Learning Content Services) which allows the creation of the course in multimedia format (text, video, sound, animation, flash, and hypertext link) diffused on the Internet.

The design and the translation of the virtual training courses of the school of The Tunisian Post office are made in partnership with external companies.

The school is a unit of human resources head office. The virtual training school via internet is administered by a director as well as by a technical team and an administrator. The school is reaching a huge insight within the professionals of the Post office since its creation.

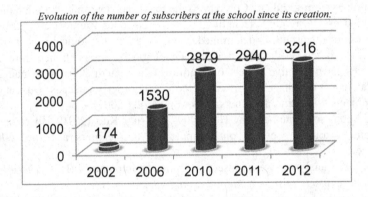

Evolution of the number of subscribers at the school since its creation:

Questionnaire Administration: The questionnaire was administered to 150 employees. The 150 respondents to the questionnaire, consist of 59 men (39.3%) and 91 women (60.7%). The scales of constructs depicted from the literature are presented on the following table:

Constructs	Scale (alpha)	Items
Effectiveness of learning (learning realization)	Warr and Birdi (1999) ($\alpha = 0.88$)	1. I was able to apply what I learnt 2. I used what I learnt in training to improve my general functioning 3. I operated certain knowledge during this training
Motivation to learn	Noe and Schmitt (1986) alpha = 0.82	1. I am motivated to learn via the e-learning 2. I would try to learn on-line as much as I could 3. I would remain actively involved throughout this learning 4. I would supply the efforts that it will be necessary to learn via the e-learning

(continued)

(continued)

Constructs	Scale (alpha)	Items
Reflexivity (task reflexivity)	Facchin et al. (2006)	1. I often revise my objectives 2. I often examine my method of work 3. I estimate regularly the efficiency of my work 4. I modify my objectives according to the changes of circumstances
E-learning quality system (effectiveness of system)	Parasuraman et al. (2005)	1. I find easily on the platform on the Internet what I need 2. Il is easy to go wherever on this platform 3. The information about this platform is organized well 4. The platform is easy to use 5. The platform allows me to reach it quickly 6. The platform is organized well

Tests of the Construct: We are concerned to study the operational effectiveness of the concepts defined in the theoretical model. More exactly, we describe the statistical properties of every construct of the model in terms of confirmatory factorial analysis and of the analysis of the reliability. These analyses are used to refine the measures scales and appreciate their dimensionality and their internal reliabilities. The most used technique is alpha of Cronbach coefficient.

As a second step we proceed to the factorial confirmatory analysis which allows the test of measure model and the analysis by the correlation and the regression. The results of the reliability analysis are very acceptable, we found alpha equal in 0.967 with a minimal required of 0.6. The analysis of reliability showed that the correlation between items retained to represent construct is clearly superior to 0.8 which prove a good internal coherence. The alpha of Cronbach is very significant. This confirms that items are strongly homogeneous and that they represent constructs very significantly.

4   Results and Interpretations

E-Learning System Quality and Realization of Learning: For the purpose to verify the significance of the regression parameters, we will interpret the regression results presented below (Table 1).

Table 1. Results of the regression analysis for the variable e-learning quality system

Coefficients[a]

Model	Non standardized coefficient		Standardized coefficient	t	Sig.
	A	Error standard	Bêta		
(constant):	4.221E−017	.082	0.62	.000	1.000
e-learing quality system	.062	.082		0.751	0.454

[a] dependant variable: Realization of learning

We used the test of Student to verify the significance of the parameters of regression and according to the results, we notice as follows:

The construct is not significant because its meaning (0.454) exceeds the 5% (probability of error) and its value of the test of Student (0.751) is lower than 1.96.

The Beta value standardized of e-learning quality system is not significant because the value of the test of Student is widely lower than 1.96 as well as its meaning is upper at the limit of 5% (t = 0.751; p = 0.454 > 0.05).

The equation of regression is presented as follows:

Y = Constant + ß1 X1
Y: e-learning realization
X1: e-learning system quality

The realization of e-learning by the learners = 0.422 and the e-learning system quality (t = 0.751; p = 0.454).

Learner Reflexivity and Realization of Learning: The analysis of regression shows that the second variable which is the reflexivity of learner explains the e-learning realization by the learners of the post office (R- Two = 0.505; R- Two adjusted 0.502). This model is very significant since that the test of Ficher is of the order of 0.000 with a probability of 12.291 (p = 0.05).

To verify the significance of the parameters of regression (the constant and the Bêta), we interpret the presented results of regression (Table 2).

Table 2. Results of the regression analysis for the variable reflexivity of variable

Coefficients[a]

Model	Non strandardized Coefficients		Strandardized Coefficients	t	Sig.
	A	Erreur standard	Bêta		
(constant)	2.098E−017	.058	.711	.000	1.000
Reflexivity of learner	.711	.058		12.291	.000

[a]Dependant variable: Realization of learning

The constant is very significant and its significance is (0.000), it is lower at the limit of 5% (probability of error) and its value of the test of Student (12.291) is superior to 1.96.

This model of regression shows that the reflexivity of learner has the highest impact on the acquisition of the skills via the e-learning.

Motivation to Learn and Realization of Learning: Based on the test of Student to verify the significance of the parameters of regression and according to the results, we notice as follows:

- The constant is very significant because his meaning (0.000) is lower at the threshold of 5% (probability of error) and its value of the test of Student (7.576) is superior to 1.96.

– The Beta value standardized of the support of motivation to be learnt is very significant because the value of the test of Student is widely superior to 1.96 as well as its meaning is lower at the limit of 5% (t = 7.576; p = 0.000 0.05).

The equation of regression spells as follows:

Y = Constant + ß1 X2
Y: the satisfaction of the learners
X2: motivation to learn

The satisfaction of the learners = 0.529 and motivation to be learnt (t = 7.576; p = 0,000).

Coefficients[a]

Model	Non strandardized Coefficients		Strandardized Coefficients	t	Sig.
	A	Error standard	Bêta		
(constant)	−1.685E−016	.070	.529	.000	1.000
Motivation to learn	.529	.070		7.576	.000

[a]Dependent Variable: Realization of learning

5 Conclusion

The results of the research highlight the importance of the reflexivity of learner on the realization of learning and the degree of transfer of the learning acquired by the employees of the post office.

The reflexivity of learner affects the acquisition of skills and the transfer of learning on environment work.

A number of managerial insights are worthy to be discussed during the implementation of the e-learning project. Thus, new mode of learning and especially its acceptance by the employees is dependent on certain factors as the head office of the company which wants to implant a project successful e-learning has to take into account.

For the post-office employees, the reflexivity constitutes an important lever of skills acquisition via e-learning. This construct turns out to be a key factor of success of the e-learning. In fact, the process of electronic learning offers to e-learner the opportunity of being autonomous in terms of new knowledge acquisition. Thus, it allows him building a skill of reflexivity during the experience of learning.

Certainly, the reflexivity is positively correlated with learner motivation. His is committed in somehow in the learning process: the knowledge acquired by the learner is translated into skills in particular working situation. Afterward, these skills acquired by the employee can be transmitted within the work place via a process of transfer.

Hence, the e-learner capacity to understand its learning as well as its capacity of continued control of its learning process. The reflexivity of the learner develops an internal learner motivation to reach learning and practicing success.

References

Ben Zammel, I., Chichti, F., Gharbi, J.-E.: Comment favoriser le transfert d'apprentissage dans l'organisation par le biais de l'utilisation du e-learning? Réflexion à partir du contexte tunisien, pp. 83–103 (2016)

Cavanaugh, C., Gillan, K.J., Kromrey, J., Hess, M., Blomeyer, R.: The effects of distance education on K-12 student outcomes: a meta-analysis. Learning Point Associates (2004). http://www.ncrel.org/tech/distance/index.html

Cavanaugh, C.S.: The effectiveness of interactive distance education technologies in K-12 learning: a meta-analysis. Int. J. Educ. Telecommun. 7(1), 73–88 (2001). http://www.unf.edu/~ccavanau/CavanaughIJET01.pdf

Giddens, A.: The Constitution of Society: Outline of the Theory of Structuration. Polity Press, Cambridge (1984)

Gilibert, D., Gillet, I.: Revue des modèles en évaluation de formation, approches conceptuelles individuelles et sociales. Pratiques Psychol. 16, 217–238 (2010)

Guerrero, S., Sire, B.: La motivation à se former chez les ouvriers et employés: approche conceptuelle et résultats empiriques. Les Notes de LIRHE (293/99), 1–21 (1999)

Ho, L.A.: The antecedents of e-learning outcome: an examination of system quality, technology readiness, and learning behavior. Adolescence 44(175), 581–599 (2009)

Ho, L.A., Kuo, T.H.: How can one amplify the effect of e-learning? An examination of high-tech employees computer attitude and flow experience. Comput. Hum. Behav. 26(1), 23–31 (2010)

Ho, L.A., Kuo, T.H., Lin, B.: Influence of online learning skills in cyberspace. Internet Res. 20(1), 55–71 (2010)

Lee, J.-K., Lee, W.-K.: The relationship of e-learner's self-regulatory efficacy and perception of e-Learning environmental quality. Comput. Hum. Behav. 24, 32–47 (2008)

Kirkpatrick, D.L.: Techniques for evaluating training programs. J. Am. Soc. Train. Dev. 13(11), 3–9 (1959)

Lim, H., Lee, S.G., Nam, K.: Validing E-learning factors affecting training effictiveness. Int. J. Inf. Manag. 27, 1–29 (2007)

Maor, D., Volet, S.: Engagement in professional online learning: a situative analysis of media professionals who did not make it. Int. J. E-Learn. 6(1), 95–117 (2007)

Noe, R.A.: Trainee's attributes and attitudes: Neglected influences on training effectiveness. Acad. Manag. Rev. 11, 736–749 (1986)

Tracey, J.B., Hinkin, T.R., Tannenbaum, S.I., Mathieu, J.E.: The influence of individual characteristics and the work environment on varying levels of training outcomes. Hum. Resour. Dev. Q. 12(1), 5–23 (2001)

Wang, Y., Wang, H., Shee, D.Y.: Measuring e-learning systems success in an organizational context: scale development and validation. Comput. Hum. Behav. 23, 1792–1808 (2007)

Warr, P., Bunce, D.: Trainee characteristics and the outcomes of open learning. Pers. Psychol. 48, 347–376 (1995)

Waxman, H.C., Lin, M.F., Michko, G.M.: A meta-analysis of the effectivenesss of teaching and learning with technology on student outcomes. Learning Point Associates (2003). http://www.ncrel.org/tech/effects2/waxman.pdf

Zhang, D., et al.: Instructional video in e-learning assessing the impact of interactive video on learning effectiveness. Inf. Manang. 43, 15–27 (2005)

E-Government and Social Media in Tunisia: An Empirical Analysis

Chaima Chaieb[(⊠)], Hadhemi Achour, and Ahmed Ferchichi

Université de Tunis, ISGT, LR99ES04 BESTMOD, 2000 Le Bardo, Tunisia
chaiebchaima@gmail.com, hadhemi_achour@yahoo.fr,
ahmad.ferchichi@gmail.com

Abstract. E-government is one of the areas that have been strongly impacted by Information and Communication Technology (ICT) in general and by the growing use of social media, in particular. Social networks are indeed, being increasingly used as an e-participation tool for a better involvement of citizens in decision-making with their governments, raising consequently important and challenging issues, such as the automatic analysis of the massive data generated on the social web. In this paper, we share the findings of a study undertaken on the official Facebook pages of the Tunisian government ministries and governorates, aiming to: (1) shed the light on the way Facebook is being currently used by government institutions, (2) to study the way Tunisian citizens are interacting on this social platform, (3) to pinpoint the specific characteristics of the Tunisian citizen-generated content on the government social pages, which will constitute an essential basis for investigating appropriate techniques and approaches to the Tunisian social web automatic analysis.

Keywords: e-Government · e-Participation · Social media · Facebook
Tunisian government · Content analysis

1 Introduction

Since the rapid growth of the Internet, many web applications have been developed in different areas such as e-commerce, industry, medicine and so on. One of the most significant developments of the web is that often known as the Web 2.0. This evolution is marked by the emergence of a set of innovative and simple tools and applications, allowing Internet users to comment, evaluate, share and interact, in a such a way that information users become also information producers by participating to the creation and the share of new web content.

With this major transformation of Internet practices, the traditional tools of communication have marked a watershed with the rise of the social networking sites. Social networking sites such as Twitter, Facebook, Google+, etc., have rapidly gained popularity as they allow people to share and express their views about topics, have discussion with different communities, or post messages across the world [1].

The shift from the mass-media era to the networked digital media has impacted several domains. E-government is one of the areas that have been strongly impacted by ICTs in general and increasingly by the use of social media, in particular. In these last

M. A. Bach Tobji et al. (Eds.): ICDEc 2018, LNBIP 325, pp. 173–184, 2018.
https://doi.org/10.1007/978-3-319-97749-2_14

years, increased interest has been shown in the way social media could be used in e-government by investigating the role of these technologies in delivering information and services, boosting relations with citizens and fostering the public engagement and collaboration. Criado et al. [2] have pinpointed the role of social media in government in term of citizen participation, openness, transparency, good governance, and trust as priorities. Other studies pointed out, the governments need for a social media strategy and policy [3] and the importance of investigating new methodologies and practices to efficient social media exploitation [4]. Important and challenging issues are consequently raised such as the analysis of the massive data generated on the social web, including the informal and unstructured textual content (such as citizens postings and comments).

In this study, we are concerned with the Tunisian government use of social media. In the past few years in fact, several governmental institutions began to be present on social networks, mainly on Facebook given the popularity of this network with Tunisian people. Indeed, according to the Medianet report published in January, 2017 [5], Facebook is the most used social network by Tunisians, with approximatively 6,300,000 Facebook users, against 1,200,000 Instagram users and 1,393,000 LinkedIn users. This increasing use of Facebook, has thus led the government to take into consideration this emerging paradigm of interaction with citizens. This paper attempts to study how Facebook is currently being used by the Tunisian government on one hand, and to explore how Tunisian citizens are involved in the government presence on the social web, on the other hand. Moreover, having as a future perspective, the automatic analysis of the citizen-generated textual content on the social web, we propose a descriptive study of the textual postings and comments published on the Facebook pages of the main Tunisian government institutions. Our main objective is to pinpoint the specific characteristics of the texts produced on the government pages, which will be helpful in investigating the most appropriate Natural Language Processing (NLP) tools and Text Mining approaches to the Tunisian social web automatic analysis.

This paper is organized in five sections, including this foregoing introduction. The second section presents a brief literature review on related studies investigating the social media use in e-government. The third section is dedicated to presenting the proposed study and its results. Finally, we conclude this paper with future perspectives of research.

2   Related Work

The use of social media tools in the public sector is among the recent waves of ICT's adoption by governments that succeeded to the wave of online e-services [6]. The growing adoption of such technologies in governments is motivated by their wide-spread usage and their ubiquity on one hand, and the benefits in terms of government efficiency and effectiveness that may be expected from using social platforms, on the other hand. In this regard, mány potential advantages, expected from the adoption of social media in government are cited in the literature, such as: improving relationships with citizens, specifically regarding information, transparency, and participation [7]; improving citizens' trust in government and enhancing its legitimacy and transparency [8, 9]. Other authors suggest the capacity of social media within the government to promote co-production of public services and policies, and crowd-sourcing solutions to social and political problems [6, 10, 11].

Several case studies have been conducted to examine and evaluate actual experiences of social media use in governments over the world. We can cite as examples, the case of Indonesia illustrated in [12], where the author examined the initiative of Jakarta City government to adopt social media for disseminating information. The findings of this study showed that citizens are eager to learn more about government activities, through the YouTube channel whereas the two other used platforms Facebook and Twitter still need necessary improvements. In [13], the case of the United States Department of Agriculture using the social media features was investigated and assessed as an open government initiative. The study results showed that social networks are used more to disseminate information than to interact with public. Chatfield et al. [14] studied a case of government use of social media during extreme events. They examined how both government agencies and citizens actively engaged in Twitter conversations, exchanging 132,922 tweets during the Hurricane Sandy in 2012 and highlighted the potential benefits of using social media for both governments and affected communities, especially during the immediate response to the catastrophe. In [15], the authors performed an analysis assessing the use of Facebook by German cities for managing their communication with citizens. The main results showed that only 48% of the largest German cities have an official Facebook page, that are mainly using this social network for delivering up-to-date information and are not well-exploiting the potential of social networks characteristics. They consequently, recommended a set of communication behaviors to increase its success.

Regarding the case of Tunisia in particular, we should note that some works have focused on social media use and impact on political participation. Kavanaugh et al. [16], for example, examined media use and sharing during the 2011 Tunisian revolution, and their impact on political information efficacy. Their findings indicate that, during crises, social media use and information sharing lead to higher sense of efficacy, strengthening consequently, political participation. Also, and in relation with the Tunisian uprising, the findings of the study of Breuer and Groshek [17], suggest that social media use has a role in shaping political attitudes of citizens, increasing political efficacy and can positively contribute to a democratic transition.

For our part, we propose in this work, a study which is also focusing on the case of Tunisia, but whose objectives are different from those targeted by the two previous studies. Our main goals are indeed, to study the way Facebook is being currently used by government institutions, the way Tunisian citizens are interacting on this social platform and to pinpoint the specific characteristics of the Tunisian citizen-generated content on the government social pages.

3 Proposed Study

3.1 Research Method

This work is based on a content analysis research method, where Tunisian Government Facebook pages are studied, in order to investigate the way they are used by both government institutions and Tunisian citizens. Content analysis is indeed an approach to research that can be carried out quantitatively as well as qualitatively [18]. It is defined by [19] as "*a procedure for the categorisation of verbal or behavioural data, for purposes of classification, summarisation and tabulation*". In our study, both quantitative data (such as the number of subscribers, number of posts, number of comments, etc.) and qualitative data (such as postings and comments) are collected.

Inspired by the content analysis research planning proposed in [20], our study was planned following these major steps: establishing the aim of the study, determining the sample and the units of analysis, choosing the data collection method and choosing the data analysis method.

3.2 Aim

Through this study, we are seeking to answer the following questions:

- To what extent is the Tunisian government present on the most used social network by Tunisian people, namely Facebook?
- How is Facebook used by Tunisian government institutions?
  - For what purposes?
  - At which pace?
  - Are they responsive to citizen's comments?
- How do citizens interact on Facebook e-Government pages?
  - Are they subscribed to these pages?
  - Are they reactive to government postings?
  - What types of comments do they post?
  - What are the main linguistic specificities of these comments (languages used, transcription alphabet, etc.)?

The ultimate goal of this study is to shed light on the way Facebook network is being used in e-Government and to prepare the ground for the automatic analysis of the Tunisian citizen-generated textual content on the social web. The research findings will be indeed, helpful in identifying what kind of useful information could be extracted automatically from these pages for assisting stakeholders in their decision-making and helping them to better serve citizens. Furthermore, they will guide us in choosing or creating NLP and text mining tools that best meet the linguistic specificities of these textual productions.

3.3 Sample

Tunisia political system is a semi-presidential system in which, the Republic President is at the head of the state and the Government President is at the head of 28 ministries. The country is divided into 24 administrative areas called Governorates. In our study, the data is collected from the official Facebook pages of Republic Presidency, Government Presidency, all the ministries and governorates. The collected and analyzed sample is limited to Facebook content during the period of 01/09/2017 to 30/09/2017.

3.4 Data Collection Method

In a content analysis based research, various kinds of data collection methods are provided by different authors without compulsory specific rules to follow [20]. These methods include interviews, questionnaires, documents, audiovisual materials, observation, etc. [18]. In our study, we used the global written material accessible on the Facebook pages of Tunisian government institutions, including government postings, citizens' comments, users' reactions, number of subscribers, etc. Much of the data was automatically collected using the tool "SocialBakers"[1].

3.5 Data Analysis Method

As mentioned above, content analysis as a research method can be performed on both quantitative and qualitative data. In the present study, quantitative data analysis summarizes the key numbers (subscribers, posting paces, users' reactions …) into statistics performed automatically using "SocialBakers" tool. As for qualitative data, it mainly concerned textual postings and comments, for which we proceeded to a content analysis, in order to categorize them and summarize their specificities. At this stage of our research, we did not use automatic text analysis tools, but we relied on observing, reading and understanding the various collected textual contents. It should be indeed pointed out that, one of the main objectives of this work is to provide a preliminary study, exploring the characteristics and specificities of user-generated textual contents on the Tunisian e-Government social web pages. It is aimed to, precisely help us to develop appropriate NLP, text mining and Information extraction tools, adapted to the linguistic specificities that would emerge from our study (such as multilingualism, code-switching, use of dialects, etc.), and able to process and mine large amounts of data that can be generated on this type of social web.

3.6 Results

Tunisian Government Presence on Facebook. We can see through Table 1, that the Republic Presidency, the Government Presidency and all the Governorates are present on Facebook with an official Facebook page. Regarding Tunisian Ministries, we have found that 26 from 28 Ministries have an official Facebook page. The two Ministries that are not yet on Facebook, are Ministry of Relations with the Assembly of People's Representatives and Ministry to the Head of Government in charge of Monitoring Major Reforms, both very recently created on August 20, 2017. Tunisian Government is thus strongly present on Facebook with 98,2% of the examined Government institutions using this social network.

---

[1] www.socialbakers.com.

Table 1. Tunisian government presence on Facebook

Type of institutions	Number of institutions	Number of official Facebook pages	Presence rate
Republic Presidency	1	1	100%
Government Presidency	1	1	100%
Ministries	28	26	92.8%
Governorates	24	24	100%
Global government presence rate on Facebook:			**98.2%**

Government Institutions Activities on Facebook. We can see through Table 2, that Government institutions are rather active with a daily pace of publication that varies on average, between almost 2 postings per day for the Republic Presidency, more than 4 postings on average per governorate and almost 6 posts per day on average per ministry.

Table 2. Statistics on government activities on Facebook during the period of 01/09/2017 to 30/09/2017

	Republic presidency	Government presidency	Average/ ministry	Average/governorate
Total Nb. of postings	54	68	176	139
Average/day	1.8	2.26	5.86	4.63

As for the nature of postings published during the period of study, by Government agencies, they are essentially news about government activities and different types of announcements (such as offers of scholarships, results of contests, etc.). Figure 1 illustrates their distribution. These postings are of different forms. As we can see in Fig. 2, photos are the most used type of postings representing 75% of the total publications. Only 7% of the postings are in the form of textual content generally written with the official language in Tunisia which is the Modern Standard Arabic.

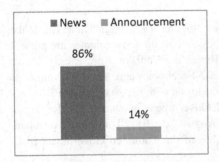

Fig. 1. Types of government postings

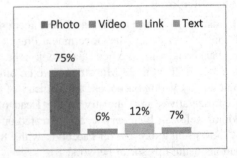

Fig. 2. Forms of government postings

While postings are more or less frequent on the pages of government institutions with an average ranging from 2 to 6 publications per day, we note however, the lack of responsiveness to the comments made by users. In fact, Table 3 shows that the average number of reactions per publication, to user comments is zero on all Facebook pages examined during the period of the study. It is on the Facebook page of only one Ministry, which is the Ministry of Higher Education and Scientific Research, that we could find a posting for which, responses were given to some users' comments about that posting.

Table 3. Government responsiveness to citizens' comments

	Republic presidency	Government presidency	Ministries	Governorates
Avg. reactions to users comments/posting	0	0	0.026	0

Citizens Involvement and Interactions in Government Facebook Pages. The number of subscribers to the different Facebook pages of the government can indicate the degree of involvement and interest of the citizens in these pages. Total numbers of subscribers are given in Tables 4 and 5. According to Table 4, at the top of the list, we find the official Facebook page of the Interior Ministry (997 730 subscribers), respectively followed be the Republic Presidency (916 646 subscribers), the Government Presidency (527 185 subscribers), the Ministry of the Education (477 052 subscribers), the Ministry of Tourism (421 111 subscribers), and the Ministry of the Public Health (316 459 subscribers). Citizens interest in these institutions pages in particular, can be explained by the events that have recently been experienced by the Tunisian country including the fight against terrorism, which explains the raised interest in the follow-up of the page of the Interior Ministry. In addition, the important changes and decisions taken towards the establishment of a democracy and the recent campaign of fight against corruption, may be reasons for the increased interest in following the pages of the Republic Presidency and the Government Presidency by Tunisian people. The Ministry of Education Facebook page is also among the most followed pages, given the latest reforms proposed in the education system.

Regarding the governorates, the numbers of subscribers given in Table 5 are lower than those found for ministries. This is explained by the fact that subscribers to governorate pages are limited to citizens of each governorate. At the top of the list, we find the governorate of Gafsa with 134 678 subscribers, followed respectively by the governorate of Tunis with 78 839 subscribers, governorate of Nabeul with 54 704 subscribers, governorate of Sousse with 52 844 subscribers and the governorate of Monastir with 40 259 subscribers.

Although the number of subscribers vary from one institution to another, they globally reflect significant level of engagement and interest in the government's strategy to inform the citizen through Facebook.

Table 4. Numbers of subscribers (republic presidency, government presidency and the top 5 ministries)

Institution	#Subscribers	Ministry	#Subscribers
Republic Presidency	916 646	Interior Ministry	997 730
Government Presidency	527 185	Ministry of Education	477 052
		Ministry of Tourism	421 111
		Ministry of Health	316 459
		Ministry of Foreign Affairs	286 879

Table 5. Numbers of Subscribers (Governorates)

Governorate	#Subscribers	Governorate	#Subscribers	Governorate	#Subscribers
Gafsa	134 678	Manouba	19 408	Ben Arous	7 832
Tunis	78 839	Kef	16 983	Kébili	7 611
Nabeul	54 704	Tozeur	14 519	Sidi Bouzid	6 725
Sousse	52 844	Siliana	13 175	Beja	5 136
Monastir	40 259	Kasserine	13 128	Mahdia	5 132
Kairouan	30 390	Sfax	11 389	Jendouba	4 576
Gabés	25 841	Médenine	10 974	Tataouine	1 546
Zaghouan	21 649	Ariana	8 866	Bizerte	1 268

Citizens involvement is also shown through their interactions within these social platforms. Table 6 gives some results and shows that Facebook pages of both the Republic Presidency and the Government Presidency are the social pages where citizens react the most to government publications and where postings are the most commented, with averages that are respectively of almost 39 and more than 32 comments per posting. Regarding Ministries, there is on average more than 8 comments per posting.

Table 6. Statistics on Citizens Involvement and Interactions

	Republic Presidency	Government Presidency	Average/ministry	Average/governorate
Nb. Subscribers	916 646	527 185	179 194	24 478
Nb. "Share"s	7 900	4 700	950	331
Nb. Reactions	28 000	19 000	2 503	159
Nb. Comments	2 100	2 500	377	206
Avg. Reactions/Post.	518.51	243.58	65.42	31.84
Avg. Comments/post	38.88	32.05	8.77	4.01

Citizens' Comments Analysis. Through the analysis of the collected comments produced by citizens on the governmental Facebook pages, we could classify the citizens messages according to the information carried by the comment as illustrated in

Fig. 3. As we can see, 56% of the comments are of the category *"Complaint"* which gathers comments that point to a problem or express a negative opinion about an issue. 27% of the comments are categorized as of type *"Gratitude"* which regroups all positive comments about a posting, thanks, whishes of success, etc. It is important to notice however that relatively few comments are about suggesting an idea, a project or an initiative (classified in the category *"Proposal"*) with a rate of 16% of the total comments and 10% of the comments are about asking for an information.

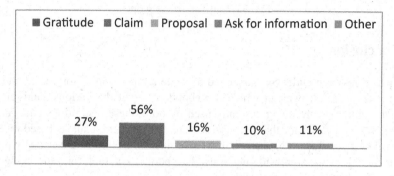

Fig. 3. Comments contents' analysis

Looking at the language and script used by Tunisian web social users to comment government postings, we can see that, contrary to Government postings which are formal and mainly written in the official administrative language of the country (Modern Standard Arabic), user-generated comments are not restricted to a single language. Indeed, Tunisian people tend to use multiple languages on Facebook as it is shown in Fig. 4. The three most used languages are Arabic (Modern Standard Arabic (MSA)), Tunisian Dialect and French, while only 3% of comments are written in English. It is thus important to note that the informal everyday spoken language of Tunisians which the Tunisian dialect, is frequently used with 17% of the total comments. Moreover, dialectal comments are written using both the Arabic and the Latin Alphabet. Figure 5 shows indeed, that almost 49% of the dialectal comments use the Latin script. In addition, 22% of users' comments are in the form of symbols and emoticons ("Other" in Fig. 5).

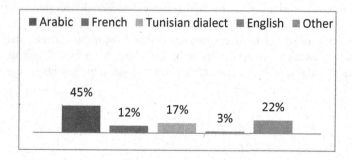

Fig. 4. Language of citizens' comments

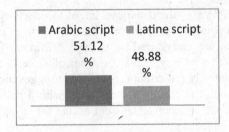

Fig. 5. Tunisian dialect script

4 Conclusion

The present research endeavor has aimed to make a kind of inventory, shedding light on the extent and the way in which, Facebook pages of the various Tunisian government institutions are being currently used by both, these institutions and Tunisian citizens. We proceeded for that purpose, to conduct a content analysis based research. The results of our study demonstrate that Government Institutions are strongly present on this social network considering thus, Facebook as a tool for reinforcing their strategy of communication with citizens.

Results show however, that this use is limited to information delivery and news posting and is not really exploiting the virtual space offered by this social media for leading discussions, animating debates that can lead to a better citizen participation.

On the other hand, the obtained results about citizens subscriptions and interactions show that Tunisian citizens are rather interested in government actions and decisions and also involved in citizen participation. This is why, it is important for these institutions to develop organizational, methodological and technological means to make the best use of these social tools, in order to encourage citizens e-participation (by opening and animating debates on given issues) and to be able to analyze citizens' exchanges on these networks and take them into account in their decision-making processes.

Our study has also shown that the automatic analysis of citizens' textual social exchanges in the Tunisian context will be a challenging task that faces difficulties to overcome in terms of developing the appropriate Natural Language Processing tools and text mining techniques, and which are due to linguistic specificities characterizing the content to be analyzed, such as multilingualism, the use of the Arabic language as well as an informal variant of Arabic which is the Tunisian dialect that is written with both the Latin and the Arabic alphabet.

Our future work will be to investigate new methodologies to efficient analysis of the massive data generated on the social web, including the informal and unstructured textual content produced by citizens through their e-participation interactions.

References

1. Kharde, V., Sonawane, S.:. Sentiment analysis of twitter data: a survey of techniques. arXiv preprint arXiv:1601.06971 (2016)
2. Criado, J.I., Sandoval-Almazan, R., Gil-Garcia, J.R.: Government innovation through social media. Gov. Inf. Q. **30**(4), 319–326 (2013)
3. Magro, M.J.: A review of social media use in e-government. Admin. Sci. **2**(2), 148–161 (2012)
4. Charalabis, Y.; Loukis, E. Transforming government agencies' approach to e-participation through efficient exploitation of social media. In: Proceedings of the 2011 European Conference on Information Systems, Helsinki, Finland, pp. 1–12 (2011)
5. Medianet: Chiffres clés web et réseaux sociaux en Tunisie et en Afrique, Janvier 2017. https://fr.slideshare.net/ihebbejimedianet/chiffres-cls-web-et-rseaux-sociaux-en-tunisie-et-en-afrique-janvier-2017?qid=c6119639-3c9d-4539-ac47-8c416e104282&v=&b=&fr. Accessed Nov 2017
6. Merger, I.: The social media innovation challenge in the public sector. Inf. Polity **17**(3, 4), 281–292 (2012)
7. Criado, J.I., Rojas-Martín, F.: Adopting social media in the local level of government: towards a public administration 2.0? In: Sobaci, M.Z. (ed.) Social Media and Local Governments. PAIT, vol. 15, pp. 135–152. Springer, Cham (2016). https://doi.org/10.1007/978-3-319-17722-9_8
8. Graham, M.W., Avery, E.J., Park, S.: The role of social media in local government crisis communications. Public Relat. Rev. **41**(3), 386–394 (2015)
9. Song, C., Lee, J.: Citizens' use of social media in government, perceived transparency, and trust in government. Public Perform. Manag. Rev. **39**(2), 430–453 (2016)
10. Bertot, J.C., Jaeger, P.T., Grimes, J.M.: Using ICTs to create a culture of transparency: E-government and social media as openness and anti-corruption tools for societies. Gov. Inf. Q. **27**(3), 264–271 (2010). https://doi.org/10.1016/j.giq.2010.03.001
11. Bertot, J.C., Jaeger, P.T., Hansen, D.: The impact of polices on government social media usage: issues, challenges, and recommendations. Gov. Inf. Q. **29**(1), 30–40 (2012). https://doi.org/10.1016/j.giq.2011.04.004
12. Tarmizi, H.: E-government and social media: a case study from Indonesia's capital. J. E-Gov. Stud. Best **2016** (2016)
13. Unsworth, K., Townes, A.: Social media and E-Government: a case study assessing Twitter use in the implementation of the open government directive. Proc. Assoc. Sci. Technol. **49**(1), 1–3 (2012)
14. Chatfield, A.T., Scholl, H.J., Brajawidagda, U.: #Sandy Tweets: citizens' co-production of time-critical information during an unfolding Catastrophe. In: 47th Hawaii International Conference System Sciences (HICSS), pp. 1947–1957 (2014)
15. Hofmann, S., Beverungen, D., Räckers, M., Becker, J.: What makes local governments' online communications successful? Insights from a multi-method analysis of Facebook. Gov. Inf. Q. **30**(4), 387–396 (2013). https://doi.org/10.1016/j.giq.2013.05.013
16. Kavanaugh, A., Sheetz, S. D., Skandrani, H., Tedesco, J.C., Sun, Y., Fox, E.A.: The use and impact of social media during the 2011 Tunisian revolution. In: Proceedings of the 17th International Digital Government Research Conference on Digital Government Research, pp. 20–30. ACM (2016). https://doi.org/10.1145/2912160.2912175
17. Breuer, A., Groshek, J.: Online media and offline empowerment in post-rebellion Tunisia: an analysis of Internet use during democratic transition. J. Inf. Technol. Polit. **11**(1), 25–44 (2014). https://doi.org/10.1080/19331681.2013.850464

18. Hashemnezhad, H.: Qualitative content analysis research: a review article. J. ELT Appl. Linguist. **3**(1), 54–62 (2015)
19. Hancock, B.: Trent Focus for Research and Development in Primary Health Care: An Introduction to Qualitative Research. Trent Focus, Nottingham (1998)
20. Bengtsson, M.: How to plan and perform a qualitative study using content analysis. NursingPlus Open **2**, 8–14 (2016)

Social Marketing in Tunisian Public Health: Case of Sahtek

Ines Daoud Mezghani$^{(\boxtimes)}$ and Marwa Meddeb

High Institute of Technological Studies in Communications, Tunis, Tunisia
ines.mezghani@edu.isetcom.tn, meddebmarwa92@gmail.com

Abstract. Non-communicable diseases such as obesity, diabetes, cardiovascular diseases and cancers have become a major health concern for most countries around the world. Different key elements as social, biological and environmental cause the non-communicable diseases. But the only way that can intentionally modified to avoid these diseases is the motivation to reduce risk factors. Several prevention strategies have been launched worldwide thorough governmental programs by implementing policies/laws. However, these programs don't integrate active communicate participation and support with the social community. This research aims to first bring out, the priority of enhancing the level of public awareness of Non-Communicable Disease in Tunisia.

This paper focus on the construction of "Sahtek", a Facebook solution developed on the fundamentals of Social Marketing, to better coach and promotes awareness of Non-Communicable Disease prevention.

Keywords: Social marketing · Health · Non-communicable diseases
Facebook · Behaviour · Tunisia

1 Introduction

A non-communicable disease is a medical condition or disease that is not transmissible from an infected individual to another [1]. In the last decade, non-communicable diseases have shown an unexpectedly evolution and a rapid spread. These can be perceived clearly from the continual increase of mortality in developing countries. Cardiovascular diseases, respiratory diseases, hypertension, osteoporosis, stroke, diabetes, and obesity are all examples of what could be considered nowadays as the invisible epidemic.

In 2017 [2], a large study directed by the World Health Organization has shown a significant increase in mortality from non-communicable diseases in developing countries in the last thirty years. These non-communicable diseases provoke the premature deaths of 15 million people aged 30 to 70 years annually. Tunisia does not escape to this global phenomenon [3], the burden of non-communicable diseases causes 82.3% of all deaths.

It is not unexpected therefore that this scourge has inspired research's interest and that the fields of research into this widespread are several and diverse. Most of these researchers are in medicine, pharmacy and public health. These various studies are providing curative actions based on heavy medical treatments, which represent a high

© Springer Nature Switzerland AG 2018
M. A. Bach Tobji et al. (Eds.): ICDEc 2018, LNBIP 325, pp. 185–195, 2018.
https://doi.org/10.1007/978-3-319-97749-2_15

cost to the society. To bring down the burden of this short-term strategy, the world health organization underscores the importance to apply a holistic approach with multi level policies. To achieve this global change, a new approach of healthy lifestyle initiatives is needed. Effective communication and meaningful practices set partnerships among stakeholders is essential.

Stakeholder association is crucial for increasing the percentage of people adopting healthy behaviours. Social marketing through social media offers a new opportunity for key stakeholders to share, to organize and to coordinate interventions. Social marketing aims to influence or encourage people to adopt specific behaviours, which are widely recognized as being beneficial through coordination efforts between the various stakeholders. The marketing research has also suggested the inclusion of an additional P, dedicate to partnership between stakeholder, to the 4 Ps of marketing: product, place, price, and promotion [6].

This article will review growing complexity in global governance for NCDs. In the absence, as yet, of a universal standard to advance multi-sectorial global health governance, the chapter will explore whether current governance mechanisms in Tunisia are capable of addressing the determinants of NCDs. In this process, the article proposes to find ways to increase public awareness of NCDs and support NCD prevention and control efforts by using social media solution. Social networks proposed initiatives for the global governance of NCDs, and the challenges and opportunities confronting health actors in their efforts to implement healthy lifestyle to all. For this, the specific objectives of the article are first to propose a social media solution with effective preventive and control policy on diet, physical activity and health, second to promote the adoption of more healthful behaviour and finally to promote the multi-stakeholder engagement.

2 Literature Review

The social marketing was introduced by kotler and Zaltman in 1971 [7] as "design, implementation, and control of programs calculated to influence the acceptability of social ideas, and involving considerations of product, planning, pricing, communication, distribution and marketing research". In the last years, changes in social marketing have been made, by integrating several features [8]. First, rely on techniques and principles of commercial marketing specially 4Ps in social marketing campaign. Second, focus on behaviour change "to create, to communicate and deliver value in order to influence target audience behaviours".

Kotler and Lee [11] highlight four main fields of researchers that social marketing have focused on: health promotion (e.g. tobacco use, drinking, obesity, cancer, blood pressure), environmental protection (e.g. water conservation, litter, forest destruction), injury prevention (e.g. women abuse, suicide, road accident), and community mobilization (e.g. organ or blood donation, vote). Social marketers strategies encompass traditional mass media, but also interactive and digital media to enhance community level outreach public's attention.

In many countries, social marketing researchers and strategies are nowadays, at the top of health development and especially in the prevention of non-communicable diseases [12]. In the United States, social marketing is increasingly being promoted as a fundamental key strategy for prompting voluntary lifestyle behaviours such as smoking, drinking, drug use and diet [13]. In the United Kingdom, the advantages of social marketing have been recognized by the department of Health, as a key success factor "to build public awareness and change behaviour". Besides these strategies, many social marketing campaigns have been launched and developed such as "let's move" (United States) supported by Michelle Obama, "Manger bouger" (France) or "Change4Life" (United Kingdom). All these campaigns apply social marketing strategies to transform lifestyle and environmental factors supporting diet and physical activity to reduce the proliferation of non-communicable diseases.

Social Marketing through community-based approaches is becoming increasingly relevant. It allows shaping markets that are more efficient and decrease the obstacles and increase motivations to behaviours that improve the quality of life for individuals and society [14, 15]. The use of traditional media such as newspapers, magazines, radio, and television are not a powerful method to reach individuals or community [16]. While, in the digital age, modern mass media, that public are passionate about like Social Media offers a number of benefits including extension of richer and responsive messages to a larger audience, convenience, cost reduction and competitive pricing.

In fact, the access for health information is problematic to low income or low education citizen. The Internet provides an incontestable way to implement and spread health related information with nationwide impact. Internet world stats estimate in June 2017 that the number of Internet users in the world is about 3,88 billion users. The same stats indicate that more than 64% of Internet users accessing social media service on line. Advances in social media are an exclusive way to prevent the spread of NCD and to change mind-sets to promote a Healthy Lifestyle.

3   Social Media in Health Care

There is a continuing spread of the use of social media generally [17] and especially in health care contexts [18, 19]. Some research highlight opportunities that social media offers among health professional [19, 21], patient [22, 23] and the general public [23, 24] to create posts, share, like, and comment on health care content through multi-sensory communication. Before focusing on social media for health communication, it is important to outline, first, the characteristics of social media. Kaplan and Haenlein [26] defined social media as "a group of Internet-based applications that build on the ideological and technological foundations of Web 2.0, and that allow the creation and exchange of user generated content". Social media encompasses interactive web and mobile platforms through where individuals and communities can share, co-create, or exchange information, ideas, photos, or videos within a virtual network. Besides, it offers opportunities for public health to communicate about health issues, including the prevention of NCDs by using social media platforms.

The main practices of social media concentrate on rising exchanges with others, and gathering, sharing, and obtaining health messages [27]. Various benefits of using social media for health communication were reported. A major advantage of social media for health communication is the accessibility and widening access of health information to a large audience, regardless of race, age, ethnicity, education or locality [28].

[29] explain, present patterns of cooperation tend to create an asymmetric relationship between health care provider and patient. This underlines a real need for health providers to develop the role within social media in the health communication. [30] have suggested that stakeholders need to recognize and understand the social media landscape by developing appropriate strategies. Specially, work out how often and when they should enter into conversations, and be aware of what others are doing and act accordingly.

This development of social media is because they are clear, understandable, accessible and affordable. Social media also encourage interaction, communication, and expansion of health-related content by way of multiple channels including Facebook, Twitter, Google, Pinterest and Instagram. According to "Statista, 2017" [31], Social Media statistics indicate an enormous evolution in 2017 as shown in Fig. 1. This clear shift is attributed towards mobile platforms. Smartphone, tablet apps and mobile web access have facilitated the constant presence of users. The incontestable leader of social media is Facebook by surpassing the 2 billions active users monthly.

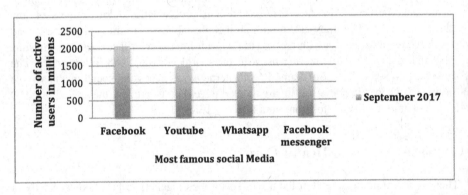

Fig. 1. Most famous mass media

Given the widespread use of social media, even among population and groups, there are opportunities to leverage these popular online platforms to support prevention of NCDs. Social media platforms such as Facebook has been gradually used for health prevention and supporting public health efforts, as demonstrated in a recent review of 73 studies [32]. To be efficient, the archetype NCDs prevention solution should be developed to reach large audiences with being accessible any times and inexpensive.

In January 2017, despite its small size, Tunisia ranks 4th in Africa in terms of the number of Internet users. 56% of the global population accessed the Internet with 7.7 million users. Facebook is extremely popular. 6,31 million Tunisians use Facebook for a penetration rate of 50.5%, making Tunisia the second country in Africa in terms of Facebook users [33]. These statistics show an obvious increase of Internet usage and validate the use of Facebook as a solution to support the implementation of a Tunisian health policy and to promote the prevention of NCDs.

This paper intends the creation of "Sahtek", a Facebook page developed on the fundamentals of Social Marketing, to better support awareness of Non-Communicable Disease prevention. The choice of this type of social media has been motivated by the fact that Facebook offers an influential platform that promotes exposure to health information. It allows the exchange of information easily, flexibly and quickly [34].

The Facebook platform "Sahtek" considers three distinctive dimensions: intensity, richness, and responsiveness of Facebook activity. First, intensity is measured by the network size. A developed flow of posts and comments could represent an opportunity to improve users' awareness and engagement [35]. The next dimension is richness, obtained qualitatively by the posts made by administer and also the quality of their Facebook page activities. The researchers suggest that messages containing text, pictures, or videos have a higher capacity to deliver information [36]. The third and last dimension is responsiveness. It is obtained qualitatively by the degree of interaction between Sahtek Facebook page and users.

The following section explores how "Sahtek" has been created to incorporate the needs of all stakeholders.

4 Creation of "Sahtek"

"Sahtek" is Facebook solution, which helps individuals, families or communities to learn how to avoid the behavioural risk factors of NCDs, through interaction with healthcare professionals as well as a sports coach. Former to the development of "Sahtek", the stakeholder needs were gathered through Focus brainstorming, Focus Group Discussions (FGD), interviews, and self-analysis of existing healthcare based Social Networks in Tunisia. After analysis of the results, it was definite that "Sahetek" will be developed as a Facebook solution developed on the fundamentals of Social Marketing.

This choice is motivated by the accessibility, the ability and the cost effectiveness of social media solution. Users of "sahtek" need minimal system requirement as Internet connection and hardware with basic personal computer or smart device. Sahtek is accessible for a range of devices as long as it is Internet enabled.

4.1 Features of "Sahtek"

Information is available to guests of "sahtek", it is essential that visitors are provided adequate information before they can become a member of the page. Therefore, a visitor is able to gather the following information before signing up as a member:

- A presentation of "Sahtek",
- Current membership of "Sahtek",
- Information on NCDs and their behavioural risks,
- The team of healthcare professionals (doctors, dieticians and Physical coach),
- In what ways "Sahtek" can help the visitor in the prevention of NCDs,
- Demonstration video describing the main features of sahtek,
- The team that manages "Sahtek" and ways in which they can be contacted.

4.2 Logo

A logo is an essential element of communication. It is used in various communication media, both to reinforce the image and to offer a personality to the brand, but also to identify and recognize it. It is a graphical representation that immediately identifies companies, products, services or campaigns in a unique way. The following figure demonstrates the key features of Logo "Sahtek" (Fig. 2).

Fig. 2. The logo of Sahtek (Color figure online)

- Name: The name Sahtek means, on the one hand, the adoption of an active lifestyle by increasing physical activity and reducing sedentary time.
- Keywords: logo "sahtek" is perceived by the patient as a balance, a change, a health, a well-being, a healthy diet, a sport and a lifestyle.
- Shape: The first half of the apple refers to healthy diet and the second half represents a person in good shape. It supposes that it is essential to eat healthy to be in good health.
- Choice of colours: First, green is about hope, well-being, balance, happiness, energy, patience, optimism, youth, and concentration. It symbolizes growth, stability, calm and nature, health, success, freshness, confidence, or security. Second, blue evokes the color of nature, the sea and the sky.
- The slogan: is the catch of our brand. This short phrase easily memorized, intended to hit the spirits and make a promise to the customer: "koul metwezen w koun sportif." Translated from Arabic as "eat balanced and be sporty". This slogan aims at counterbalance the current Tunisians behaviors by changing their eating habits, plus their sedentary lifestyle, which are responsible for NCDs.

4.3 Facebook Content of "Sahtek"

To increase users' awareness of NCDs with the opportunity to communicate efficiently, it is crucial to focus on the quality of the messages and posts. The content of the different posts emphasis sport activity the perception and the choice of food and the importance of sport activity. The style of writing was friendly to reach the maximum of users. The Table 1 below, summarize the different posts and pictures created for the first 2 weeks.

Table 1. Sahtek's Facebook content for the first 2 weeks

First week		
Monday	Wednesday	Sunday
Follow us to know who we are	J-3 you may save the date	We are new: Sahtek
Second week		
Monday	Tuesday	Wednesday
Fruits want you good	Healthy lifestyle ? The choice is yours.	One apple a day keeps the doctor away
Thursday	Friday	Saturday
Be in good shape is easy	We all need vitamin C	Ride a bike and enjoy your Weekend
Sunday		
A new day has just started!	What's your collation today?	You are what you eat. Eat healthy

In Tunisia, according to a study made by MEDIANET in 2016, the effectiveness of publications on Facebook is during the period between 10 h and 15 h with a peak at 11 h (Fig. 3). It is more relevant to post the publications in this time interval.

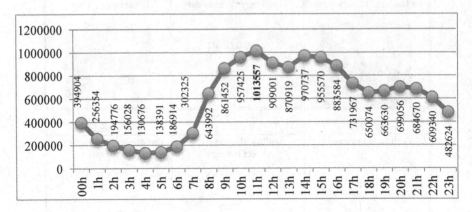

Fig. 3. The effectiveness of publications on Facebook in Tunisia

5 Discussion and Implications

The current study examined preventive and health-related predictors of NCDs by the use of Facebook in an effort to better understand who is accessing and being reached through these emerging communication channels. The results showed that this form of social media have distinctly different use patterns and user characteristics, hence different health communication implications. Among the forms of social media, Facebook by far attract the most users in Tunisian context, making them an obvious target for maximizing the reach and impact of health communication and NCDs prevention. Furthermore, with increasing prevalence of personal wireless devices, communication scientists commonly expect the popularity of social networking applications to continue to grow worldwide.

Compared to social media, a much smaller percentage of Tunisian Internet users have reported writing in a blog, twitter or Instagram suggesting a lower prevalence of these media. However, reading and commenting on Facebook may have been a more reliable measure of Internet penetration due to its higher popularity in Tunisian context. Moreover, Facebook presents a tremendous opportunity for NCDs prevention. Particularly so, because Facebook users have been observed to act as important communication stakeholders, not only are they information disseminators, but they play a crucial role in developing the awareness of NCDs through Facebook content and comments.

A key finding of this study offers new and important implications for NCD communication in this digital age: among Internet users, Facebook is found to penetrate the Tunisian population regardless of education, race, ethnicity, or health care access. Considering implications of NCDs prevention communication efforts, the results of this study suggest that in the future, social media promise to be a way to reach the target population regardless of socioeconomic and health-related characteristics. If stakeholders efforts can enable wilder and more equitable Internet access (e.g., increasing broadband access or Free wireless mobile access), thus reducing the digital divide, the potential for impacting the health and NCDs prevention behaviour of the general Tunisian population through social media will be remarkable.

6 Conclusion and Future Works

NCDs are the prominent cause of death worldwide. Preventive action must be taken to stop the number of deaths through NCDs. Several biological, environmental and social factors are the main cause of this spread. Specially, the lifestyle adopted by people provokes the majority of theses diseases. The best NCD prevention action must influence a wide audience to change their behaviours before it is too late. Social marketing is a strategic key to incite individual's voluntary behavioural changes with the support of social community. Nowadays, traditional social marketing campaigns are insufficient. Therefore, it is fundamental to reinforce them through modern media such as social media. It is in this context that sahtek was developed as a Facebook solution based on the fundamental of social marketing. Sahtek's ultimate contribution is to enhance the awareness and inspire individuals to adopt a healthy lifestyle. It provides personalized and specific plans and programs through consulting with healthcare professionals. This Facebook solution can be sustained by value added services such as online consultation with doctors or physical trainer or the incorporation of other social networks Twitter or google+. Future studies may take into consideration the users individual factors as gender, age, and perceived risk of adopting a sedentary lifestyle. More studies are needed to uncover the variable behind the spread of NCDs in Tunisian context to better target their spread.

References

1. National Institutes of Health: Understanding Emerging and Re-emerging Infectious Diseases (2007)
2. World Health Organization: Non-communicable disease Progress Monitor (2017)
3. World Health Organization: Health profile, Tunisia (2015)
4. Atun, J., Jaffar, S., Nishtar, S., et al.: Improving responsiveness of health systems to non-communicable diseases. Lancet **381**, 690–697 (2013)
5. Arena, R., et al.: Healthy lifestyle interventions to combat non-communicable disease. Eur. Heart J. **36**, 2097–2109 (2015)
6. Lee, N., Kotler, P.: Social Marketing, Influencing Behaviors for Good, 4th edn. Sage Publications Inc., Thousand Oaks (2011)
7. Kotler, P., Zaltman, G.: Social marketing: an approach to planned social change. J. Mark. **35** (3), 3–12 (1971)
8. Fench, J., Blair-Stevens, C., Merritt, R., McVey, D.: Social Marketing and Public Health, Theory and Practice. Oxford University Press, Oxford (2010)
9. Kotler, P., Lee, N.: Social Marketing: Influencing Behaviors for Good. Sage Publications, Thousand Oaks (2008)

10. Grier, S., Bryant, C.: Social marketing in public health. Annu. Rev. Public Health **26**, 319–339 (2005)
11. Kotler, P., Lee, N.: Social Marketing Influencing Behaviors for Good. Sage Publications, Thousand Oaks (2008)
12. Douglas, E., et al.: Childhood obesity prevention in South Africa: media, social influences, and social marketing opportunities. Soc. Mark. Q. **15**, 22–48 (2009)
13. Stead, M., Gordon, R., Angus, K., McDermott, L.: A systematic review of social marketing effectiveness. Health Educ. **107**(2), 126–191 (2007)
14. Newton-Ward, M., Andreasen, A., Hastings, G.: Positioning social marketing. Soc. Mark. Q. **10**(3), 17–22 (2004)
15. Andreasen, A.: Social marketing: its definition and domain. J. Public Policy Mark. **13**(1), 108–114 (1994)
16. Brooks, R.: The basics of social marketing: how to use marketing change behaviours, University of Washington, United Stats of America (2000)
17. Boyd, D., Ellison, B.: Social network sites: definition, history, and scholarship. Comput. Med. Commun. **13**, 210–230 (2008)
18. Thackeray, R., Neiger, B.L., Hanson, C.L., McKenzie, J.F.: Enhancing promotional strategies within social marketing programs: use of Web 2.0 social media. Health Promot. Pract. **9**(4), 338–343 (2008)
19. Dawson, J.: Doctors join patients in going online for health information. New Media Age (2010)
20. Hu, Y., Sundar, S.: Effects of online health sources on credibility and behavioral Intentions. Commun. Res. **37**, 105–132 (2010)
21. Sanford, A.A.: "I can air my feelings instead of eating them": blogging as social support for the morbidly obese. Commun. Stud. **61**(5), 567–584 (2010)
22. Nordqvist, C., Hanberger, L., Timpka, T., Nordfeldt, S.: Health professionals' attitudes towards using a Web 2.0 portal for child and adolescent diabetes care: qualitative study. J. Med. Internet Res. **11**(2), e12 (2009)
23. Liang, B., Scammon, D.L.: E-word-of-mouth on health social networking sites: an opportunity for tailored health communication. J. Consum. Behav. **10**(6), 322–331 (2011)
24. Denecke, K., Nejdl, W.: How valuable is medical social media data? Content analysis of the medical web. Inf. Sci. **179**, 1870–1880 (2009)
25. Kaplan, A.M., Haenlein, M.: Users of the world unite! The challenges and opportunities of social media. Bus. Horiz. **53**(1), 59–68 (2010)
26. Freeman, B., Chapman, S.: Is "YouTube" telling or selling you something? Tobacco content on the YouTube video-sharing website. Tob Control. **16**(3), 207–210 (2007)
27. Chou, W.Y., Hunt, Y.M., Beckjord, E.B., Moser, R.P., Hesse, B.W.: Social media use in the United States: implications for health communication. J. Med. Internet Res. **11**(4), e48 (2009)
28. Moen, A., Smørdal, O., Sem, I.: Web-based resources for peer support - opportunities and challenges. Stud. Health Technol. Inf. **150**, 302-6 (2009)
29. Sedereviciute, K., Valentini, C.: Towards a more holistic stakeholder analysis approach. Mapping known and undiscovered stakeholders from social media. Int. J. Strateg. Commun. **5**(4), 221–239 (2011)
30. https://www.statista.com/statistics/272014/global-social-networks-ranked-by-number-of-users/
31. Capurro, D., et al.: The use of social networking sites for public health practice and research: a systematic review. J. Med. Internet Res. **16**(3), e79 (2014)
32. Tunisia Digital Summit (2017)

33. Mozas-Moral, A., Bernal-Jurado, E., Medina-Viruel, M.J., Fernández-Uclés, D.: Factors for success in online social networks: an fsQCA approach. J. Bus. Res. **69**(11), 5261–5264 (2016)
34. Vlachvei, A., Notta, O.: Greek food manufacturing firms' social media efforts: evidence from Facebook. Procedia – Soc. Behav. Sci. **175**(1), 308–313 (2015)
35. Daft, R.L., Lengel, R.H.: Organizational information requirements, media richness and structural design. Manage. Sci. **32**(5), 554–571 (1986)

Author Index

Printed in the United States
By Bookmasters